Teaching Multicultured Students

Studies in Inclusive Education Series
Series Editor: Roger Slee, Dean of the Graduate
School of Education, University of Western Australia

Teaching Multicultured Students

Culturism and Anti-culturism in School Classrooms

Alex Moore

London & New York

First published 1999
by Falmer Press
11 New Fetter Lane, London EC4P 4EE

Simultaneously published in the USA and Canada
by Falmer Press
Garland Inc., 19 Union Square West, New York, NY 10003

Falmer Press is an imprint of the Taylor & Francis Group

© 1999 Alex Moore

Typeset in Times by Taylor & Francis Books Ltd
Printed and bound in Great Britain by Biddles Ltd,
Guildford and King's Lynn

British Library Cataloguing in Publication Data
A catalogue record for this book is available from the British Library.

Library of Congress Cataloguing in Publication Data
Moore, Alex
Teaching Multicultured Students/Alex Moore
(Studies in Inclusive Education series)
Includes bibliographical references and index
1. Education, Bilingual–Great Britain Case studies.
2. Minorities–Education–Great Britain Case studies.
3. Inclusive education–Great Britain Case studies.
I. Title. II. Series.
LC3736.G6M66   1999
370.117′0941–dc21   99-28143

ISBN 0–750–70826–3 (hbk)
ISBN 0–750–70825–5 (pbk)

Contents

Figures

Acknowledgements

People too numerous to mention have helped in the production of this book, in all kinds of ways. Particular thanks, however, must go to Peter Woods, Jane Miller, Josie Levine, Keith Kimberley and Alex McLeod for helping me, at various points, to develop and organize the central ideas; to the staff at the case-study schools for allowing me into their working lives as a critical friend and for responding so constructively to my analyses of their practice; to the students at those schools, whose voices continue to shine through with such vividness and candour; to my family and friends – and in particular my wife Anna – for keeping me at it and restoring my often flagging confidence; to Roger Slee and Falmer for seeing the potential for a book in the first place – and for making me believe that I could write it; to Mike Quintrell at King's College and Andy Hudson at the Institute of Education for their endorsements and encouragement; and to all those colleagues at Goldsmiths College who, in their different ways, helped me to find the time, the energy and the faith to complete the project – in particular, Susan Sidgwick, Clyde Chitty, David Halpin, Nola Turner, Dennis Atkinson, Gwyn Edwards, Paul Dash and Shirley Chapman.

Alex Moore
July 1999

Series Editor's Preface

As Ira Shor quite correctly observes, 'Knowledge is not exactly power'. He explains, 'Knowledge is the power to know, to understand, but not necessarily the power to do or to change ... while their [alienated students'] writing and thinking developed, the testing policy remained the same' (Shor 1992, p.6). Alex Moore confronts the multidimensional politics of knowledge production and transmission for multicultured students in 'the long shadow' of the 'British' National Curriculum and its attendant cultural rituals and practices. A book for all educators, *Teaching Multicultured Students* takes up the micro- and macro-pedagogic struggles for inclusive schools.

You will find the complex web of theoretical and political issues enveloping multilingual, bilingual and bidialectal children and their teachers in schools are mediated through a number of actors in the text. The cast includes students such as Nozrul, Abdul and Mashud, teachers such as Mr Geddes, Mrs Green and Ms Montgomery, an extensive array of researchers and theoreticians, and those who establish the policy field in which the stories are set. The objective is clear, to identify, support and extend approaches to teaching which are genuinely inclusive. In this context, as in many others, inclusive education refers to pedagogic practice, curriculum and school organization that legitimizes the culture and language of children whose principal language is not English. And, I hasten to add, what a particular rendition of English it is. I will leave it to John, Carrie, Jason, Steven, Lynette and their teacher to tell you whose English it is. Just as important is the recognition of those forms of theory, pedagogy and curriculum – vestiges of the 'humanist Victorian missionary' – that continue to visit the sins of culturism on children in classrooms. This latter objective helps keeps our cultural wits about us so that we do not leave the 'back door' ajar for exclusionary visitations in the inclusive school.

Alex Moore makes a number of major contributions to this series:

1   He demonstrates the maxim *cultural politics is cultural politics,* no matter what we do to describe it otherwise. Here I refer to this book's implicit counter to the tendency to seal our project of inclusive education within

the community of our own marginalized group of constituents. As a series editor I have intentionally sought work that represents a range of struggles and experiences of educational exclusion and inclusion for different groups of people. There is much to be gained from providing a forum where we gain access to the work of others in the project of inclusive education.

2 He demonstrates the centrality of theory-making to the shaping of education practice. This is particularly important in an age of pragmatism when we are told that theory is an academic indulgence. Unsurprisingly, this charge most often is levelled by those whose theory remains unexplicated, submerged in lock-step recipes and tips for teachers. Somehow we are supposed to accept that theory is rendered redundant when it remains unacknowledged. Associated with this problem is the tendency to demean teachers through the denial of the messiness of the world in which children, schools, their work and education policy are situated and thereby to trade in superficiality. This book elaborates and explains theory as an essential part of refining our pedagogic practices in polycultural schools. It does so respectfully by recognizing the pressures that beset teachers in the carriage of their work. Returning to Shor, teachers struggle with the field of education policy characterized by national standardized testing, league tables and problematic inspection schedules. This book proposes different sites for different kinds of related struggle.

3 *Teaching Multicultured Students* has firm footholds in ordinary schools and classrooms. Alex privileges us with visits into classrooms he has been observing over an extended period of time and allows the voices of the students and their teachers to illuminate the theoretical narrative. Like others in this series, the author draws our attention to the fundamental question of the form of enquiries into inclusive education. As Clough and Barton (1995) continue to impress upon us, we need to make difficult the research process itself and ask questions about the relationship between the researcher, the subjects of research and the outcomes of the research.

I invite you to add to this list upon conclusion of a book that subscribes to the proposition that inclusive education is not simply a technical problem for experts in particular educational fields: it is a project for educators as cultural transgressors of the hegemonic educational form.

Roger Slee

References

Clough, P. and Barton, L. (eds) (1995) *Making Difficulties: Research and the construction of SEN*, London, Paul Chapman.

Shor, I. (1992) *Empowering Education: Critical teaching for social change*, Chicago, University of Chicago Press.

1 Themes and Perspectives

[L]egal slavery may be in the past, but segregation and subordination have been allowed to persist.

(Hacker 1995, p.229)

Introduction: A Biographical Note

My active interest in bilingualism and bidialectalism started in April 1969, when I took up my first teaching post at an inner-London secondary school. Having received no formal teacher training and having had only a very limited experience of secondary schooling after attending a boys' grammar school from the age of eleven to eighteen, I took into this post a common-sense and, with the benefit of hindsight, profoundly flawed notion of what teaching and learning ought to be about. This included perceiving surface errors in my students' written work as symptoms of laziness, slovenliness or plain stupidity (at any rate, as unsightly blots deserving of the most rigorous red-inking at my disposal), and seeing any differences at all between my students' performance and 'standard' English practices as deviations that must be rectified instantly and without explanation. Mine was an unquestioning acceptance of the received cultural practices of school and academic life as the only right cultural practices, and of other cultural practices as simply gone-wrong versions of that standard.

Fortunately, my students did not allow me to get away with this sort of thinking for too long. Under their determined, sometimes brutally frank guidance, my uneducated practice gradually gave way to more appropriate forms of pedagogy, linked to a much clearer understanding not only of how the learning process worked but of what was actually going on in the schools I worked in and the world I lived in. When I moved on to posts in other schools, working first with large numbers of bidialectal students and then with even larger numbers of bilingual students, that process gathered speed and focus. I still made mistakes, of course, the way all teachers do, and in many ways this book is about those mistakes and about the lessons they taught me. However, I like to think that the mistakes receded as the voices of my students continued to advise me and as I listened, increasingly, to voices wiser than my own within the profession.

Those voices taught me many things. They taught me, for instance, to value and appreciate my students' 'non-standard' cultural practices and artefacts, rather than to respond to them in terms of correctness or incorrectness. Such a reorientation led me, in turn, to reconfigure my central pedagogic task, away from eliminating and replacing those non-standard practices, towards fostering and developing them in ways that simultaneously promoted expertise in the 'standard' practices my students would need to reproduce if they were to succeed academically – a pedagogic function I later came to understand as *extending students' cultural–linguistic repertoires*. The voices of my students also reminded me that bilingual and bidialectal students are not minorities but minorit*ized*, that they are not unicultured or even uncultured, but multi-cultured, and that although dominant educational systems and practices do marginalize and coerce large numbers of school students (in much the same ways as I had done in my initial practice), schools are not just sites of coercion, oppression and straightforward cultural reproduction: they are also, to quote Giroux and McLaren, 'sites that contain the promise of counterhegemonic struggle' – places where teachers and marginalized students, working together, *can* promote, albeit within the constraints imposed upon them by the larger society, alternative agendas that involve a recognition of and deliberate opposi-tion to the culturist practices to which large numbers of our students are habitually subjected (Giroux and McLaren 1992, p.xiii).

Each of these lessons has been underpinned by an understanding that schools do not exist independently of the larger society and are not seen, by students, as doing so. As Cummins has argued, 'power relations in the broader society' are inevitably

> reflected in the organization of schooling ... and in the mindset that educators bring to the teaching of culturally diverse students. These educational structures and the role definitions that educators adopt directly affect the interactions that culturally diverse students experience in schools.
>
> (Cummins 1996, p.136)

It seems not unreasonable to suppose that if students' cultures are marginal-ized in the classroom, those same students are likely to feel that their presence and contribution will be considered marginal in the wider community. It is also reasonable to suppose that many students, because of their awareness of the marginalizations to which they and their cultures are subjected, may be fundamentally suspicious of teachers – including those who purport to share their understandings and who openly commit themselves to a joint struggle for improvement: not all students, for example, may wish to accept their (typically white) teachers' understandings of coercion and marginalization, or their strategies for 'empowerment'.

Sources of Field Data: The Investigation of Symbolic Exclusion

In exploring in this book the issues related to these important lessons, I have continued to draw on my own experience of classroom practice. In particular, I have made use of data and analysis arising from my involvement in two interrelated research projects. The first of these was work undertaken with bidialectal students and their teachers at a school in which I originally worked as an English teacher (Moore 1987b). I knew these students well and had tracked their progress unofficially through the third and fourth years of their secondary schooling. The project was undertaken when they were in their fifth year at the school (Year 11), working towards public examinations, and arose from a growing awareness on the part of one of their teachers not only that there were huge differences between what these young people considered to be good writing and what their teachers and examiners considered to be good writing, but also that the students themselves had remained unhelpfully unaware of these differences throughout their school careers. A practical sharing of examination assessment criteria with the students illuminated the precise ways in which, through formal assessment procedures, the students' preferred cultural practices and skills were marginalized, as well as highlighting the potential advantages and inherent difficulties of developing marginalized students' language repertoires in this particular fashion. A flavour of this work and of work subsequently carried out with much younger bidialectal students is given in Chapters 7 and 8.

The second project arose from working with bilingual students and their teachers at a neighbouring school. These students were arriving in the UK at secondary-school age, typically with little or no spoken or written English and occasionally with no first-language literacy (students described in the jargon of the time as 'Stage 1 bilingual learners').[1] Given that it is likely, in current circumstances, for such students to take between five and ten years to 'catch up with' their monolingual peers adequately enough to be able to benefit equally from main-language engagement with the curriculum (Klesmer 1994, Cummins 1996), large numbers of these students were clearly at risk on arrival. As James Cummins has observed, young bilinguals of this kind, who arrive in a new country after the age of twelve, 'often [run] out of time before they [can] catch up academically in language-based areas of the curriculum' (Cummins 1996, p.61; see also Collier 1987). What teachers do with their limited and very precious time with such students is consequently of critical importance.

While one of my initial research interests was in comparing different kinds of *provision* or organization for bilingual students – in particular, comparing the relative merits and demerits of working with bilingual students in mainstream classes alongside majority-monolingual peers and of withdrawing bilingual students for specialist language support (Moore 1995) – it quickly became apparent that examples of effective and ineffective pedagogy could be found in either organizational system. It was also evident that much ineffective pedagogy was ineffective because it was fundamentally *culturist* in nature – that is, it treated alternative cultural practices not as signs of difference, but as indications of inadequacy or deficit – while much of the most effective teaching took a deliberately *anti-culturist* stance – recognizing and valuing alternative cultural practices and seeking ways of adding to or extending them. In the culturist classrooms, bilingual students – and often bidialectal students – were effectively 'ghettoized' in much the same way that Sharp and Green have described the ghettoization of 'low ability' students in so-called mixed ability classrooms (Sharp and Green 1975): that is to say, not only were the bilingual students treated very differently – often quite patronizingly – by their teacher and given radically different work to do; they were also allowed to become isolated *physically* from the rest of the class, with whom they consequently had little or no communicative contact. In the anti-culturist classrooms, by contrast, teachers had high expectations of their bilingual students, valued their cultures and previous language and learning experiences, and sought actively to involve their students in interactions with other students in the class.

As a consequence of these observations, and in the light of what has already been said about the 'catch-up' situation of developing bilingual learners, my interest turned away from organizational issues, first toward practical pedagogic issues, then to the philosophical underpinnings of pedagogy and to the relationships between pedagogy and the views and perceived needs of the larger society. This shift of emphasis in my own research may be seen to reflect a corresponding history of deliberate exclusion and subsequent partial inclusion of bilingual and bidialectal students in mainstream British education – a history explored in a little more depth in Chapter 2. This movement, which began with the total physical exclusion of newly arrived bilingual students in off-site centres, has now moved, via on-site withdrawal classes, to students being supported by EAL (English-as-an-additional-language) experts in mainstream classes alongside monolingual peers. My own research evidence suggests that although the physical inclusion of bilingual and bidialectal students may have been achieved in many institutions, such students typically continue to be excluded and marginalized in other ways, partly through the persistence of a culturally biased school curriculum but also through forms of pedagogy that render students and their existing cultural experiences 'invisible'. I have called this kind of exclusion *symbolic exclusion* for two reasons. First, I want to distinguish it from physical exclusion, which involves an act of bodily displacement such as sending someone home or to another room (symbolic exclusion excludes pupils not by physically removing them from the classroom but by invalidating major 'non-standard' aspects their cultures and/or languages). Second, I want to stress that through such processes students effectively have their own favoured and familiar *symbolic systems* (systems through which they have constructed understandings and interpretations of the world) excluded from the classroom by a privileging of the arbitrarily dominant symbolic systems of the school. (They may also, of course, be effectively excluded from access to those dominant systems – such as when they are ignored by the teacher.) We could say that symbolic exclusion represents the exclusion *through* a dominant symbolic system of 'alternative' symbolic systems and processes.

Prioritizing Pedagogy: 'Micro-oriented' and 'Macro-oriented' Resistances

If, as I am suggesting, education *systems* continue to marginalize students, chiefly through the imposition of culturally fixed assessment criteria (Apple 1979, Atkinson 1998, Moore 1998), what can teachers do (1) to combat culturism in their own classrooms, and (2) to militate, with any degree of hope or success, for attitudinal change *within* that larger marginalizing system and within the larger society within which it is sited?

James Cummins is quite clear on this issue: it is not only incumbent on teachers to adopt – as far as they are able – anti-culturist practices within their own classrooms, but to militate for changes within the culturist system itself, through a willingness 'individually and collectively, to challenge aspects of the power structure of the wider society' (Cummins 1996, p.iii). This is a view predicated upon a belief that educators 'have considerable power to affect change in the lives of those they interact with' (Cummins 1996, p.222). It is a challenge that begins with a renewed self-belief on the part of hard-pressed teachers that they still comprise the social group 'most dedicated to democratic values, most knowledgeable about cultural trends, and in the most strategic position to direct social change' (Hunt and Metcalf 1968, p.278; see also Lucas, Henze and Donato 1990, McCarty 1993).

The kinds of pedagogic action implicit in Cummins' call to arms might be categorized as 'micro-oriented' and 'macro-oriented'. Micro-oriented action relates to what we can do with our students in the classroom, within the constraints of the larger system as it currently operates – and, typically, in line with the existing ethos and policies of our particular school (these policies and ethos may be multicultural, anti-culturist or even culturist in nature):[2] oppositional action, that is, which focuses on arming students, as far as is possible within the given 'rules', with the necessary political understandings and insights to challenge coercive societal practices *independently*. As the case studies will show, this does not necessarily involve acts of great daring or courage on the part of teachers, or place upon their shoulders the unreasonable burden of changing dominant ideologies single-handedly.

More often than not, it is a matter of teachers adjusting their own cultural orientations (both individually and collectively) through processes of 'cultural distancing', and fashioning their pedagogic choices and approaches accordingly: that is, processes of problematizing or 'making strange' practices and procedures that are perceived and experienced as the natural way of things, and of beginning to see them as simply one *possible* set of practices or procedures among many.[3] One potentially very useful way of achieving such (re)orientation is through the detailed study of the practice and experience of other teachers, leading to what Bourdieu has called 'an awakening of consciousness and socioanalysis' (Bourdieu 1990a, p.116). Other ways include the (re)development of whole-school policies that take radical stock of the way in which the individual institution promotes or resists culturist practices that may be embedded in its own micro-culture.

The second kind of pedagogic action – which may be practised simultaneously with the first – is more specifically and more consciously oriented away from the institution, towards the larger social system itself. Here, the challenge is for teachers – working with their students, with colleagues in their own and other institutions, with parents, governors, councillors and any other interested parties – to seek to militate more directly for ideological, hegemonic changes that will produce a fairer, more pluralistic system of education and assessment for all students. This activity – included, like the former, in what Giroux has called 'border pedagogy' (Giroux 1992, pp.28–9) – involves the active occupation, within existing legal frameworks, of whatever negotiation- and action-spaces are available, in order to ensure teachers' own empowerment and to make their own wise, professional voices heard. Such activity might include efforts, channelled through (for example) teachers' unions or subject-based pressure groups, to promote a return to the more pluralistic assessment procedures that were beginning to emerge in the UK in the 1980s (Moore 1998). It also, however, includes classroom-based activity (more normally associated with micro-oriented pedagogies) that actively seeks to empower and 'activate' students themselves in ways that are overtly political (a prime example would be explaining to students exactly how they are marginalized within the larger system). As Cummins puts it:

> [C]oercive relations of power can operate only through the micro-interactions between educators and students. Thus, educators, students and communities can challenge this coercive process. Although educational and social structures will impose constraints on resistance, these structures can never stifle the pursuit of empowering interactions on the part of educators and students. In short, educators always have options in the way they negotiate identities with students and communities. ... Culturally diverse students are empowered or disabled as a direct result of their interactions with educators and schools.
>
> (Cummins 1996, pp.139, 141)

While accepting in broad terms this double-faceted nature of anti-culturist teacher action, there are two caveats that need to be added. The first is that, as Cummins implies, only so much can be achieved in the classroom within the existing constraints of the larger system and society: as long as public examinations retain their culturally biased character, for example, teachers will always be constrained, to a greater or lesser degree, to reproduce that bias – however critically and self-consciously – through their own teaching. In this respect, we might say that a certain 'action threshold' is reached, even in cases of the very best pedagogic practice, to move beyond which requires a hegemonic change in the wider society. Such a change involves a radical rethink of how we perceive not only cultures themselves but the very purposes and nature of formal schooling (Freire 1970, Giroux 1992, McLaren 1995). The second caveat is that 'projective' teacher action – even that which is primarily 'school-based' – is not easy to achieve and is not getting easier. Increasingly, teachers are finding their working lives absorbed by the legal and bureaucratic demands of examination syllabuses, national testing, school-inspection criteria and national curricula. Thus, however much they might want to mount a 'challenge' to the coercive powers and conditions within the larger society and however 'strategically equipped' they might be to do so (Hunt and Metcalf 1968, p.278), they are also among the people who have the least time and energy to sustain the kind of 'counter-hegemonic struggle' that is required (Giroux and McLaren 1992, p.xiii). Furthermore, although 'action-spaces' still can be found within the ever-tightening grip of national curricula, these, too, are becoming increasingly difficult to locate.

It is partly because of this difficulty in mounting and sustaining 'projective' resistance that I have chosen to focus, in this book, on 'introjective' resistance – that which is more immediately 'do-able' and over which we still have some measure of control. Another way of looking at this is to say that I have focused on what most of us recognize as *pedagogy* – that is to say, on that which we do *with* our students *in* the classroom.

The 'Missing Concept'

There are, of course, other reasons for wishing to focus on pedagogy in a book such as this. One of these is that pedagogy has become, as Levine has pointed out, something of a 'missing concept' in official educational discourses (Levine 1992). The current UK National Curriculum, for instance, specifically (some might say mercifully) does not presume to tell teachers *how* to teach (only *what* to teach),[4] while the highly influential Office for Standards in Education and Teacher Training Agency both appear more concerned to assess teaching by measurable *outcome* and evidence of *preparation* than by the quality of teacher–student *interaction* (see, for example, TTA 1998). With reference to bilingual students, the absence of the pedagogic perspective is particularly noticeable. In its recent document 'The Assessment of the Language Development of Bilingual Pupils', for example, the Office for Standards in Education (UK) is principally concerned about the validity and usefulness of ascribing 'levels' to bilingual students (see Note 1) over and above the levels already available through the National Curriculum (OFSTED 1997). While examples of 'good classroom practice' are offered in this document, none of these apply to the group of bilingual students about whom teachers often express the greatest concern (Moore 1995): that is to say, students who arrive in the country fluent in one language but possessing little or no visible knowledge of the main language of the classroom ('Stage 1 learners'). Nor is there any obvious acknowledgement, in what is essentially a competence-driven picture of good practice (for example, OFSTED 1997, p.9), of the importance of the teacher–student *relationship*: an acknowledgement, that is, that for bilingual students 'to invest their sense of self, their identity, in acquiring their new language and participating actively in their new culture, they must experience positive and affirming interactions with members of that culture' (Cummins 1996, p.73).

To a certain extent, the absence of an informed pedagogical perspective from 'official', centralized educational discourses (at the very time when, as I shall argue, classroom teachers themselves should be focusing far more on pedagogical issues) has been mirrored in a corresponding absence at the local level. In the area of continuing professional development for teachers, for example, there is a still a tendency for the prime focus to be on *teaching materials* for bilingual students, while in books and published research there remains an emphasis on decontextualized theory rather than on the application of this theory to analyses of actual teaching and learning events.[5] No one would want to deny the immediate value of classroom materials for teachers of beginner-bilingual students, many of whom are denied any consistent support in the classroom, in the form either of an experienced EAL teacher or of appropriate and adequate training related to working with bilingual students: certainly, the provision and development of appropriate – as well as usable – classroom materials has offered an invaluable lifeline to many a teacher on the brink of despair. Furthermore, the need to develop such materials, as well the bases upon which they are developed, is often underpinned by serious theory and research in the area (I am thinking, for example, of Krashen's work on 'comprehensible input' [Krashen 1982]). However, the difficulty with an emphasis on classroom materials, if it is at the expense of professional development related more specifically to pedagogy (that is, not just 'Here is something you can give your bilingual students' but 'This is how you might work with bilingual students' or 'This is how you might go about producing your own materials for bilingual students'), is (a) that it only produces a quick-fix, short-term solution to a more abiding difficulty; (b) that it deflects teachers' attentions away from the real issues at stake, which are to do with how bilingual students are marginalized and silenced, and how teachers can best help those students to overcome such marginalization.

Placing such an emphasis on pedagogy is, I am aware, a potentially risky business, since it inevitably quotes, describes and critiques practice which is manifestly ineffective, counter-productive or downright hostile, in addition to practice which is effective, helpful and sympathetic. It may also, as in the case of this book, offer examples of practice which take a realistic, pragmatic view of the place of teaching within the wider social context and within the grammar of that wider context[6] alongside examples of practice that appears to operate only within the limited grammatical context of the particular classroom or school situation within which the teacher is operating. Whereas the latter practice may often – though not exclusively – be characterized by its essentially *reactive* nature ('this is what needs to be done in relation to this student or set of students in order to maintain discipline, make them more likely to achieve their best grades, and so on'), the former is more typically characterized by its essentially *responsive* nature ('this is what needs to be done in relation to this student or set of students in order to maximize their opportunities – and the opportunities of all people – in the wider social context in which they must operate'). To borrow, from the main body of the text, an example of what I mean by this, we have the case of a teacher who is confronted with a work of art by a newly arrived bilingual student – a work which plainly does not conform to any of the preset, externally fixed criteria by which the student will subsequently be adjudged to be a competent artist. The teacher's response to this student, as someone who is simply not conforming to acceptable artistic practice, leads her to treat the student exclusively in terms of the amount of time and effort he is likely to demand and of the unlikelihood of his ever being able to achieve the necessary skill to pass a public examination in the subject. Her pedagogy in relation to this student consequently becomes one dominated by the need for containment and surveillance rather than by an emphasis on development. Against this, we have the teacher who, on encountering an almost identical situation, assesses the student's work (a) within the possible frames of reference of a hypothetical alternative set of cultural practices and preferences ('This may not conform to the criteria by which the student's competence will be judged *here*, but could they perhaps conform more closely to those that apply somewhere else?'), *as well as* (b) within the context of the skills and generic expertise the student will need in order to be adjudged competent within the terms of reference of the new symbolic (value-)system within which they are now operating ('What [additional] skills will the student need to acquire in order to be successful in the public examination in this subject?'). As we shall see, these two quite different perspectives on and interpretations of bilingual students' work, partly caused by divergent, autobiographically rooted views as to what the teacher's role should be, can lead to two quite contrasting pedagogies and contribute to two very different learning outcomes.

The risk in making such identifications and comparisons of teachers' practice lies partly in its immediate openness to misinterpretation. There is always the possibility, for example, that the critical analysis of certain episodes of classroom practice will be read as a *general* criticism directed towards all teachers, suggesting that they have a personal and exclusive responsibility for everything that goes wrong with a student's education – a view too often emanating from the official views and agendas of central government.[7] There is also the danger that case studies can oversimplify the 'messy complexity of the classroom' and its never more than 'partially apprehendable practice' (Goodson and Walker 1991, p.xii), or that they can distract attention from where – and in whose hands – the larger problems lie (problems related to the culturally biased curriculum, the ever increasing and ever undermining burden of bureaucracy in teachers' working lives, the endemic culturism and racism that continue to characterize the larger society, and so forth). On the other hand, teachers are, I believe, very keen to improve the quality of their work and find it as useful to reflect upon examples of ineffective practice as to reflect upon examples of practice that appear to be 'good'. Perhaps it needs to be said that the many teachers with whom I have already shared some of the examples used in this book have had no difficulty recognizing their illustrative purpose and have been very happy to use them as a way into the interrogation and refinement of their own practice. It is in this spirit, I hope, that the studies will be received by others. Teachers do not need to be protected from notions of improvement. Indeed, to treat them as if they do is as insulting as to believe that their existing experience and expertise should be ignored.

Theoretical Perspectives

As will already be evident, in seeking and offering explanations of the classroom interactions and phenomena that will be described in the book, I have drawn eclectically on a range of theory, none of which I have the space to explore in great detail. While the book describes the school-based activities of some bilingual and bidialectal students and their teachers, it does not claim to be a book *about* bilingualism or bidialectalism; nor does it pursue many interesting and salient issues that the reader might feel inclined to follow up independently as an adjunct to anything of value they may find in these pages (I am thinking, for example, of the fascinating work being conducted with bilingual students and their *families* by researchers such as Eve Gregory [1996, 1997], the work on *identities* being carried out by writers such as Giroux [1992] and Cummins [1996], or the growing literature on teachers' biographies and how this affects their work with a whole range of students [for example, Goodson and Walker 1991]). Rather, this is a book which seeks to present one unified interpretation of some of the critical educational *experiences* of students who are bidialectal or sequentially bilingual:

critical in the sense that they appear to have contributed either to the subsequent linguistic–cognitive successes or failures of such students, or to the development of their self-esteem, or to the reconfiguration of their identity in the school situation.

I have chosen, in doing this, to write about a range of students: primary and secondary, bilingual and bidialectal, across a range of subject areas. In the vast majority of examples, I was able to spend at least one day a year with the students and teachers involved. However, I had the pleasure of working with Winston and his friends, whose experiences are described in Chapter 8, for a period of almost three years. All the material has been drawn from close observation made at various points over a period of some ten years, including work undertaken on a number of research projects.[8] Each of these projects has contributed greatly to my central argument, as have a number of key commentators whose work will figure prominently – sometimes explicitly, sometimes implicitly – in the pages that follow. The book could not have been the same, for example, without the groundbreaking sociolinguistic work of James Cummins (1978, 1979a, 1979b, 1980a, 1980b, 1984), or the profound sociological insights of Pierre Bourdieu (1977, 1990a, 1990b) and Basil Bernstein (1971a, 1971b, 1977).[9] Others to whom I am indebted are Mikhail Bakhtin (1981, 1984a, 1984b, 1986) and Valentin Volosinov (1986) for their theories of utterance and repertoire; Gunther Kress (1982) for his seminal work on the nature of genre; Lev Vygotsky (1962, 1978) for his elaborations of the interrelations between language and thought, and for reminding us all so eloquently that learning, like teaching, is a fundamentally social activity; Michael Apple (1979) for his exposition of the way cultural bias operates arbitrarily through a range of educational discourses and assessment criteria; William Labov (1972), Michael Stubbs (1976, 1983) and Peter Trudgill (1983), who have all shown us, in their different ways, that 'non-standard' linguistic forms are intrinsically just as valid and useful as 'standard' ones; Valerie Walkerdine (1982) and Neil Edwards and Derek Mercer (1987) for suggesting how classroom-based discourse analysis can connect with 'larger' explanations of human characteristics and behaviour; Peter Woods (1977), Robert Burgess (1984) and Stephen Ball (1981) for demonstrating the value and discipline of ethnographic research that takes researchers into where 'the action is' (Stubbs 1976, p.88); Shirley Brice Heath (1983) and Barbara Tizard and Martin Hughes (1984) for their important empirical research into cultural mismatches between in-school and out-school cultures, and the ways in which these are prone to misinterpretation along the lines of deficit rather than difference; and, of course, the staff and students at the three schools from which my major exemplars have been drawn. Though I have been critical of some individual instances of practice at these schools, the staff there know how much I valued their work. They also know that I have drawn on examples of what seems to me to be very effective practice as a way of indicating some of the strategies that teachers might adopt in order to begin to challenge, albeit locally at first, the culturally discriminating culture in which they operate. For the examples of symbolic *in*clusion that consequently abound in the book, we have these institutions and teachers to thank.

In addition to the general support and inspiration offered by the above writers and texts, several of them have contributed in varying degrees to the key theories that I have suggested drawing out from the case studies. The notion of Variable Underlying Proficiency (VUP), which I use to explore intercultural variations in *genre*, makes little sense, for example, without Cummins' well-known elaboration of *Common* Underlying Proficiency (CUP) and language transfer (Cummins 1979a, 1984). Cultural Mismatch Theory,[10] which relates to the ways in which teachers misrecognize genre variations as deficiencies, emerges in turn from Walkerdine's work on psychosemiotics (Walkerdine 1982) and Kress's work on genre (Kress 1982). The notion of cultural–linguistic *repertoire extension* explores ground initially opened up by the work of writers such as Bakhtin (1981, 1986) and Volosinov (1986),[11] as well as later work by Stubbs (1976), Trudgill (1983) and Labov (1972) on language in its social context. The notion of the 'arbitrariness' of signs and genres has been developed from a wide range of writers – not only Stubbs, Trudgill and Labov, but also, centrally, Apple (1979) and Barthes (1973). Bourdieu's conceptualizations – in particular those of cultural capital, symbolic violence, pedagogic action and authority, and habitus and field – have also contributed significantly to the notion of symbolic exclusion, as well as (along with Bernstein 1971a, 1971b) shedding light and offering perspectives on analyses of student and teacher activity in the light of dialectical relationships between the 'objective conditions' within which teachers and students work (for instance, cultural bias in the school curriculum and in government policy, or inequalities of access to academic-related aids and materials) and the 'subjective' or 'internalized' orientations they bring to their work.

As I have indicated already, this is *not* a book 'about' bilingualism and bidialectalism, but about cultural practice and reproduction – about working with multicultured students. I have not, therefore, assumed on the reader's part either a deep background knowledge of issues and theory related to bilingualism and bidialectalism, or a complete lack of such knowledge. Rather, I have sought to offer concise references and explanations of bilingual and bidialectal theory as and when these seem relevant, in ways that are both challenging and easy to follow regardless of pre-existing knowledge.

Structure of the Book

Leaving aside the final chapter, the book consists of two parts. The first part, comprising Chapters 1 to 4, is mainly issues-based. Although relevant theory is introduced and there is some reference to empirical data, these are used to support and illustrate the key points that are being made rather than vice versa. The second part of the book, comprising Chapters 5 to 8, consists of case studies of classroom practice. While there is a compelling logic to exploring – and sharing – key issues first and then seeing how these issues manifest themselves in practice, the book can equally well be read 'in reverse order', beginning with the case studies and using these as a 'way in' to a more theoretical consideration of the issues.

As has already been indicated, some of the case studies presented in the second half of the book have been previously written up. Earlier versions of some chapters, or parts thereof, have appeared as follows:

Chapter 5   'Responding to bilingual pupils in the art classroom', *Journal of Art and Design Education*, 15(2), 179–88; ' "Bad at art": Issues of culture and culturism', in Dawtrey, L., Jackson, T., Masterton, M. and Meecham, P. (eds) *Critical Studies in Modern Art*, Yale University Press, pp.98–105.

Chapter 6   'A whole language approach to the teaching of bilingual learners', *Occasional Paper No. 15*, Center for the Study of Writing, University of California, Berkeley/Carnegie Mellon University; 'A whole language approach to the teaching of bilingual learners', in Goodman, Y., Hood, W. and Goodman, K. (eds) *Organizing for Whole Language*, Heinemann/Irwin, pp.231–47; 'Genre, ethnocentricity and bilingualism in the English classroom', in Woods, P. and Hammersley, M. (eds) *Gender and Ethnicity in School*, Routledge, pp.166–90.

Chapter 7   'Assessing young readers: Questions of culture and ability', *Language Arts*, 73(5), pp.306–16.

Readers might find it useful to refer to these alternative versions, most of which contain additional material.

Notes

1   In UK schools, bilingual students are still, typically, categorized using Hester's 'stages'. These are Stage 1 ('New to English'), Stage 2 ('Becoming Familiar with English'), Stage 3 ('Becoming Confident as a User of English') and Stage 4 ('A Very Fluent User of English in Most Social and Learning Contexts'). For more detailed descriptions, see Hester 1989. The need for these levels in the context of existing National Curriculum levels of attainment applicable to *all* students has recently been called into question in the UK by the Office for Standards in Education (OFSTED 1997, p.2).

2   I am using broad categories here which inevitably result in some measure of oversimplification. Both micro-oriented and macro-oriented teaching, for example, can take place in direct opposition to the parent school's own ethos and policies. An example I recently came across of a teacher taking micro-oriented action which was legitimate within the larger legal framework but which opposed the

parent school's policy involved that teacher refusing to put grades or marks out of ten on her students' essays, insisting that she would only append comments.

3   The notion of 'distancing' finds one elaboration in the work of Garfinkel (1967, pp.37–8), who discusses the possibility of making visible the 'seen but unnoticed' expectancies of social behaviour by employing techniques which 'produce reflections through which the strangeness of an obstinately familiar world can be detected'. See also Burgess 1929, p.47, on 'the secrets of human nature and society', and Mason 1994 on 'noticing'. Another approach to understanding the distancing process can be made through Ricoeur's work on metaphor and narrative (for example, Ricoeur 1978, 1984, Brown 1998).

4   It is, however, true that to a considerable extent curriculum content suggests or determines pedagogic style. The more teachers and students have to 'get through', for example, the less time they may have to dwell and explore.

5   Notable exceptions include Bleach and Riley (1985), Burgess and Gore (1985).

6   Another way of looking at this difference is through considerations of the 'metaphoric' and 'metonymic' axes of teaching. For this particular interpretation of metaphor and metonym, extrapolated from Jakobson's 'Two aspects of language and two types of aphasic disturbances' (Jakobson 1971), I am grateful to Valerie Walkerdine (Walkerdine 1982). Building upon her reading of the terms, we might suggest that teachers operating along the metaphoric axis are able to 'insert' their own practice and working conditions into wider social practices and conditions, and vice versa. Teachers working on the metonymic axis, by contrast, will only relate personal classroom experiences – including perceived difficulties – to other classroom experiences. At its crudest, this might result in one teacher approaching an 'underachieving' child from the perspective of that child's general social experience and the power relations within which they have to operate, while another teacher might simply resort to available sanctions, on the basis that the child's behaviour connects only tenuously with extra-institutional circumstances. For alternative interpretations of the terms metaphor and metonym, and different applications, see Culler 1983, Wright 1998.

7   As I have argued elsewhere, the blaming of individual teachers or institutions has become a very handy and effective way of masking difficulties that exist within social and economic *systems* (Moore 1996a; see also Hargreaves 1994).

8   Principally, these include my own MA dissertation (Moore 1987b) and PhD thesis (Moore 1995), carried out under the invaluable supervision of Keith Kimberley and Josie Levine in the first case, and Peter Woods and Jane Miller in the second; the DES-funded ImpacT project, investigating school-based IT work, at King's College London, where I was fortunate to work with Stephen Ball and Margaret Cox; and a small research project funded by Goldsmiths University of London, on issues related to bilingualism and Key Stage 3 testing.

9   Though I have been equally indebted to the work of Bernstein and Bourdieu, these two commentators have not always been equally appreciative of one another's work: see, for example, Bernstein 1996, pp.182–3.

10   The notion of cultural mismatch is not, in itself, an unfamiliar one (Phillips 1972, Au 1980, Guthrie and Hall 1983). Guthrie and Hall, for example, remind us that 'cultural differences in language use do exist' and that the teacher's difficulty lies in identifying them since 'these differences are subtle and largely unconscious' and consequently 'not available to the casual, or even interested, observer' (Guthrie and Hall 1983, p.73). Mismatch theory has tended to focus, however, on issues of behaviour (Phillips 1972) or been suggestive to teachers of an unacceptable deficit model of bilingualism and biculturalism. My own use of the expression describes critical breakdowns in classroom interaction that are caused by differences in perception, understanding or habit between the student and the teacher,

often involving issues of representation and genre. In such situations, it is clearly the teacher's responsibility to identify the mismatch and to structure their pedagogy accordingly.

11 Although active in the USSR between the Wars, Bakhtin and Volosinov were not really 'discovered' in Western Europe and America until much later.

2 Marginalizing Bilingual Students

Physical and Symbolic Exclusion

From Physical to Symbolic Exclusion

In this chapter I want to provide an overview of recent developments in teaching bilingual students in the UK, suggesting that in organizational terms we have witnessed a gradual (though by no means tidy) progression from the physical isolation and exclusion of such students to their physical inclusion – but continued symbolic *ex*clusion – in mainstream education (Figure 1). I shall argue that in order for the full inclusion of bilingual students to take place – that is to say, both their physical *and* their symbolic inclusion in mainstream education and in the larger society – changes need to be made to the way in which culture, bilingualism and indeed the purposes and functions of education itself are perceived and understood in that larger society, and in consequent changes in official state policy on these issues. Clearly, this has implications for curriculum change, but also for how 'bilingual education' itself is configured and perceived. As Giroux has argued with reference to the education of multicultured students in the United States:

> [T]he problem within our educational system lies ultimately in the realm of values and politics, not in the realm of management and economics. Consequently, educational reformers and other cultural workers need to address the most basic questions of purpose and meaning. What kind of society do we want? How do we educate students for a truly democratic society? What conditions do we need to provide teachers … and students for such an education to be meaningful and workable?
>
> (Giroux 1992, p.241)

While teachers have much to contribute to these debates and to the larger project of effecting a 'hegemonic shift', it would plainly be unreasonable and unrealistic to expect them to effect fundamental societal changes single-handedly and without either adequate resources or an appropriate 'starting status' in the eyes of policy-makers and the public. When urging ourselves to take an oppositional stance, therefore, we must never lose sight of the broader contexts and constraints (including the legal constraints) within which teachers work. Nor must a much-needed emphasis on pedagogy overlook the necessity for genuine curriculum change as a prerequisite for a fairer and more effective educational system.

As Figure 1 suggests, organized provision for secondary-age bilingual students in the UK in the last quarter of the century has moved from the development of off-site centres, where such students experienced much – or in some cases all – of their early UK education physically removed from the mainstream education environment, to school-based provision which included large measures of physical withdrawal from mainstream *classes*. A further, more recent development has seen the increasing inclusion of these students in mainstream classes, alongside monolingual peers, where their learning is supported by specialist 'EAL' ('English as an Additional Language') teachers. This movement, as has already been suggested, cannot be regarded as a tidy one. Not all local authorities, for example, provided off-site centres in the first place, while throughout the 1980s some education authorities were still running such centres even as neighbouring authorities

Figure 1 The shift from exclusion to partial inclusion

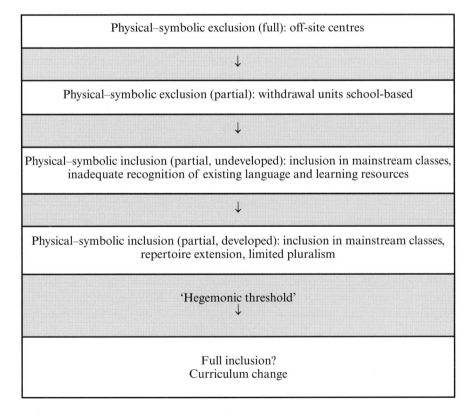

Physical–symbolic exclusion (full): off-site centres
↓
Physical–symbolic exclusion (partial): withdrawal units school-based
↓
Physical–symbolic inclusion (partial, undeveloped): inclusion in mainstream classes, inadequate recognition of existing language and learning resources
↓
Physical–symbolic inclusion (partial, developed): inclusion in mainstream classes, repertoire extension, limited pluralism
'Hegemonic threshold' ↓
Full inclusion? Curriculum change

were returning to a policy of including early-stage bilingual students in mainstream schools. In some schools in those authorities, bilingual students were experiencing very large amounts of physical withdrawal, while in others they were included almost exclusively in mainstream classes. Even today, though off-site centres are out of favour, there still exist in schools often furious debates as to whether or for what proportion of the day or week bilingual students should be physically withdrawn from mainstream classes.

There remain, too, unresolved issues about what teachers should be doing with bilingual students, and whether or not their first languages should be encouraged and actively maintained by the school. This debate, which is simultaneously organizational, pedagogic and micro-curricular, leads to a range of methods of working with bilingual students who have been physically included in mainstream classrooms. In some of those classrooms, students may find that their second-language and cognitive development is being supported with little or no reference to their existing linguistic skills, cognitive levels, experience of life and cultural preferences. These classrooms I have described under the category 'inclusion (partial, undeveloped)'. In other classrooms, teachers will seek to 'plug into' their bilingual students' existing skills, knowledge, experiences and cultures, both as a way of extending these students' knowledge and cultural–linguistic repertoires, and in order to make their bilingual students' cultures and experiences an integral part of the learning processes for *all* students in the class. These classrooms I have included under the term 'inclusion (partial, developed)'. Again – as the shaded areas in Figure 1 indicate – these are not neat divisions. Even individual teachers, for example, may fluctuate in their teaching between developed partial inclusion and undeveloped partial inclusion, according to the prevailing circumstances and pressures at any given point in time: thus, when public examinations or standardized national tests are imminent, there may well be an irresistible pressure, even on the most generally inclusive of teachers, to resort to measures which are more culturally coercive. Furthermore, although the physical circumstances may alter for bilingual students, and although one set of physical arrangements (for example, withdrawal from mainstream classes) may *suggest* one particular form of pedagogy (for example, the 'decontextualized', essentially transmissive teaching of language and concepts), examples of very exclusive *pedagogy* are still to be found in ostensibly inclusive *arrangements* and vice versa. One of the worst-case scenarios in the partial-inclusive *system*, for example, is the class teacher repeatedly ignoring their bilingual students' very presence, let alone their cultural–linguistic skills and preferences. Such an approach represents a very public marginalization, unlikely to challenge any racist assumptions on the part of other students.

The difficulty for schools and teachers wishing to move – or, more accurately, to support moves – beyond models of partial inclusion towards *full* inclusion is indicated in Figure 1 by solid lines representing the threshold of intra-institutional development in this area. This threshold is created by pre-vailing hegemony, itself supportive of and generated by larger socio-economic circumstances. Hegemonic change, promoted or supported by appropriate educational *policy*, must occur if further progress toward full inclusion is to be achieved. Teachers may be active in supporting and promoting such change: however, the crossing of the threshold (in terms of classroom *practice*) is something that cannot be achieved by teachers without 'outside' assistance.

The movement away from full physical exclusion to the partial inclusion of bilingual students in the UK has also, I believe, been accompanied – and is partly, no doubt, resultant on – a corresponding shift in debate and educa-tional research (Figure 2) from matters of organization and curriculum (*where* and *what* should bilingual students be taught?) to issues of pedagogy (*how* should bilingual students be taught?). Again, the further shift required to bring about full inclusion and genuine *empowerment*, requires an extra-institutional engagement (represented by the shaded area) with policies and policy-makers, and with public opinion: in other words, a qualitative shift of action from the pedagogic to the more directly political. For this reason, we can say that, while the organization debate has given way relatively easily to the pedagogy debate (the self-empowerment of many black and Asian local councillors, for example, made it impossible for the inherent racism of off-site centres to continue unchallenged), the movement into the empowerment debate is more difficult, both because of the challenges it presents to teachers and because of the degree of external opposition that it can be expected to activate. In addition to direct political activity on the part of teachers, this shift suggests a renewed emphasis on sociological and cultural *theory* in rela-tion to bilingual and bidialectal students, to run *alongside and complementary to* existing debates about pedagogy.

The overlapping, uneven nature of these developments, which I have found difficult to capture in diagrammatic form, can be illustrated by summarizing the position at three different, geographically close institutions at one particular point in time – the autumn of 1988 (see also Moore 1995).

Figure 2 Principal debates and informing theoretical perspectives

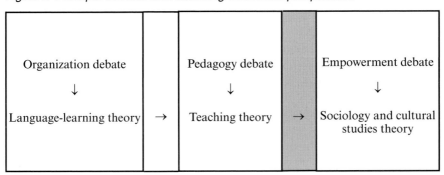

One of these institutions, School A,[1] was already in the process of moving away from a previous system of the heavy withdrawal of bilingual learners towards far more in-class support, involving a dramatic change in the way both EAL[2] and subject teachers perceived and configured their work. A recognition of the value of first-language maintenance had led to certain languages being offered on the curriculum as well as via twilight classes, while the school's English department, which generally valued the presence of bilingual and bidialectal students in the classroom, had developed a public examination mode that enabled students simultaneously to sit both examinations in the then two-tier system ('O' level GCEs and CSEs) and, to a certain extent, to include in the coursework element of their exam-submissions work written in forms of non-standard English. In support of these initiatives, a raft of whole-school policies had been drafted, which emphasized equality of opportunity and the importance of valuing the cultures of all the students. Thus, the policy for the Arts was able to argue that:

> Historically, Britain has based its critical values and aesthetic standards around western European art forms. Too often, our perceptions and understanding of arts from non-European cultures have been channelled through the perceptions and value judgements of colonial administrators.... It is our responsibility as educators to [provide] an arts education that gives positive recognition to the differences of culture and heritage, and that respects and affirms the identity of each individual child.

Such statements provided clear evidence of a movement at this particular school away from internal debates about withdrawal/support toward an engagement with issues of pedagogy and even with the wider political agenda.

Less than a mile down the road, another school, School B, was still teaching its Stage 1[3] bilingual students almost exclusively in withdrawal groups, allowing them into mainstream classes only for 'practical' subjects such as P.E. and Art. Here, the pedagogy debate had not yet taken root, since the teaching of early bilingual students was generally regarded – conveniently, perhaps – as a matter of expertise sited exclusively within the EAL department and qualitatively quite different from the teaching of monolingual students. Teachers at School B still complained when bilingual students were eventually 'released' into the mainstream curriculum – inevitably still some way short of being able to perform as competently as their monolingual peers – with the result that the only major debate at the school was one of organization: that is to say, the length of time that such students should remain in – or out of – the mainstream classroom. A secondary pedagogical debate had been activated at this school, but this focused on the question of *what* the bilingual students should be taught during their time *away* from the mainstream, rather than on *how* they should be taught or how the mainstream subject teachers should adapt and develop their own teaching skills in order to be most useful to bilingual students once they had been allowed to attend their lessons.

A further two miles away, situated in another local authority, School C was an off-site language centre – one of the few left in the country and itself under threat of closure. Here, early bilingual students were removed not only from mainstream classrooms but from mainstream schools for the whole of the school day, often remaining for a year or more until their English was deemed good enough for them to be able to cope in normal schools. First-language use was effectively banned from the classroom, on the basis that (to quote the deputy headteacher) the students would 'never learn English if they were allowed to always take the easy way out'. Students were taught a modified version of the standard school curriculum, with cognitive levels pitched at levels of proficiency in English.

Thus, within the space of three miles there existed one institution oper-ating a system of full (physical–symbolic) exclusion, one operating partial exclusion and one moving into a system of partial *in*clusion. In each case, of course, teachers could argue that the arrangements made for their bilingual students were in the students' own best interests. Both School A and School C, for example, cited 'student empowerment' as rationales for their approaches, although each institution had its own idea of what empowerment comprised. At School C, for instance, student empowerment stopped at basic literacy – or rather basic literacy was seen as an essential 'first base' whose achievement nothing else must impede – while at School A a different notion of empowerment held sway, along the lines that true empowerment was achievable not just through basic 'functional' literacy but through cultural and critical literacy *in combination with* basic literacy. Such a view emphasized the importance of bilingual students intermingling and inter-acting with monolingual peers from very early stages in their bilingual development, in order that their presence in the classroom might appear both normal and valid (Moore 1995). Consequently, efforts were made not just to include bilingual students physically, but also to make that inclusion social and symbolic. As we shall see, these efforts at some times met with more success than at others.

As Figure 3 indicates, huge differences existed – and still do exist – in the manner in which, in the continuing absence of a coherent, properly funded national policy, different institutions respond to the presence of their bilingual students (see also Bourne 1989, pp.140–64). An obvious consequence of this is that bilingual students will have very different experiences of formal education, depending on where they are lucky or unlucky enough to find places.

Even *within* the institutions described, however, there was by no means unanimity of philosophy or practice. At School A, for example, where (as one might expect) such variations were particularly pronounced, there continued to be very heated debates about how much withdrawal there should be and from what lessons, what the students should do in their withdrawal lessons,

*Figure 3 Comparison between basic provision for newly arrived bilingual
students at neighbouring institutions*

	School C	School A
L1 use	Use of first languages discouraged. Quasi-immersion model of second language development.	Use of first languages encouraged. Mainstream and twilight classes for further development of first languages.
Curriculum	Students taught modified curriculum, restricted in content and range: levels determined by second-language proficiency.	Students follow mainstream curriculum but miss some elements through out-of-class support. Existing levels of cognition recognized.
L1 input	Several teachers bilingual but bilingualism rarely made use of in class.	Very few bilingual teachers. One Bengali speaker to promote first-language development. No curriculum area taught through a minority language.

and whether the use of first languages should be allowed or encouraged. These debates in turn sought support in a range of theory (Cummins' work being frequently cited, for example, in the support of first-language maintenance, Levine's in support of the value of students being taught in mainstream classes) as well as in local authority policy on working with bilingual students and on any connections between this and published anti-racist or multicultural policy. As the case studies will show, intra-institutional differences of opinion could have a quite profound effect on the bilingual students' experience of school and on their self-esteem.

Full Exclusion: The Off-site Centre

The actual and potential horrors of full physical–symbolic exclusion in North America have been well documented (Platero 1975, Tschantz 1980, Cummins 1996). In these cases, Native Americans were withheld in special isolation units away from 'civilized' white schools, in order to *be* 'civilized' until they were considered safe to be accommodated within white social institutions. Such 'civilization' – effected with the help of the severest punishments for non-compliance – included the attempted elimination of such cultural preferences as religion, as well as of first languages, and their replacement with mainstream white cultural preferences and language: that is to say, physical exclusion by the removal of the body from the presence of other bodies, supported by cultural–symbolic exclusion through the attempted genocide of 'non-compliant' cultures.[4]

These accounts of the experiences of Native American children are not unreminiscent of the treatment of Welsh children earlier this century, when, again, a colonizing people sought to eliminate the primary cultural practices of existing tenants which involved processes of physical exclusion and coercion (see, for instance, Williams 1985). In the more recent history of the UK, however, different circumstances have applied which have prompted the dominant cultural groups to take different measures to assert their superiority. As with 'non-indigenous' multicultured students in North America (for example, Hispanics), the issue for the dominant classes in the UK has not, in recent times, been a matter of invading races feeling they have to marginalize and subordinate existing cultural and linguistic groups in order to legitimize their own presence and to normalize and justify their own usurped dominance: rather, the situation has been one in which immigrant communities have been allowed into the spaces – or the margins of the spaces – occupied by an already dominant group, on the tacit understanding that they will repay this enormous favour by making certain cultural–linguistic 'adjustments'.

These adjustments have varied historically and, along with the variations, the attendant accommodatory arrangements have changed. In the 1950s and 1960s, the desired adjustment was an almost total rejection of one's existing cultural–linguistic styles and forms in favour of approximations to the dominant ones of the new society into which one had moved (Coard 1971, Dalphinis 1988). The prevailing view of politicians seemed to chime pretty closely with the common-sense view of the person on the street: 'If they want to come over here, they've got to learn to fit in' – where 'fitting in' meant, effectively, assuming a completely new identity and rejecting any 'old' ones. Though the kind of savage isolation units described by Cummins, Platero and Tschantz might not have existed, it did become common policy for off-site language centres to be established for bilingual children – not to mention 'special schools', which seemed to be populated, in urban areas at least, by disproportionately large numbers of black youngsters of Afro-Caribbean origin (Coard 1971). At language centres, children typically received no instruction in or through their first languages. The focus was, rather, on providing them with the basic English skills they would need to 'cope with' a curriculum taught exclusively in standard English in main-stream schools (ILEA Division 2 1985, p.12). If such an approach did not require the same kind of brute coercion as in the North American institutions for Native Americans, it resulted nevertheless in a more avuncular form of racism, rooted in the worst kind of Victorian liberal humanism (see also Levine 1985, p.1).

Such an approach, which has much the same end result as more obviously brutal ones – that is, the subordination of minoritized cultural practices and their 'replacement' by dominant ones – seeks to consign minoritized groups' struggle 'to master-narratives that suggest that the oppressed need to be remade in the image of a dominant white culture' (Giroux 1992, p.116).

This particular power relationship, underpinned by an unquestioning belief in the superiority of white, Western, middle-class values, skills and practices, continues to dominate in many institutions, where in recent times it has been encouraged and accentuated by the refugee status of large numbers of multi-cultured students. In this relationship, the dominant social groups and their 'representatives' set themselves up as *benefactors*, hoping to discover in their victim-students[5] not merely progress but gratitude. Since the sole purpose of the off-site centres was to 'give' newly arrived students English, the students' previous experiences of language and learning were considered irrelevant – a view which has managed to survive, to an alarming degree, in the new, more inclusive arrangements for bilingual students.[6]

Some of the later UK off-site centres, it is true, did begin to seek alternative ways of working with their students that required less drastic accommodations, attempting, for example, to teach not just language but curriculum content at levels appropriate to the students' cognitive abilities, or even encouraging the development of first languages so that cognitive development could take place 'normally' while second-language proficiency was being developed. The physical withdrawal of students, however, was anathema to large numbers of teachers, local councillors and politicians, who quite rightly found it indefensible both on humanitarian and educational grounds.

The demise of such centres was already imminent, and indeed many had already fallen by the wayside, when, in 1986, the damning Calderdale Enquiry hastened their disappearance from the UK scene with dramatic effect. This enquiry, carried out by the influential Commission for Racial Equality (CRE), investigated provision for bilingual students within one UK education authority – Calderdale, in West Yorkshire – where the policy was to provide specialist help for recently arrived bilingual students by withdrawing them into specialist language units. The Calderdale Enquiry concluded that

> Calderdale's arrangements for ESL [English as a Second Language] teaching amounted to an indirectly discriminatory practice contrary to the Race Relations Act 1976

recommending that

> funds under Section 11 [money set aside specifically to provide additional support to immigrants from the 'new commonwealth'] of the Local Government Act 1966 for ESL teachers should only be made available to [Local Education Authorities] whose system for teaching ESL either is, or is moving towards, a system integrated with mainstream schooling.

Among a range of objections to the establishment and running of the Authority's language units, the report highlighted specific organizational problems compatible with those described by Levine and others (Levine

1983) in relation to the withdrawal of students from mainstream schools: in particular,

> their curriculum is not always as extensive or of the same depth as the curriculum of children in mainstream schooling

and

> [t]heir language development and learning process are hindered by not taking place in an environment where they learn alongside native speakers of English with a full curriculum.
>
> (Commission for Racial Equality 1986, pp.5, 17)

Partial Exclusion: Withdrawing Students in School

The Calderdale Enquiry not only sounded the death-knell for off-site language centres in the UK, it also impacted upon the way learning was organized for multicultured students in mainstream schools – in particular lending strength to the argument that students should be fully integrated into mainstream *classes* since to withdraw them from these was, effectively, little better than withdrawing them from ordinary schools altogether. Thus, in 1985, Silvaine Wiles of the Inner London Education Authority's Centre for Urban Educational Studies was able to offer the following advice to English teachers in UK schools:

> Research has shown that the more you take children out of the main-stream class for help with their English the less progress they are likely to make in the learning of the language. Although surprising at first, this finding is consistent with what we know about the factors which are conducive to language learning. The main problems of a withdrawal system are these. Firstly, it removes children from natural models of the target language, the native English speakers in the class, and gives them the adult teacher as the only available model; by doing so it promotes a form of communication which is tiring and difficult to handle naturally – and for this reason the sessions tend to be adult-dominated and, from the learner's point of view, relatively unproductive. Secondly, the system is difficult to organize: you tend to end up with groups of children of similar age but varying linguistic levels (in which case, why withdraw?) *or* with groups of children at the same linguistic level but of varying ages (in which case there are problems in relating the work of the group to differing curriculum demands). Thirdly, the social arguments against separate reception units apply to some extent to the withdrawal system; withdrawal is often associated by pupils themselves with abnormality.
>
> (Wiles 1985a, p.21)

In spite of this recognition of the relevance of the argument against off-site exclusion to on-site exclusion, the large-scale withdrawal of bilingual students remains a popular option with many schools: indeed, in some institutions teachers continue to militate – apparently from the best of motives – for moves *back towards* increased withdrawal of bilingual students, away from policies forged in the 1970s and 1980s of increasing their inclusion in mainstream subject classes (Moore 1996b). Given that, in the wealth of literature on this issue (for example, Brumfit and Johnson 1979; Dulay, Burt and Krashen 1982; Krashen 1982; Levine 1983, 1990; Wiles 1985a, 1985b), there is no cohesive argument in favour of withdrawal, we might speculate that the motives behind such moves are concerned primarily with emotive rather than educational concerns.

Such a view is given some support by the recorded views of teachers themselves. The following exchange of views, for example, occurred via an internal questionnaire organized by the head of one EAL department (Moore 1995):

Teacher 1: *Removing pupils from mainstream classes is racist. It cuts them off from large areas of the standard curriculum, from exposure to the ordinary language of their monolingual peers, and, most importantly, from monolingual peers themselves. It creates ghettos.*

Teacher 2: *What is the point of putting non-English-speaking pupils straight into the mainstream if they can't even understand what is going on? That is not 'exposure' to the curriculum: it's just demoralizing. It's also racist. What you end up with are ghettos within the classroom, with the pupils' lack of English simply being exposed to the other pupils and becoming the object of ridicule.*

What is interesting in these divergences of view within the same educational establishment is the rationale behind them. With Teacher 2, for instance, it isn't simply a matter of washing one's hands of the situation: here the preference for withdrawal appears to emerge from a genuine professional concern as to what is best for bilingual students given the prevailing circumstances. The same is equally true of Teacher 1. Indeed, in this case both teachers claim to have the best interests of their bilingual students at heart, each condemning the other's position as both impracticable and *racist*.

What emerges from internal debates such as these is that there not only exists a polarity of views within the organization debate, but also a wide spectrum of opinion – and indeed no shortage of confusion and contradiction – between these polarities, which often counterbalance teachers' professional views as to what, in an ideal world, is *desirable* ('of course bilingual students should follow exactly the same curriculum as monolingual students') with what the same teachers consider *possible given current circumstances* ('they simply don't understand a word of what I'm saying'). These contradictions, which are reminiscent of Edwards and Mercer's examples of teachers overtly espousing one educational philosophy while finding themselves constrained covertly to practise another (Edwards and Mercer 1987), find their partial explanation in Keddie's account of the differences between 'educationist' and 'teacher' contexts (Keddie 1971): that is to say, the notion that what seems like good practice in theory, away from the actuality of classroom interaction, may be rejected for alternative practice in the classroom itself, where more practical, immediate concerns ('How can I get these children to be quiet?') or even different sorts of questions altogether ('What will other people think of what I'm doing?') are prioritized in the teacher's mind.[7]

It is important to note, in the light of observations I have already made about teachers' and schools' culturist practices, that teachers are genuinely concerned about these issues, not just collectively but individually, and that they do lose sleep over them. That such tensions exist 'within' individual teachers' minds (intrapersonally) as well as *between* teachers (interpersonally) is demonstrated by the following examples, also cited in Moore (1995), drawn from questionnaire responses at a school in which there had been a radical shift of emphasis away from withdrawal towards increased mainstream support, resulting in teachers in all subject areas seeing a lot more of the school's bilingual students than had hitherto been the case. Though the argument about withdrawal-versus-support seemed to have been moving toward resolution at the institutional level in this school, leaving the way open to more rigorous reappraisals of pedagogy, individual opinions on the wisdom of such a shift continued to be very varied and were to remain so for a period of two years.

Teacher A (English): *I have one support teacher once a week for an English class that is nearly fifty per cent non-English-speaking. A lot of our work is based on literature: it has to be. So what am I supposed to do? Ignore the literature side to the detriment of the English-speaking children, or press on with it knowing that for fifty per cent of the class it's a complete waste of time – time that could be better spent with a specialist [EAL] teacher learning the language? Give me more support and I'd be delighted to have a class full of bilingual children. The way things are, it's not fair to anyone.*

Teacher B (Mathematics): *I'm supported in my [Year 7 class] for every lesson, and from my point of view it works very well. I mean, I don't know how I'd cope without it, to be honest. But I'm not convinced it's best for the children. What they really need is not just an [EAL] teacher[:] I think for real support*

| | *they should have a bilingual teacher in with them – even one maths lesson a week would be okay. That way, you could make sure they were getting the basic concepts, which at the moment I'm not sure they always are.* |
| *Teacher C (Science):* | *I've no objections at all to ESL children doing their science or any other subject with the other children – as long as they are getting something out of it. But at the moment it's just a matter of sink or swim, which in my view is not good for anybody. Unless there are sufficient resources to make life in mainstream classes more productive for them, I think we should use the limited resources we have in a different way.* |

Statements such as these go some way toward explaining some of the unhelpful pedagogies and confusions we shall examine in subsequent chapters – where, for example, teachers claim to value marginalized students' cultures but, in the classroom situation, are constrained to *support* the marginalization of such cultures. They are also, however, often illustrative of a gulf between teachers' private views regarding the education of bilingual students and their public views as expressed in a range of whole-school policies that they either subscribe to or are instructed to subscribe to. The school from which the above examples are drawn, for instance, did much to demonstrate publicly the valuation of its multicultured student intake, greeting visitors to the school with welcoming signs in a variety of languages and making repeated reference to its 'rich linguistic and cultural mix' in its prospectus, in its range of formal policy statements (for the Arts, for Numeracy, for Literacy and so on) and in the details sent to applicants for teaching posts at the school. In all such statements, bilingualism in particular was described in positive terms and cultural pluralism was promoted as central to the school's ethos.

One explanation of these seeming contradictions has been put forward by Josie Levine in a particularly important contribution[8] to the support-versus-withdrawal debate in British schools. Taking a strong 'anti-withdrawal' perspective, Levine argues that everything we know about language and learning development points to the efficacy of a policy of bilingual children being educated in mainstream classes alongside monolingual peers (Levine 1983, 1990). Since this is the norm of educational provision for all children, the onus, she argues, is on the 'withdrawers' to demonstrate the case for deviating from such a system. Such a case Levine finds unproven. Taking the withdrawers' central argument that bilingual children experience mainstream classes as 'places of incomprehension and racism', Levine suggests that 'special language classes can be equally poor places of learning' since neither the children nor the teachers have access to a wide enough curriculum, socially the children are ghettoized, and the specialist provision (with honourable exceptions) is too much based on the linguistic structures in isolation from the natural contexts in which they occur.

(Levine 1983, p.1)[9]

Levine concludes that the withdrawal of bilingual students from mainstream classes for specialist language work has come about not so much out of observations and understanding of such students' needs and learning processes, or out of related research, as out of a prioritization of *teachers'* needs, including the pleas of mainstream teachers (examples of which we shall visit towards the end of this section of the book) to get on with their 'normal work' without having to deal, additionally, with non-English-speaking students. Such an analysis offers one reason why a synthesis or resolution of contradictory views on support-versus-withdrawal has proved so difficult: that is to say, *the official location of the debate in the area of students' needs* ('I support this arrangement because it's in the students' best interests') *may have been fundamentally dishonest* – a way of taking emphasis away from the real, less acceptable reasons for withdrawal within a profession that prides itself on being caring and accommodatory.[10] Levine herself (Levine 1992) suggests that the organizational support–withdrawal debate in schools has acted – deliberately or incidentally – as something of a diversion from what ought to be the central issue: that is, not the *where* of teaching but the *how* – a dimension which inevitably forces the issue of institutional racism and culturism that the physical withdrawal of multicultured students denies on a day-to-day basis. (Put bluntly, when multicultured students spend a large proportion of their time in withdrawal groups, it often, for the subject teacher, becomes a case of 'out of sight, out of mind'. When such students are in the classroom on a regular basis, the pedagogical debate, which is also an ideological debate and a political debate, is inevitably activated.)

Levine's analysis is not meant to imply that mainstream classroom teachers simply do not care about bilingual students. Nor is such an implication borne out by evidence. For instance, over 90 per cent of teachers interviewed at School A (representing roughly 60 per cent of the staff as a whole) expressed, in various ways, genuine anxiety and even desperation over the education of the bilingual students in their classes. At the same school, everyone interviewed (67 per cent of the staff as a whole) valued the EAL support that was available to them and wanted more of it. Additionally, all these teachers agreed that full bilingual support (that is, the presence of first-language teachers working in the mainstream classroom alongside subject teachers) would represent the ideal situation. *Such data suggest the need to provide professional development for teachers that, among other things, reduces the tendency to panic when confronted by feelings of inad-*

equacy. (Most secondary-school teachers, for example, will be familiar with the sorts of feelings engendered by the contradiction of needing to get beginner-bilingual students through examinations in two years when the expected 'catch-up time' may be three times that long, and of the rejection of good practice precipitated by those feelings.) Such development would need to demonstrate to teachers that, however problematic inclusive education may seem, it is still preferable to large-scale withdrawal. It would also provide education for teachers on the processes by which early bilinguals *develop* their bilingualism – that, for example, the appearance of non-involvement typically demonstrated by such students in their early months in a new educational environment should not be treated as evidence that the student is (to quote another teacher) 'simply not learning anything [and] not able to cope'.

Towards Inclusion: Changing Attitudes towards Bilingualism

I have already indicated that while my initial research interest was in comparing different kinds of *provision* for bilingual students (in particular, comparing the relative merits and demerits of working with bilingual students in mainstream classes alongside majority-monolingual peers and of withdrawing bilingual students for specialist language support), it quickly became apparent that examples of effective and ineffective pedagogy could be found in either organizational system and that this was a factor in my switching my interest to strictly pedagogical issues. Without wanting to backtrack on that observation, it needs to be stated quite clearly that *although good pedagogy can exist in withdrawal situations, (a) this does not, in itself, render the system of withdrawal non-problematic, (b) good pedagogy can only ever be a very limited kind of good pedagogy, isolated within the individual practice of a particular teacher or teachers and constantly undermined by larger system of physical exclusion to which the student is subjected.* As Cummins has argued, occupying territory explored elsewhere by McLaren (1995) and having much, too, in common with the work of Foucault (for example, Foucault 1977), the act of physical exclusion of multicultured students effectively denies – or seeks to deny – the negotiation of those students' developing *identities*, turning the potential interaction space of the classroom, where teachers and students might cooperate within a framework of mutual accommodation, into a place of one-sided action and *in*action perfectly suited to cultural–linguistic *coercion* (Cummins 1996). While we might argue that the desires and wills of the individual actors normally render such efforts only ever partially successful (McLaren 1995), the impact on the student is still, typically, one of demoralization, low self-esteem and underachievement.[11] In such situations, the classroom fails to become a site of struggle and hope, engaging the mutual efforts of students and teachers, becoming instead a place of struggle *against* teachers as well as against systems, where hope is dented, and where identities are first fixed and then pathologized if they do not conform to certain base criteria.

The large-scale withdrawal of bilingual students from mainstream lessons is still the norm at some institutions. However, an awareness of the potential harmful effects on multicultured students of such withdrawal – coinciding, it must be added, with financial issues and the increased control of some schools over their budgets – has led to an increasing number of schools shifting their work with multicultured students towards the partial inclusion of 'mainstream support': that is to say, a situation in which bilingual students spend most of their time in the 'normal classroom' alongside monolingual peers, attempting much the same work but with some level of in-class support provided by a peripatetic EAL specialist. Such a shift (towards what I have called partial inclusion because, as we shall see, it typically includes high levels of *symbolic exclusion*) has been accompanied, inevitably and for the reasons cited above, by an opening or reopening of debates about pedagogy (Figure 4). Not surprisingly, this shift of debate *within* schools has been paralleled by a similar shift – albeit rather shadowy and uncertain – within the areas of research and theory.

If there had never been much research to support high levels of withdrawal of bilingual students, even when such an arrangement was the norm, there was, by contrast, even as off-site centres continued to exclude students permanently from normal society, a growing body of literature arguing for comprehensive packages of in-school reforms in the teaching of bilingual students in British schools (see, for example, Brumfit and Johnson 1979; Dulay, Burt and Krashen 1982; Krashen 1982; Wiles 1985a, 1985b). These included not only the integration of bilingual students into mainstream classes, but provision and time for them to develop skills in their own first

Figure 4 Paradigms of provision for bilingual learners and shifts in educational focus

Paradigm	Primary focus	Secondary focus
Full exclusion/ partial exclusion	Organization	Curriculum/pedagogy
↓	↓	↓
Partial inclusion (u)	Pedagogy	Curriculum/organization
Partial inclusion (d)		
↓	↓	↓
Full inclusion	Curriculum	Pedagogy(/organization)

languages, and calls for new pedagogies that gave primacy to previous and ongoing learning and language experiences, focusing on what such students already could do rather than on what they could not (see also Selinker 1974, Miller 1983). Much of this theory had arisen out of a radical change in how bilingualism was perceived, away from the view quoted by Appel and Muysken (1987, p.104) that 'human beings have a certain potential, or perhaps neural and psychological capacity, for language learning' so that 'knowing one language restricts the possibilities for learning other languages', towards a belief that bilingualism is, on the contrary, a potential linguistic and academic *advantage* to those who develop it. This view had, in turn, been supported by a range of published research suggesting clear benefits for bilingual students, both in terms of second-language acquisition and, over monolingual peers, in terms of general cognitive development, *provided such students were given opportunities to develop skills in their first languages alongside the learning of a second language*: that is, an *additive* conceptualization of bilingualism, akin to the *repertoire extension* concept of bidialectalism that I describe in the later chapters of this book. (See, in particular, Peal and Lambert 1962, Liedke and Nelson 1968, Ianco-Worrall 1972, Bullock 1975, Ben-Zeev 1977, Swain and Lapkin 1982, Swann 1985, Wright 1985.)

An increasing awareness among researchers and experts that, as the organizational issues appeared to resolve themselves in favour of mainstream support, pedagogy should be prioritized, is evident in the work of several theorists (for example, Levine 1992), some of whom have begun to examine classroom practice from the perspective of both teachers and learners (Bleach and Riley 1985, National Writing Project 1990, Warner 1992, Moore 1993). The notion is also central to much of the earlier work of the linguist James Cummins, to whom we shall return later (see, especially, Cummins 1984, p.109). In developing his argument in favour of prioritizing pedagogy over such matters as the relative merits and demerits of 'maximum exposure' and 'linguistic mismatch' approaches to the education of bilingual students, Cummins suggests that teachers often – *regardless* of the specific arrangements in place – have lower expectations of bilingual students, and adopt different pedagogies when working with them, than is the case with monolingual students. In developing this argument, Cummins quotes Moll (1981, pp.439–40), who contrasts observations of high-level comprehension-oriented literacy activities taking place among a 'high ability' reading group in a Spanish (L1) lesson, with activities undertaken by the same group in an English (L2) classroom. In the latter classroom, the students are refused access to the higher-level comprehension activities, through being compelled to focus on 'the mechanical tasks of practising decoding skills, word sounds or lexical meaning'. This pedagogical mismatch is attributed by Moll to the English teachers' apparent assumption (implicitly questioned by the author) that 'decoding is a prerequisite to comprehension' and that 'correct pronunciation is the best index of decoding' (Moll 1981, p.439).

Partial Inclusion: Undeveloped and Developed Varieties

The movement of the 'bilingual debate' away from matters of organization to matters of pedagogy also suggests a shifting of the debate away from a view which pathologizes the learner (Walkerdine 1990), towards one which focuses on in-service training and professional development for teachers, and which reconceptualizes the school experiences of both bilingual and bidialectal students in terms of race and ethnicity. In the early 1980s, when the shift was experienced by teachers and schools with particularly dramatic force, this movement was to find critical support in both likely and unlikely places. In one London borough in the early 1980s, for example, the quick dismantling of an off-site unit by a local council was swiftly followed by the establishment of a team of experienced teachers whose task was to re-educate schools to teach bilingual and bidialectal students within a specifically anti-racist paradigm. At the same time, it was possible for a student of Afro-Caribbean origin who had spent the first three years of his schooling in 'remedial' classes aimed at 'rectifying his poor use of language' to achieve a pass in the 'O' level GCE examination in English Literature[12] through an enlightened Oxford and Cambridge Examination Board that allowed him to submit his coursework essay – worth up to 50 per cent of his overall mark – not only *about* Caribbean poetry but in a written version of a Caribbean dialect *of* English (Moore 1987a).

Following the euphoria of such apparent revolutions, we are now in a phase of less radical practice in the UK, in part engendered and very powerfully supported by an education policy that bears all the appearance of a fundamentalist revival.[13] Thus, while bilingual students are generally (though not exclusively) included *physically* both in schools and in individual school classrooms, we can begin to trace two strands of inclusive classroom practice and two parallel areas of theory and research. The former of these, which I want to categorize as *undeveloped* partial inclusion, articulates with mainstream teaching-and-learning theory and with what has come to be known as multicultural education. Its main field of debate is that of pedagogy. The latter – which I shall call *developed* partial inclusion – leans more towards the sociology of culture for its support. It is more actively anti-racist and, hence, more directly and consciously *political*. Its main field of debate is that of empowerment (Figure 2).

In terms of actual classroom practice and teaching philosophy, the two forms of partial inclusion can most easily be identified with reference to the notion of *symbolic* inclusion and exclusion. Symbolic exclusion, it will be remembered (see Chapter 1), is characterized by an abiding determination of the social system, often manifested in the deeds of individual actors, to identify certain groups as cultural minorities and then to refuse to acknowledge or validate the non-dominant skills and accomplishments of those groups, or to recognize, accept and embrace *difference. Typically, this includes the denial or marginalization of minoritized students' first languages: not just the words, sounds and visual appearance of those languages, but also their proto-cols, their styles and their genres.* In classroom situations, such exclusion means that although multicultured students may be physically present, they may regularly find themselves on the wrong end of routine symbolic marginalizations. Even when encouraged to feel welcome in the classroom (through smiles, through help with their work, through the publicizing of their strongest languages and so on), they are likely to find that their own cultural skills, values and practices are rendered largely invisible and invalid, while the dominant culture's skills, values and practices, which they must acquire if they are to succeed academically within UK schools, are presented and treated not as mere alternatives to their existing skills, values and practices but rather as the 'right and only' skills, values and practices (Apple 1979). As Giroux, providing a particularly illuminating description of the way in which hegemony operates at the local and personal level, has argued and as will be graphically demonstrated in the case studies that follow:

> Multiculturalism is generally about Otherness, but it is written in ways in which the dominating aspects of white culture are not called into question. ... [T]he norm of whiteness [becomes] an ethnic category that secures its dominance by appearing to be invisible.
>
> (Giroux 1992, p.117)

Even in the physically inclusive classroom, multicultured students can expect to experience exclusion through the kind of 'double invisibilization' described by Giroux: on the one hand, their existing cultural experiences and expertise are rendered invisible by a refusal to allow them to penetrate a curriculum which is resistant to genuine change (Moore 1998); on the other hand, that curriculum is presented – is made to appear to 'present itself' – as a handed-down item received equally by all members of society regardless of who they are or what positions of power they occupy – that is, those who have manufactured the curriculum hide, like cat burglars, all evidence of their part in its construction: innocent bystanders who just happen to be handily placed to help initiate others into its emancipatory wonders.

In partial inclusion this is the view that is implicit in practice, even if it is not the view expressed and supported by the often hard-pressed teacher, who may find they can do little more than assume the role of clearing up and making themselves generally useful after a particularly distressing accident. There are, however, two kinds of partial inclusion: one which finds its roots in the kinds of pedagogy that tended to be found in off-site centres and in withdrawal groups (Wiles 1985a) – what we might call the undeveloped model of the 'basics discourse' – and one which has far more in common with some of the multicultural, student-centred practices associated with mixed-ability teaching and, at its best, with anti-racist teaching (Figure 5).

The undeveloped variety of partial inclusion provides the fewest difficulties for teachers, since it suggests the least ambivalence. This kind of approach, which owes much in terms of its form and content to TEFL (the teaching of English as a *foreign* language), concentrates on 'providing pupils' (as the head of School C put it) with 'the language skills they will need in order to cope with the curriculum' (Moore 1995, p.87). These are the basic academic and social skills of English grammar and vocabulary, seasoned with a generous pinch of spelling and punctuation. The purposes to which those skills will be put – that is to say, matters to do with the nature and content of the curriculum and of formal assessment processes – are not an issue in this discourse. Teachers may – and more often than not do – introduce 'multicultural exemplars' in teaching students within this discourse, and may make efforts to discover and build on existing experience and expertise; however, the prime function of their practice is to introduce, in a simple, incremental, 'no nonsense' (and therefore, necessarily, uncritical) way the basics required for potential success within the British educational system. The key pedagogic identity associated with such an approach, which often characterizes – for the reasons outlined by Wiles (1985a) – the kind of teaching we might expect to find in withdrawal classes, I want to describe as 'the teacher as pedagogic missionary'. This identity often results in a highly selective use of cognitive–linguistic inputs on the teacher's part (Wiles 1985a), leading, as we shall see in the following chapter, to the bilingual student's exposure to unnatural language forms that dictate the cognitive–academic levels at which they are encouraged to operate.

The *developed* variety of partial inclusion – which, I shall argue, results in more effective teaching and learning but often engenders more *angst* in the teacher because of the questions and issues it raises – can be divided into two varieties: the 'multicultural discourse', which has, as it were, one foot

Figure 5 Models of partial inclusion (undeveloped and developed)

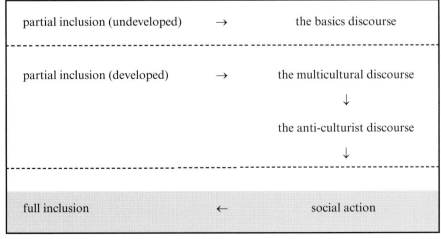

still in the undeveloped version of partial inclusion, and the 'anti-culturist discourse', which pushes close up against the boundaries of what can be achieved by individual schools and classroom teachers without recourse to social action. The multicultural discourse variety involves the physical inclusion of multicultured students in the mainstream classroom and goes some way towards symbolically including such students through all or any of the following broad strategies:

- Allowing and encouraging the use of the student's strongest language or languages where this enables them to tackle appropriately demanding tasks in a way denied them by an insistence on the use of English.
- Giving the students the same work to do – as far as seems reasonable and appropriate – as monolingual anglophone students in the class.[14]
- Acknowledging cultural difference in a limited way through such activities as the selection of multicultural teaching materials and exposing students' first-language speaking and writing skills to the class as a whole.

As we shall see in subsequent chapters, such strategies have a limited capacity for including multicultured students, but continue to marginalize them within the classroom through various forms of symbolic exclusion. Typically, these symbolic exclusions take the form of treating *difference* in cultural practices and expertise (a particular way of drawing a map, for example, that is significantly different from the conventional format used within dominant Western cultures) as examples of deficiency, failure or lack of understanding on the student's part. Thus, when a bilingual student writes a story, in English, in which the element of parable is more important than characterization or 'plot', the teacher may perceive – and effectively dismiss – the work as deficient or 'wrong', rather than seeing it as simply belonging to a different set of cultural preferences – a different raft of *genres* – than those espoused by UK public examination criteria. Such activities may be viewed as specific manifestations of the ways in which, to quote Perera and Pugliese describing the situation in Australia, 'assimiliationist ideologies and practices … continue to underpin the core structures of multiculturalism' (Perera and Pugliese 1998, p.162).

The 'anti-culturist' discourse seeks to take as full account of difference as is possible without claiming an expert's knowledge of the full range of cultural practices of all the multicultured students in the classroom. In the evaluation and analysis of students' work, on which it structures ongoing pedagogy, it begins by asking: *what does this student's work tell me about their existing cognitive–symbolic skills, including the way in which their existing practice may differ from the kind(s) of practice in which they will need to develop expertise if they are to succeed within a culturally biased education system?* As we shall see in Chapter 5, such a question can lead to more helpful pedagogic practices, often leading, particularly in the case of bi-dialectal students (Chapters 6 and 7), to cooperative interrogations on the part of students and teachers of the existing power relations, discursive in/exclusions[15] and consequent curriculum bias within which all school students operate. I shall argue in Chapters 4 and 5 that in order for teachers to operate in this way they must first develop an understanding of hegemonic practice in general educational terms, and in its particular manifestations in the classroom setting, leading to an understanding of culturist practice in terms of 'the creation and reproduction of a society in which the voices of the center appear either invisible or unimplicated in the historical and social construction of racism as an integral part of their own collective identity' (Giroux 1992, p.116). A prerequisite of the development of such an understanding is that teachers first make visible to themselves the 'voices of the center', both as they are manifested in the arbitrariness of the school curriculum and formal assessment criteria, and as they are manifest within their own individual classroom practice and assessment procedures: what we might call a process of ethnic or cultural decentring (Moore 1993). It is hoped that the case studies included in these chapters, along with those in Chapters 6 and 7, will support teachers in their efforts to achieve such a decentring, and in so doing to support improved teaching *practice* within the constraining culturist frameworks within which they have to operate.

It is precisely those constraining frameworks which present the limits beyond which individual classroom action cannot pass without joining others in collective, extra-classroom action. Teachers can, to an extent, express their personal valuations of 'alternative' cultural forms and practices, for example, but they cannot, in an instant, do anything about sets of National Curriculum or public examination criteria that clearly devalue such forms and practices. As I have argued elsewhere (Moore 1998), although we have witnessed considerable developments in multicultural education and consequent pedagogic practices in the UK during the last twenty-five years, the formal criteria by which students are assessed, with their inbuilt cultural bias, have remained largely unaltered. A similar point has been made by Cummins, who (with reference to North American education systems) refers to studies which suggest that 'despite the appearance of change with respect to nondiscriminatory assessment, the underlying structure has remained essentially intact' (Cummins 1996, p.161; see also Perera and Pugliese 1998). In Cummins' analysis, this is because '[m]ost of the [recent educational] reforms have focused on cosmetic modifications to surface structures, leaving intact the deep structures that reflect patterns of disempowerment in the wider society' (Cummins 1996, p.v). Cummins suggests that the move from individual pedagogic action to collective social action, through which practitioners militate for changes in those deep structures, involves the need for teachers to replace an existing 'legitimating' function (that is, one of acceptance of current assessment criteria and curriculum content) with one of 'advocacy' (one of reasoned, professional challenge) (Cummins 1996, p.162).

The Future: Social Action and the Promise of Full Inclusion

It is through collective social action – which (as needs to be stressed again) is not to be confused with a call to teachers to take up arms and singlehand-edly right society's wrongs (a variation of recent UK government-speak – although this, of course, seems to imply that teachers are largely to *blame* for society's ills) – that teachers can begin to see a way of moving beyond the constraints of dominant educational ideologies and their imposed frame-works, towards militating for a change in those ideologies and frameworks. Such militations – which involve serious, critical engagement with questions about what public education should look like both now and in the future – challenge existing forms of curriculum and assessment, and are infused with a realistic, post-Enlightenment version of an educational discourse of eman-cipation 'concerned above all with liberating individuals and groups from constraints which adversely affect their life chances' (Giddens 1991, p.210). For Giddens, 'emancipatory politics' combines the effort 'to shed shackles of the past, thereby permitting a transformative attitude towards the future' with the aim 'of overcoming the illegitimate domination of some individuals or groups by others'. In so doing, it 'makes primary the imperatives of *justice, equality* and *participation*'. If successful, emancipatory politics leads to 'life politics', which 'presumes (a certain level of) emancipation': a 'poli-tics of choice' (Giddens 1991, pp.211–12).

The notion that educators might promote (practically and philosophi-cally) both equality and difference in ways that radically challenge existing 'wisdom' (indeed, the notion that educators can effectively promote equality and difference *only* by mounting an effective challenge to existing wisdom) is potentially a very exciting one. It is also, however, a very daunting one, if only because of the resistance it is likely to be met with *by* that existing wisdom – or rather by those powerful social groups in whose best interests that wisdom operates. As Chomsky has observed:

> In most fields [society wants] students to be obedient and submissive. ... Now teachers can try, and do break out of that, but they will surely find if they go too far that as soon as it gets noticed there'll be pressures to stop them.
>
> (Chomsky 1995, p.141)[16]

Without underestimating the difficulties of social action, there are educa-tional commentators who express a guarded optimism in this area, engendered partly by a recognition that the world is already changing in quite rapid and radical ways – some of which sit relatively comfortably with the kinds of educational reform being proposed by social activists – and that the future of educational practice is inextricably tied up with the future of the human race. For such commentators, it is important to find congruencies of philosophy and interest *as a way of celebrating difference and promoting change.* Cummins, for instance, has suggested that 'the economic and diplomatic realities of our independent global society in the 21st century demand enormous critical literacy and problem-solving abilities and the constant crossing of cultural and linguistic boundaries' (Cummins 1996, p.220), suggesting that

> coercive relations of power have reached a point of diminishing returns, even for those socially advantaged groups whose interests they are intended to serve. The fiscal and social costs of maintaining the current structure of privilege and resource distribution far outstrip the costs that would be involved in shifting to more collaborative relations of power.
>
> (Cummins 1996, p.222)

Cummins' view of the world, in contrast to that embedded in – and in a sense preserved by – the current curriculum in UK schools, suggests that nations which persist in validating only very narrow ranges of cultural expertise are in danger of financially and culturally collapsing in upon themselves, since

> cultural diversity is the norm in both the domestic and international arenas. Around the world we see unprecedented population mobility and intercultural contact. ... Educators concerned with preparing students for life in the 21st century must educate them for global citizenship.
>
> (Cummins 1996, p.224)

If such analyses are correct then radical, critical teachers can take heart that, although their desires for a better education constructed on fairer, more equitable principles may be met with immediate scorn, and though they may themselves be pathologized as crazy, overly idealistic, dogmatic or naive, they may well find some measure of support in the broader global trends for the oppositional arguments they put before elected representatives and other interested parties. Those arguments will support new forms of pedagogy that are more genuinely empowering and that move the attack to the final obstacle in front of genuine pluralism: that is, the entrenched, ethnocentric cultural imperialism and coercion of dominant social groups, as enshrined in such aspects of the legal framework as National Curricula and public examinations. They will do this taking full account of the fact that as long as there is a system of universal public examination incorporating future-influencing grades, and as long as that system retains its cultural bias, partial inclusion is all that schools and teachers can, in them-selves, expect to achieve.

In the meantime, there are forms of pedagogy that teachers *can* engage in, inside the classroom and within the current constraints, that go beyond the recognition and valuation of multicultured students' cultural practices and experiences, towards sharing with them an understanding of how – and why – such practices and experiences came to be marginalized in the first place. This kind of teaching – sometimes known as 'transformative pedagogy'[17] – centralizes what McLaren and others have called critical literacy (McLaren 1988): that is, the development of sophisticated reading and writing skills in ways that not only help multicultured students become functionally and culturally literate in more than one language (what Cummins 1996, p.74, has called '[e]ffective instruction that will give students access to the power of language and accelerate their academic growth') but that empower them to challenge the status quo that represses and coerces them.

Notes

1   School A is also referred to as 'Company Road' in Moore 1995.
2   'English as an Additional Language'. This term continues to replace ESL ('English as a Second Language') in UK schools, indicative of a growing under-standing among educators that bilingual students may, in addition to English, be fluent in two or more other languages.
3   For an explanation of this term, see Chapter 1, Note 1.
4   See also Perera and Pugliese's account of the treatment of indigenous peoples in Australia (Perera and Pugliese 1998).
5   See also Ryan (1972). The notion of the multicultured student as victim is a dangerous and misleading one, not only when applied in the circumstance quoted, but when used in arguments supportive of radical pedagogies. Multicultured students are, of course, on the receiving end of cultural bias. They also, however, are living, thinking, active citizens who, by and large, refuse to surrender meekly to the symbolic enslavement of dominant cultural groups. A parallel danger is in teachers viewing *themselves* as victims, and the kinds of message this can send to their students. As one EAL teacher put it to me in inter-view: 'If you feel victimized yourself, you just develop a siege mentality and then the victimization gets passed down the line to your students. They pick up on your frustrations, get a sense that you don't like the situation – which to them is like you don't like working with *them* – and this damages their self-esteem irreparably.' Such a view was borne out at this teacher's school by numerous observations from students themselves – for example, 'Miss So-and-So, she don't like teaching us [Bangladeshi] kids.'
6   The recent UK OFSTED document *The Assessment of the Language Development of Bilingual Pupils*, for example, offers as exemplary the practice of '[o]ne L[ocal] E[ducation] A[uthority]' which 'carries out initial interviews and assessments in both the pupil's first language and English ... in order to build up a full picture of prior attainment and current need' (OFSTED 1997, p.5). That only 'one' authority is cited as meeting what would seem a fundamental human right is as alarming as the offering up of the case as 'good' rather than *compulsory* practice.
7   See Keddie (1971, p.139) on attitudes to streaming: also Sharp and Green's distinction between 'teaching perspectives' which are 'situationally' specific and

'teaching ideologies' which relate to wider issues including 'the role and functions of education in the wider social context' (Sharp and Green 1975, pp.68–70). Both Edwards and Mercer and Keddie, however, were interested in *unconscious* contradictions, rather than in teachers deliberately weighing situations up. At all the institutions cited in this book, there was abundant evidence of teachers making both conscious and unconscious decisions. In the case of unconscious classroom decisions, these often appeared to contradict what teachers said and thought they were doing.

8   Important, that is, because the contribution was aimed specifically at practising teachers.

9   See also Wright (1985, p.6) and, for a more comprehensive survey of the support–withdrawal debate, Levine 1990.

10 For a related argument, suggesting that schools use student-focused 'formal equality' as a 'cloak and a justification' for practices which actually promote inequality, see Bourdieu 1974.

11 Or, of course, revolution and resistance of a kind that seldom leads to the sort of academic success that such exclusion purports to achieve on behalf of those being excluded. See, too, Willis 1977 on the school experiences of white working-class students.

12 The General Certificate of Education (GCE) 'O' (Ordinary) level examinations represented the higher tier of a two-tier system then in operation in the UK for (typically) sixteen-year-olds. 'O' level examinations were available in a number of subjects, including English Language and English Literature. Successful candidates might go on to sit GCE 'A' (Advanced) level examinations – usually in three or four subject areas. The particular examination sat by this individual comprised 50 per cent coursework and 50 per cent end-of-course examination.

13 Advances in teaching multicultured students are clearly endangered by such policies, whose dominant 'back-to-basics' ideology is profoundly suspicious of anything that challenges the status quo.

14 An interesting and important issue here concerns the way in which teaching and learning are organized within the institution as a whole. I have tended to assume so-called mixed-ability groupings. However, in schools which set, band or stream their students – as many in the UK increasingly do – the bilingual student is likely already to have been subject to some form of symbolic exclusion prior to their allocation to a class or classes – that is, at the assessment stage. Thus, in some schools bilingual students will find themselves in mixed-ability groupings where all students are expected and encouraged to follow the same curriculum, while in others bilingual students may find themselves assigned to 'lower ability groupings' where they may be given simpler work – especially where a tiered examination syllabus is being used.

15 There is, of course, an argument that, to a considerable extent, all socialization is about the selective and phased exclusion and inclusion of human beings from and into certain formalized discursive practices. As with any club, this is carried out sometimes according to age, sometimes according to notions of conformity which might include such issues as 'Do we think this person has the skills and interests we are looking for?', 'Does this person have the kind of appearance we find acceptable?', 'Is this person within the right age-group for us?', 'Is this "our kind of person" in terms of their cultural interests and practices?' and so on. In education, the notion of levels or stages of development and achievement, rules of conduct, examination criteria and so forth may be said to illustrate and signal just such an in/exclusive discourse.

16 See also Willis's observation in relation to 'progressivism' that changes in education have neither been brought about nor been caused by any 'real shift in basic

philosophies' (Willis 1977, p.178), Bourdieu's claim that changes in educational systems tend to be 'morphological', affecting 'nothing essential' (Bourdieu 1976, p.115), and Bruner's observation that 'educational reform confined only to the schools and not to the society at large is doomed to eventual triviality' (Bruner 1976, p.114).

17 Cummins (1996) identifies three broad kinds of pedagogy: 'traditional', 'progressive' and 'transformative'.

3 Bilingual Education Theory
In Support of Inclusion

Principles of Good Practice

I have already indicated that this is not a book 'about' bilingualism. However, because the bulk of the book looks at cultural issues through examining the experiences of young learners who are bilingual, because it is necessary to provide some theoretical context to support our understanding of these experiences, and because the bulk of current theory and research works oppositionally to much classroom practice – including the physical and symbolic withdrawal of students and the missionary approach to teaching – it is necessary to provide some brief background, and in particular to outline the principal arguments, drawn from research, that have informed my own presentations and analyses of classroom events. Having summarized these arguments as a way of simultaneously suggesting some basic principles of effective classroom practice, I will consider in a little more detail the possibilities of three particular strands of bilingual education theory for promoting greater physical–symbolic inclusion in the school classroom. These three strands are:

- notions of language-in-context
- distinctions between 'everyday' and 'academic' language
- the 'transferability' of language skills

The following, then, are the central research arguments to which this book subscribes:

1   There is an impressive – one might say irresistible – body of research evidence to show that bilingualism has the *capacity* to be linguistically and cognitively advantageous (and therefore *should* be linguistically and cognitively advantageous), provided it is allowed to be so by monolingual-dominated schools. (This research has included several longitudinal studies, including those by Malherbe 1946, Phillips 1972, San Diego City Schools 1975, Carey and Cummins 1983.) While it is true that not all theory and research has pointed to academic advantages for bilingual

students (for example, Coleman et al. 1966, Christopherson 1973, Skutnabb-Kangas and Toukamaa 1976), the weight of argument leans very heavily the other way. Furthermore, as Cummins has argued, any actual problems related to bilingualism are less readily attributable to 'bilingualism per se' than to 'the social and educational conditions under which minority students acquire their ... languages' (Cummins 1984, p.103; see also Little and Willey 1981, Miller 1983, Wright 1985).

2　It is becoming increasingly accepted that the cognitive levels of work undertaken by bilingual students must, as with all other students, be *cognitively demanding* (Vygotsky 1962, Cummins 1996) and not allowed to become cognitively *un*demanding by being 'led' by the simple forms of language which are often used by teachers in the early stages of a students' developing bilingualism (Moore 1995).[1] While it is clearly a major challenge for schools to provide work at appropriate cognitive levels given the monstrous shortage of funds and resources to support such work, it is a challenge that equally clearly cannot be ignored or denied.

3　It is important for bilingual students to be allowed and encouraged to use their 'first' language or languages in learning situations in addition to their developing additional language. This implies an 'additive' model of bilingualism (Cummins 1996, p.147), in which students learn additional languages and cultural practices while at the same time continuing to develop those they are already versed in, rather than a 'subtractive' model which suggests that only through the abandonment of an existing language and culture will people ever succeed in developing expertise in a new one. As Lucas and Katz have stated with reference to classrooms in which first languages were used alongside developing additional ones:

> In practice ... the classrooms were multilingual environments in which students' native languages served a multitude of purposes and functions. They gave students access to academic content, to classroom activities, and to their own knowledge and experience; gave teachers a way to show their respect and value for students' languages and cultures; acted as a medium for social interaction and establishment of rapport; fostered family involvement; and fostered students' development of, knowledge of, and pride in their native languages and cultures.
> (Lucas and Katz 1994, p.545)

In translating these basic principles into broad strategies for classroom practice, James Cummins has usefully suggested a 'four-phase instructional framework'. Within this framework, teachers of bilingual students (be they EAL teachers or mainstream subject teachers who have bilingual students in their classes):

- Activate prior knowledge/build background knowledge
- Present cognitively engaging input with appropriate contextual supports

- Encourage active language-use to connect input with students' prior experience and with thematically related content
- Assess student learning in order to provide feedback that will build language-awareness and efficient learning strategies

(Cummins 1996, p.75)

This instructional framework is structured around four basic components geared to give students 'access to the power of language and [to] accelerate their academic growth'. These components are:

- Active communication of meaning
- Cognitive challenge
- Contextual support
- Building student self-esteem

(Cummins 1996, p.74)

As we shall see in the case studies that follow, the most effective pedagogy contains each of these components. My own studies, however, suggest that it is the particular issue of *contextual support* and how this is perceived by teachers that is the key to effective pedagogy, since the other three components tend to flow naturally from it.

Contextual Support: The Argument for Physical and Symbolic Inclusion

Levine has argued persuasively against attempting to teach bilingual students 'linguistic structures in isolation from the natural contexts in which they occur' (Levine 1983, p.1). In her model of what might be called *language-in-context*, the natural context within which classroom language of all kinds[2] is best learned is classroom language itself: the bilingual student, that is, is immersed in the deep pool of language and learning activities in which the monolingual students bathe in the normal classroom and, often with the help of an experienced EAL teacher working *in situ*, learns to bathe *with* them – an approach which, of course, demands the bilingual student's physical inclusion in the classroom. Hand-in-hand with this approach stands an overall strategy that seeks to take full account and advantage of bilingual students' *existing skills and experience*, and, in particular, of the fact that 'consonant with their age and experience, [bilingual students] already have a more developed use of at least one other language' (Levine 1993, p.191) – a strategy which demands not only the bilingual students' physical presence in the mainstream classroom, but their *symbolic inclusion* too: that is to say, the inclusion of their existing linguistic–cognitive skills and their existing experiences and perceptions of the world – what we might call, collectively, their existing *voices*. This existing experience provides a 'second context' for the

45

bilingual student's cognitive–linguistic development, since '[i]t makes both human and pedagogic sense to use the natural features of pupils' lives to build an educational context out of what they already have access to and out of what they already know and can do' (Levine 1993, p.192; see also Wiles 1985a, p.20, and 1985b).

Levine's model of language-in-context, used to support the inclusion of bilingual students in mainstream school classrooms, finds strong support in the writing of L.S. Vygotsky (1962, 1978). Like Levine, Vygotsky does not attempt to separate out language and cognition as separate entities, but rather views 'word meanings' as the elemental illustration of how, from a very early stage in a child's life, thought and language operate together as essentially two aspects of the same indivisible whole (for example, Vygotsky 1962, p.3). Thus, teaching students to recognize and reproduce vocabulary separate from a true understanding of that vocabulary *can* be achieved by the teacher (just as students can – often usefully – learn to recite their times-tables); however, it is, in the general run of things, a hollow, pointless achievement, accomplishing nothing but 'empty verbalism, a parrotlike repetition of words by the child, *simulating* a knowledge of the corresponding concepts but actually covering up a vacuum' (Vygotsky 1962, p.83; my emphasis). With young people who are sequential bilinguals, perhaps only beginning to learn an additional language at the age of eleven or so, it is important to remember that while, on the one hand, much vocabulary-learning may be a case of learning new labels for *existing concepts*, the inseparability of thought from language that already characterizes their cognitive–linguistic development and achievement is not suddenly put into abeyance for some other, separatist mode of development to take over.

The second way in which Levine's model of language-in-context draws support from Vygotsky's lies in its refusal to perceive language merely in terms *of* vocabulary and grammatical structures: that is, it refuses to limit its notion of language to 'the sentence' which, as it were, can enjoy a kind of life 'outside' of context.[3] Rather, language is viewed by Levine as *language-in-use* – that is to say, as the making of individual and collective *utterances* within the constraints of particular *discourses* (Bakhtin 1986). In this view of language, text (what is said or written) is inseparable from context (the 'situation' in which it is said or written), and language and learning are approached as *social* phenomena in whatever site they are located. It is insufficient, in this model, for the bilingual student to be able to recognize and reiterate appropriate words and grammatical structures: they must also be aware of language in the broader sense of the complexities and protocols of intersubjective exchanges within the 'normal' classroom setting, both between student and teacher and between student and student. Teachers must also be aware of the importance of accumulative confidence development in additional-language development – and of the ways in which classroom and textual protocols can undermine this. To *remove* bilingual students from the mainstream classroom for language work is, according to this view, precisely to (attempt to) *decontextualize* it, *regardless of what other contextual framework might be provided.* The context for learning the normal language of the classroom can only be normal classroom language itself, as experienced in the normal classroom.

A second definition of language-in-context, that may be read as an elaboration and development of Levine's 'second context', is provided by James Cummins. With reference to bilingual children in the early stages of developing competence in an additional language, Cummins has suggested that

> the more initial reading and writing instruction can be embedded in a meaningful communicative context (i.e. related to the child's previous experience), the more successful it is likely to be. The same principle holds for L2 instruction. The more context-embedded the initial L2 input, the more comprehensible it is likely to be, and, paradoxically, the more successful in ultimately developing L2 skills in context-related situations. *A central reason why minority students have often failed to develop high levels of L2 academic skills is because their initial instruction has emphasized context-reduced communication insofar as instruction has been through English and unrelated to their prior out-of-school experience.*
>
> (Cummins 1984, p.141; my emphasis)

With the addition that instruction through English has often, in these situations, also been unrelated to students' *previous in-school experiences within different educational systems* (a point which becomes particularly significant when we examine classroom interactions in detail in Chapters 5 and 6), I would want to support Cummins' suggestions that:

1   Cognitive development needs to be contextualized within previous cognitive development and this cannot happen if instruction is solely through a language which the student is only just beginning to learn.

2   The learning *of* that language of instruction will be facilitated if cognitive development is allowed to develop through the use of the student's initially strongest language. Precisely this view was adopted, as we shall see, at one institution – School A – where students were allowed to write stories and discuss topics in their 'first language', but not at another – School B – where first languages were effectively banned from the classroom. The exclusion of first languages at this institution inevitably resulted in students following a curriculum designed for cognitive levels far below those they actually possessed. At School A, by comparison, different issues applied. Here, although first languages were included in one sense, elements of language-related cultural practices were often, as we shall see, excluded.

Cummins' definition of language-in-context, which implicitly supports the policy and practice of repertoire extension (not seeking to replace a student's first language with a second one, but helping the student to add second-language skills to existing first-language skills through building upon them) is not incompatible with Levine's. The first argues for the importance of bilingual students' experiencing of 'natural' classroom language alongside monolingual peers, the other for the need for instruction in and through the bilingual students' strongest language. Cummins offers a further argument, however, not just for instruction *through* first languages, but, especially in the case where students have poorly developed first-language skills (for example, students who may be very competent orally in their first language[s] but less so in terms of basic literacy), for continued instruction *of* that first language. (This might comprise, for example, continuing to develop first-language literacy skills rather than focusing only on the development of oral and literacy skills in the additional language as if starting 'from scratch'). As Cummins argues,

> for children whose L1 skills are less well developed in certain respects, intensive exposure to L2 in the initial grades is likely to impede the continued development of L1. This will, in turn, exert a limiting effect on the development of L2.

(Cummins 1979a, p.233)[4]

To summarize the language-in-context approach to teaching bilingual students, the context both for bilingual students' cognitive development and for their second-language development lies in what they already know and can do: in their prior experience and knowledge both of language and of the world. It is not merely a matter of providing them with contrived 'meaningful situations' in which to learn new language structures and vocabularies.

'Everyday' and 'Academic' Language: Cummins' BICS/CALP Hypothesis

At both of the main institutions from which I have drawn my case studies of bilingual students and their teachers, James Cummins' BICS/CALP theory was well known by all EAL support-teachers as well as by the headteachers and several mainstream subject teachers. Indeed, headteachers at both institutions were sufficiently familiar with the theory to be able to include it centrally in policy decisions related to organizational provision for bilingual students (Moore 1995), while at one institution the theory provided the topic for a staff-development session given by the EAL department to the rest of the school.

'BICS' is the acronym for Basic Interpersonal Communication Skills, a phrase offered by Cummins oppositionally to 'CALP', which stands for

Cognitive–Academic Language Proficiency (Cummins 1979b, 1984). Cummins' suggestion is that there are two different *kinds* of language-in-use: that which exists in the domain of everyday, personal ('social') interaction, and that which is involved in higher-order ('academic') thinking and concept development. Such a distinction is clearly problematic – tending to leave unexplored such matters as the essentially social nature of formal reasoning itself, or of the differences (if any) between 'language' and 'thought' – but it is, at the same time, not without potential advantage in arguing for a more inclusive approach to the teaching of bilingual students and indeed it may be said to have arisen partly from a desire to achieve such an end (Cummins 1984).

Basic Interpersonal Communication Skills (BICS) are defined by Cummins in terms of 'the manifestation of language proficiency in everyday contexts'. Cognitive–Academic Language Proficiency (CALP), on the other hand, is conceptualized in terms of 'the manipulation of language in decontextual-ized academic situations' (Cummins 1984, p.137; see also Skutnabb-Kangas and Toukamaa 1976). That is to say, these terms propose an essential difference (in parallel to Vygotskyan notions of 'everyday' and 'scientific' concepts [Vygotsky 1962]) between language which is used unconsciously or unreflect-ingly (the language of everyday social interaction, such as 'playground talk') and language about which one has to think (the language of learning; see also Vygotsky's notion of 'deliberation' [Vygotsky 1962, pp.100, 105], and Walkerdine 1982 on the development of 'formal reasoning'). In Cummins' formulation, the former kind of language is typically context-embedded,[5] with the ready availability of a wide range of non-verbal cues and clues (physical gestures, shared experiences and so on). It is also relatively un-demanding. The latter kind, by contrast, is 'context reduced' and more cognitively demanding, requiring reflections that are often internalized rather than obviously interpersonal.[6] Assessed on the basis of everyday, 'visible' language, Cummins argues, some bilingual students may be deemed to have reached relatively high levels of proficiency in their second language; that is to say, they converse quite fluently with their monolingual peers in social or 'non-academic' situations and discourses. Assessed on the basis of 'academic' language, however – that is, in the context of academic tasks – those same students' second-language proficiency, often confused with their general cognitive–linguistic proficiency, may be found seriously wanting.

The obvious advantage of Cummins' distinction, and one that has clear appeal to educationalists dedicated to combating institutional racism, is that it potentially shifts judgements of bilingual students' perceived academic failures in schools away from 'inherent' cognitive deficiencies, over which schools may find it relatively easy to claim to have no significant influence, towards issues of linguistic development for which the institution itself must clearly accept a major measure of responsibility. When bilingual students given IQ tests through the medium of their second language do badly, says

Cummins, too often cognitive reasons – for example, learning disability or retardation – are given for their poor performance, on the grounds, based on previous assessments of L2 proficiency in face-to-face 'social' situations, that they have already achieved levels of language proficiency sufficient to be able to cope with the tests on a purely linguistic level (Cummins 1984, p.130; see also Gonzalez 1993).

To recontextualize this within the British school system, where IQ tests are rarely used, such a misunderstanding can lead to the following argument:

> *I know from watching Student A chatting to her friends in English that she is L2 proficient: so when she did badly in her Science test it was certainly not attributable to any linguistic deficiency. Student A is clearly deficient academically.*

Such an argument can lead all too easily to:

> *I am not qualified to teach such a student: she needs special help in the classroom or needs to be withdrawn from the classroom for her own good*

and to the subsequent marginalization of the student, either within the teacher's classroom where she may be left to fend for herself, or in a withdrawal group where she will miss the company and language of her peers as well as exposure to the normal school curriculum.

Against this easily acquired deficit model of the bilingual student's perceived developmental difficulties, Cummins' argument suggests that initial assessments of Student A's linguistic proficiency may have been faulty because they failed to recognize that there are different *kinds* of proficiency required for different situations: that is to say, they only describe linguistic competence in one set of circumstances, where the competence is notably 'visible' (BICS), and not in another, where it is less visible and therefore less easy to assess (CALP). Not even the most impressive linguistic performance in the area of BICS, suggests Cummins, should lead the teacher to expect high academic performance; for that to occur, students need to be equally skilled in CALP, and CALP skills need to be developed *in addition to* BICS.

Common Underlying Proficiency and Language 'Transfer'

If the BICS/CALP hypothesis can be used in support of more inclusive education for bilingual students, so too can Cummins' elaborations of Common Underlying Proficiency (CUP) and linguistic transfer (Cummins 1979a, 1984).

The notion of Common Underlying Proficiency suggests that all languages have a great deal in common and that many of the skills already acquired in one language are 'transferable' to one or more other languages. One way of looking at this is to say that anyone about to learn an additional language already knows a lot about that language (in the sense that they know a lot about language*s* and about language-use in general) and already possesses the majority of the basic skills they will need in order to develop expertise in that language. This notion, which is extremely important in the context of the arguments I shall be making with respect to both bilingual and bidialectal students, stands in direct opposition to the Separate Underlying Proficiency (SUP) model of additional-language development still favoured by many linguists and, indeed, by many parents, students and teachers.

The SUP model, critiqued by Appel and Muysken, argues that

> human beings have a certain potential, or perhaps neural and physiolog-
> ical capacity, for language learning. If an individual learns more than
> one language, knowing one language restricts the possibilities for learning
> other languages. More proficiency in one language implies fewer skills in
> the other ones.
>
> (Appel and Muysken 1987, p.104)

In the SUP model of language development, skills – particularly language skills – learned in one language are considered to be not readily transferable to another, and consequently (from, of course, a purely academic–pragmatic point of view)[7] there may be little point in developing them if this takes up time and 'mental space' that would be better devoted to developing second-language skills and to learning concepts through those skills. It is evident that such a view supports the 'remove-and-replace' approach to bilingual students' first languages that has been popular in the past (Moore 1998), rather than the repertoire-extension approach implied by Cummins' and Levine's notions of language-in-context.

In opposition to this view, Cummins supports the 'developmental inter-dependence hypothesis', which states that

> there is an interaction between the language of instruction and the type
> of competence the child has developed in [their] L1 prior to school.
>
> (Cummins 1979a, p.233)

In an argument not dissimilar to Shirley Brice Heath's observations regarding the in- and out-school experiences of working-class American children (Brice Heath 1983), Cummins suggests that bilingual children can reach high levels of competence in their second language (L2) if their first language (L1) development, especially the use of linguistic functions relevant to school and to the development of 'scientific' vocabulary and concepts, is strongly promoted *outside* school (and, we might wish to add, *inside* school).

A high level of proficiency in L1, argues Cummins, makes possible a similarly high level of proficiency in L2. On the other hand,

> for children whose L1 skills are less well developed in certain respects, intensive exposure to L2 in the initial grades is likely to impede the continued development of L1. This will, in turn, exert a limiting effect on the development of L2.
>
> (Cummins 1979a, p.233)

Thus, in direct opposition to the philosophy and practice at some institutions, intensive 'EAL work' in the area of CALP can, according to Cummins, actually *hinder* a bilingual student's L2 development, as well as slowing down their cognitive development. (This may be seen as an argument in favour of bilingual rather than EAL support.) In Cummins' view, it is more important that CALP, in the early stages of bilingual development, is *promoted in and through the students' first language* – effectively excluded, of course, from many mainstream and withdrawal classrooms.

Cummins' argument leads him to propose the hypothesis that speaking, reading and writing skills learned in one language can subsequently be 'transferred' to another – as long as there is adequate exposure to the second language and sufficient motivation to learn it. Cummins develops this particular strand of his theory in Chapter 6 of his book *Bilingualism and Special Education: Issues in assessment and pedagogy* (1984) (see also Cummins 1996, pp.109–17). Using a variation of Shuy's iceberg metaphor (Shuy 1978), he demonstrates (Figure 6) how two languages – for example, English and Swahili – may appear very different on the surface (different characters, different sounds and so forth), but beneath the surface possess and demand the same basic requirements (for example, the ability to decode and interpret print, to argue a case, to tell a story, to interpret and respond to speech, to understand the differences between spoken and written language).

The most obvious example of literacy-related skills involved in Common Underlying Proficiency, argues Cummins, is conceptual knowledge. To illustrate this point he refers to the migrant child arriving in North America aged fifteen, who has an understanding of the concept 'honesty' in their own first language and, according to Cummins, needs only acquire a new label for it: the signifier 'honesty'. This student is contrasted with perhaps younger children who arrive in the same country with no properly developed concept of 'honesty', and who may have to acquire that concept through a second, initially weaker language. A clear implication is that certain concepts can only be acquired once a certain level and kind of language proficiency has been reached, and that for students weak in the language of instruction but strong in another language, at least some early learning and instruction – involving concept development – should be carried out in that language.

Figure 6 The 'Dual Iceberg' representation of bilingual proficiency

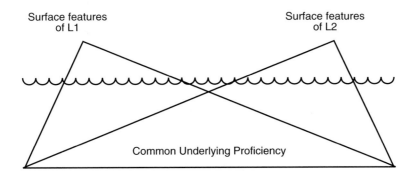

Cummins is not, perhaps, quite this explicit: however, his concluding observations leave us in little doubt as to his position:

> [W]e can predict that students instructed through a minority language for all or part of the school day will perform in majority language academic skills as well as or better than equivalent students instructed entirely through the majority language. For minority students academically at risk there is evidence that strong promotion of L1 proficiency represents an effective way of developing a conceptual and academic foundation for acquiring English literacy.
>
> (Cummins 1984, p.143)

Cummins' overall hypothesis of Common Underlying Proficiency provides useful initial guidance for teachers on which to structure pedagogies with bilingual students in more helpful, less marginalizing ways. Such guidance involves:

- Not rushing to dismiss students as cognitively deficient when there may be an ongoing issue of language and culture for the school to address.
- Ensuring that early learning of and in L2 is context-embedded – including embedding it in existing cultural experiences.
- Making sure that true concept-development takes place, where possible, by encouraging the use of L1.
- Recognizing the transferability of many language skills, in order to build on existing strengths rather than to highlight areas of weakness.

The notion of transferability is particularly important, not least because of its implications for the *status* of non-majority languages in the classroom.

Some Problems with Theory: Misappropriation and the 'Macro Blot'

If the potentially demarginalizing theories of language-in-context (BICS and CALP) and Common Underlying Proficiency are so well argued and so well known in schools, why, we may ask, should any teacher or school still entertain a tendency to *remove* bilingual students from mainstream classes, to routinely marginalize them when they *are* in the mainstream classroom and to underprivilege their existing experience, knowledge, language skills, understanding and cultural preferences? Part of the answer to this lies, certainly, in what Bernstein (1996, p.56) has called the 'macro blot on the micro context' – that is to say, the manner in which conditions 'outside' the institution constrain and direct activity within it. As Bernstein suggests, this is partly a financial matter: in the case of bilingual education, for example, L1 development cannot be provided if money is not made available by central government for schools to hire appropriate and sufficient bilingual teachers. It is also a matter, however, of symbolic repression in the wider society – the manner in which, for example, public examination systems are constructed to support cultural–linguistic uniformity rather than cultural–linguistic diversity (Moore 1998).

It is not in the scope of this book to explore in any depth the effects and implications of the 'macro blot' – although it is important to recognize the extreme financial and moral pressures and conflicts that confront teachers, and the extent to which these contribute to classroom decision-making. There is often great pressure on EAL teachers, for example, to 'get students into the mainstream as quickly as possible' or 'to give them as much English as possible in the shortest time, so that they don't miss out on the curriculum'. Similarly, classroom teachers' very understandable anxieties about getting bilingual students through public exams have only been exacerbated by the introduction of academic 'league tables', by increased competition for student numbers and by standardized national testing against National Curriculum criteria. As I have already indicated, what I am more concerned with here is first the extent to which teachers can improve practice within existing social, economic and cultural constraints in the macro–micro setting, and second the extent to which they can begin to militate for qualitative change in that broader setting. I want to suggest, however, that the macro blot does constrain teachers very considerably and that one of the effects of this constraint is a certain kind of misunderstanding or misappropriation of some of those very theories that challenge the dominant cultural practices and perceptions of 'the blot'; in other words, those theories can get transmuted into forms which can be accommodated within a marginalizing system, through being 'filtered' (Ginzburg 1980) through the grille of existing social conditions and teachers' consequent perceptions of their own practice and possibilities for practice. I also want to suggest, however, that for all their demarginalizing potential there are possible areas of weakness in some of these theories themselves – particularly the BICS/CALP hypothesis and Common Underlying Proficiency – that render them particularly *susceptible* to misinterpretation.

BICS and CALP: The Cultural Context

Of BICS and CALP, Cummins himself has suggested that 'any dichotomy oversimplifies the reality' and that the terms BICS and CALP have 'the potential to be misinterpreted' (Cummins 1984, p.138).[8] One of the obvious oversimplifications, which will be looked at in more depth in the next chapter, is the very differentiation of language into qualitatively different types, leading to a corresponding 'split' between language development and cognitive development – a simplification which often results in the pursuit of what we might call the *language-led curriculum*, whereby students' perceived levels of L2 competence are allowed to dictate the content and pace of their cognitive development. Such a pursuit inevitably ignores or marginalizes students' existing conceptual development and understandings, pitching curriculum content at levels that are patronizingly or insultingly low.

There are, however, other difficulties with BICS and CALP. One of these is that the dichotomy rather overlooks, in its implied focus on the universals of cognitive–linguistic development, the more broadly *cultural* aspects of bilingual students' school experience and performance. There are important questions left unasked, for example, about whether certain forms of language really are *intrinsically and universally essential* for effective engagement in 'higher order' academic achievement (an argument mirroring the debate we shall consider in Chapter 7 concerning 'standard English'), or whether such language-uses have been deliberately[9] contrived for academic settings, as a way of excluding minoritized students *from* high academic achievement. If this is the case, then the issue for teachers does not stop at helping students to achieve academic success within given systems, but (as Cummins implies in his more recent work) in actively challenging those systems in order to render them more equitable (Cummins 1996; see also Giroux 1988, 1992, Stanley 1992, McLaren 1995).

A further difficulty with the dichotomy – again, an essentially cultural rather than an essentially linguistic issue – relates to the fact that 'everyday' language (typically, talk) is not just different from 'academic' language (typically, writing) on linguistic grounds or even because of any differentiation in the nature of the concepts being considered and discussed: additionally, it takes place in *socio-cultural contexts* (for example, the playground or the classroom) which are often, qualitatively, very different from one another. Bilingual students may find it a much more comfortable *experience* engaging in (for them) L2 discussions in the playground with monolingual and bilingual peers, where there will exist common areas of interest as well as a common age, where they can employ a familiar *register* and where the symbolic order itself is more familiar and routine, than being in a classroom dominated by a controlling adult with whom they may feel they have relatively little in common. Furthermore, the learning situation itself – the culture-specific symbolic order of the less familiar classroom, with its own very special rules and protocols, its own view of what formal learning 'looks like' and how it should be managed – may prove daunting and ultimately far more undermining to the bilingual student than academic language *per se* (Dulay, Burt and Krashen 1982). The culture of the classroom itself can make it particularly difficult for bilingual students who actually do possess very complex L2 linguistic skills from showing those skills or bringing them to bear on tasks which may themselves appear strange or unhelpful: that is to say, there may be a difficulty, created by the classroom situation (regardless of how 'welcoming' the individual teacher may be), of translating linguistic 'competence' into cognitive–linguistic 'performance'.[10] To home in on language as a cause of apparent arrested development may certainly, as Cummins suggests, help teachers to avoid misdiagnoses of students' cognitive development; however, too much emphasis on language alone can easily absolve the teacher from the requirement to make any kind of adjustment to standard cultural practice within the classroom. It can also lead to a continued pathologization of the student (that is, describing the 'arrested development' in terms of deficient linguistic competence) rather than considering the possibility that there may *be* no arrest in development, but that the learning context – including the teacher's own (largely 'given') role and behaviour – may be having an adverse impact on the student's *performance*. As the case studies will suggest, in the best practice teachers deliberately do make adjustments and accommodations which themselves discourage pathologizations of the individual, whether those pathologizations relate to cognition or to language.[11]

It is not my intention to suggest that the BICS/CALP distinction is not a valid one. What I do want to argue, however, is that the manner in which the distinction should be viewed needs to be given very serious attention and that teachers using the distinction to inform their practice need to ensure that they do not, in that process, lose sight of other important theories of learning and development or allow themselves to adopt an oversimplified view of the distinction. Those other features include the suggestions that

- Learning itself is essentially a social activity that demands successful student–student and student–teacher dialogues.
- There is an indivisible and complex interrelationship between language and thought.
- Language used in embedded, 'recreational' contexts may not always differ *fundamentally* from language used in formal, disembedded contexts.

(Moore 1995)

Teachers who lose sight of these other theoretical perspectives may well find themselves drawn into the pursuit of an unhelpful extension of the social/academic split implied in Cummins' basic hypothesis. As I have already indicated, the BICS/CALP distinction can prove very useful in preventing bilingual students from becoming marginalized as cognitively deficient on the basis of poor performance in formal tests. The difficulty is, however, that because of its developmental spine (that is to say, the persistent notion that BICS as it were 'precedes' CALP) exactly the same kind of incorrect diagnosis can be made from the perspective of the BICS/CALP hypothesis itself. If 'academic' language, for example, is perceived by teachers as harder or more advanced than 'social' language, the danger is that they will continue to dismiss many bilingual students as 'backward' on the grounds that they have reached a language threshold beyond which, *for intrinsic, cognitive reasons*, they are unable to proceed further: in other words, they have been 'bright enough' to gain expertise in the simpler, social forms of a new language, but not bright enough to graduate to its more complex forms. In this way, one falsely perceived manifestation of student inadequacy (performance in tests) is merely replaced by another one (apparent inability to learn the more complex forms of a language).[12] As in Cummins' original configuration, the teacher is easily absolved from blame in this perception, since they can point to existing success in getting students to a particular language threshold and argue that if the student cannot get beyond it then the fault must be the student's. Further encouraged by a separation of language from context, teachers who follow such a road may be all too willing to attribute poor academic–linguistic performance to student deficiencies rather than to their own pedagogies and diagnoses or to those of the institutions in which they work.

Common Underlying Proficiency and the Question of Cultural Variations

We have considered the ways in which one of Cummins' central and best-known theories – that of BICS and CALP – can be misappropriated and misunderstood. I now want to suggest that standard CUP (Common Underlying Proficiency) theory, which again can be used to support inclusive classroom practice, is also open to criticism, and that this criticism – as with BICS and CALP – stems from questions about the extent to which the theory makes sufficient reference to cultural dimensions, including *cultural variations*.

This particular difficulty has already been flagged through reference to Cummins' selection of the concept 'honesty' to illustrate his point about the different problems confronting bilingual students at different stages of their bilingual development (Cummins 1984, p.143). Whatever else 'honesty' may be, it is clearly a concept that cannot claim universality or, therefore, easy interlinguistic transferability: using the concept in an additional language might involve not just a simple matter of acquiring a new signifier, but gaining familiarity with a new 'signified' – that is, a matter of *conceptual* rather than merely *linguistic* extension and exchange. Furthermore, we should not imagine that a concept like honesty is only taught – or indeed taught at all – in school. It is very likely that the bilingual student will have acquired and will continue to acquire and develop such a concept in the *home* environment and through their first language. What is interesting is the possible *mismatch* between these concepts and the fact that when students use the English word 'honesty' it may be to refer to a concept significantly different from that suggested by the equivalent word in their own strongest language. This same kind of 'cultural mismatch' can occur, as we shall see, in all sorts of situations where teachers do not take sufficient account of the possibility that people sometimes do – and perceive – things differently from people brought up within other cultures.

It is precisely this kind of mismatch – and teacher responses to it – that causes the difficulties we shall see in the following case studies and points to a certain 'lack' in CUP theory. At School A, for example, the notion of linguistic transfer was accepted (as was BICS/CALP theory) and the theory was used to support some of the positive classroom strategies we have already touched on (in particular, encouraging bilingual students to use their first languages to complete assignments when their second language was considered insufficient for the task). However, as with the adoption of BICS/CALP theory at School B (examples of which will be considered in Chapter 4), CUP theory was adopted only partially at School A and in ways that allowed for the same kinds of misdiagnosis warned against by Cummins in relation to the BICS/CALP hypothesis. Specifically, the adoption of the theory ignored the possibility implied in the difficulties over 'honesty', that while some aspects of languages may indeed be transferable, others may not. (For further work in this area, see Gonzalez 1993, who suggests that bilingual students construct two representational systems: one that is 'universal' and another for symbolic and verbal conceptual categories that are unique to a particular language and culture.) Thus, at School A, although the theory of Common Underlying Proficiency was fully supported in terms of stated policy, difficulties still arose due to teachers taking insufficient account of their bilingual students' existing linguistic, cognitive and creative skills. Such practice, I shall argue, suggests the need for further development of the notion of Common Underlying Proficiency and language transfer, in ways that encourage teachers to seek to extend their culturally marginalized students' affective–linguistic repertoires rather than treating their 'alternative' cultural products as merely incorrect. Part of this may involve replacing misleadingly restrictive words like 'bilingual', bidialectal', 'multilingual' and 'bicultural' with the generic term 'multicultured'.

Notes

1   This argument is implicit in the second argument, since the best way to ensure appropriate cognitive levels with Stage 1 bilingual students is to facilitate such development through a language in which they are already fluent.

2   By this, I mean both formal, academic language and the less formal language used by students with one another as they share work and ideas.

3   We can, for instance, take a sentence like 'The cat sat on the mat' and discuss it, teach it or learn it in terms of its internal grammatical and lexical relations. The sentence itself – or variations of it – may subsequently be used in a variety of situations as appropriate. The trouble is, not many potentially *useful* sentences lend themselves quite so readily to this kind of decontextualization.

4   See also Perozzi et al. (1992) who, with reference to the learning of L2 grammatical features, argue for the benefits of initial instruction in this area through students' L1.

5   There is a different notion of context here; however, the real issue is how this squares with Cummins' language-in-context model.

6   For a fuller account of the differences between BICS and CALP, see Cummins 1984, pp.136–8.

7   Such a view ignores, for instance, other possible reasons – social and cultural – for schools and students wanting to continue to develop a first language. It is for this reason that SUP theory may be firmly situated within the broader *integrationist* discourse which focuses exclusively on how best to acquire L2 and C2 ('second-culture') expertise for the benefit of the wider (intransigent) society, rather than on personal development, happiness or empowerment.

8   This broad oversimplification of the BICS/CALP hypothesis can lead to a number of specific misunderstandings, of which the following are chief:

   (a) BICS and CALP are perceived as *always* separate – with the corollaries that language is sometimes social and sometimes not, and that everyday language plays no great part in concept development.

   (b) The terms BICS and CALP are used to describe language *varieties* rather than thought–language *relationships*.

   (c) BICS is seen as somehow 'easier' in developmental terms (implied in the word 'basic'): a view which can lead to inappropriate assessments of bilingual students' development and to their marginalization as cognitively deficient when in fact there may be critical socio-cultural factors to explain apparent lack of cognitive–linguistic development, locating the problem within school practice rather than within the individual student or their cultural background. Furthermore – and not unrelated to this – such an interpretation too easily implies support for the notion of the intrinsic superiority of standard English – a notion which finds one of its most persuasive contradictions in the work of William Labov. Labov (1972) has demonstrated that the 'nonstandard' English used in everyday social communication (we might say, the BICS) among black working-class American youngsters is as complex and rule-governed (that is, as 'difficult') as standard English, which comes closest to the academic English demanded in formal learning situations. Labov argues that it is not that their vernacular is inadequate or inferior that leads these youngsters to perform badly in school: rather, it is that they have not acquired sufficient expertise in those alternative speech styles and genres that are shaped and demanded by the etiquette and interests of the dominant social classes. In other words, their learning is effectively excluded from the conferment of success because of the terminology in which it is couched and presented. (See also Kress 1982 on linguistic 'etiquette', Bourdieu and

Passeron 1977 on the notion of 'cultural capital', and Stubbs 1976, p.73, for his important reminder that high-status information manuals have been successfully published in creoles. For an example of academic writing that deliberately and very effectively eschews 'standard' linguistic forms and styles in favour of 'non-standard' ones, see hooks 1994, pp.83–90.)

9   As elsewhere, I have used the notion of 'deliberate' in the Freudian sense, where it may refer to both conscious and unconscious decision-making.

10   If, indeed, the separation of academic from everyday language and of scientific from everyday concepts is arbitrary, we might not unreasonably ask whether this offers another explanation of failure: for example, students may come from cultural backgrounds in which such separations are *not* made, but be denied opportunities for learning in their favoured ways through the arbitrary impositions that are made upon them.

11   There is another very important question that needs to be brought to models of language-in-context, and that concerns what we actually mean by the term 'concept'. In his own writing on this subject, Vygotsky is very clear about the distinction between what he calls 'everyday' concepts and 'scientific' concepts (Vygotsky 1962, p.84). 'Everyday' concepts are those acquired as it were spontaneously, during the expected course of a child's life: concepts such as 'house' (the kind one literally lives in), 'tree' (the kind that grows in the park), 'parent' (one's mother or father), even 'square' (the geometrical shape). Scientific concepts, by contrast, are of a 'higher order', a greater degree of complexity, often characterized by levels of abstraction. Such concepts have to be 'deliberately' taught and learned.

Vygotsky's dichotomy is highly problematic. (For example, the word 'square' to define a particular *human type* is arguably a complex one but probably not taught 'scientifically'. We might also ask whether 'scientific concepts' are *intrinsically* more complex, or whether they are just determined to be so by adults and schools.) However, it provides useful assistance in understanding the view of learning that underpins much that is done in the name of EAL teaching. At Schools B and C, for example, there was plainly an implicit recognition on the staff's part that there were, indeed, two *different conceptual categories*, just as they believed there were two different language categories. Thus, when the Head of Science at School C talked of 'teaching students the language first and the concepts later', the concepts he referred to were clearly the higher level 'scientific' concepts: that is to say, he was not suggesting that a word such as 'liquid' could be taught in isolation from any meaning it might have, but rather that the 'everyday' concept of liquid – the word including a certain basic level of meaning which might or might not already be possessed by the students in their own first languages – should be taught first, in order that more complex concepts embedded in the word 'liquid' might be developed subsequently. To illustrate this approach with reference to Mr P's planned lessons on squares illustrated in the following chapter, we might say that the teacher seeks first to graft on signifiers (the words 'square', 'triangle' and so on) to everyday concepts – or, where necessary, teaches those everyday concepts simultaneously with teaching the signifiers – and then, at some future date, makes use of those everyday concepts, possessed now in the student's second language, to develop 'higher order' concepts including a more complex kind of language.

The difficulty with such an approach occurs, as we shall see, in ignoring not just the existing concepts of students, but the levels of complexity of those concepts – let alone the possibility of *cultural variations* in concepts between languages (often the case with abstract nouns such as 'honesty' or 'duty'). This is an occurrence which becomes inevitable once first languages are banished from the classroom and once, at the same time, cognitive 'levels' are set according to second-language (as opposed to general linguistic) proficiency. The contrasts between Mr P's planned lessons on squares and that at School A described in Chapter 6 is illuminating. At School A, bilingual students were encouraged to use existing everyday and scientific concepts as the basis for exploring ever more complex conceptual domains, while *simultaneously* developing the L2 signifiers they would need within the English school system. This suggests a more 'organic' approach to bilingual students' needs, that defies representation in a linear, neatly progressive way.

12 This echoes the point about competence and performance made earlier in the chapter. Cummins seems to suggest that competence is the issue here rather than performance.

4 Symbolic Exclusion

The Denial of Experience

Routine Marginalizations

There are many ways in which, in physically inclusive micro-systems, bilingual students are routinely marginalized and excluded symbolically. These include, *inter alia*:

- Schools absenting students' first languages from public display (for example, public notices, welcoming signs, or classroom/corridor wall-displays of students' work)
- Teachers ignoring bilingual students' presence in the classroom (for example, avoiding eye contact, not offering help, not allowing or encouraging students to ask questions in whole-class discussion)
- The systemic imposition of a curriculum that is culturally biased and which is unproblematically reproduced locally through tasks and worksheets
- Schools assessing students' capabilities and achievements on entry through a language in which the student is not yet fluent
- The provision of support for the development of students' second-language skills (for example, through the provision of EAL teachers) but not for supporting the development of first languages or for promoting cognitive–linguistic development *through* those languages (for example, through the provision of bilingual support teachers)

Without wishing to underestimate the impact of such marginalizations on bilingual students' development and self-perception, it is my central purpose to evaluate teaching–learning situations in which teachers themselves *do* make positive efforts to help their bilingual students and to avoid their marginalization. The intention of such an evaluation is that it may help teachers who already operate in this way to be more *effective* in their operations and to be aware that, even within the overtly inclusive classroom, marginalizing culturist practices can sneak in 'through the back door'.

I have already implied that withdrawing bilingual students for 'decontextualized' language work immediately suggests a certain kind of pedagogy and is underscored by a certain view of how language and learning development occur. Specifically, such work tends to 'shelve', in varying degrees, bilingual students' existing cognitive–linguistic skills, in order to focus not so much on what they already have as on what they are perceived to lack (Bernstein 1996). While such shelvings are admittedly less sweeping in some withdrawal situations than in others, a certain amount of shelving is inevitable: otherwise, there would be no justification – however misguided – for withdrawing students in the first place. Furthermore, shelving is not necessarily confined to the withdrawal situation: it can often enter the mainstream classroom in a less invasive but still marginalizing guise through in-class support or through inadequately taught teachers seeking to follow particular strands – perhaps only partially apprehended – of EAL practice.[1] In this chapter, I shall give further consideration to the rationale and some of the consequences of pursuing such an approach at one institution, School B. Such a consideration will be of assistance in subsequent analysis of pedagogy at School A, where what I shall call the 'language-led' approach was specifically eschewed.

The Language-led Curriculum

At School B – as at School C – James Cummins' theories of BICS and CALP were adhered to unquestioningly and they contributed in no small measure both to the way in which bilingual students' learning was organized and to the justifications for such organization. At this school, the term 'social language' was liberally employed, being used variously by teachers to refer to 'everyday language', 'playground talk' and 'classroom chatter'. It was a term that was usually applied to oral language and almost always to language in informal situations. 'Academic' language, on the other hand, was normally spoken of with reference to written language in formal settings, comprising essentially the absorption and usage of specialist vocabulary, style, and forms of presentation of knowledge and thought: that is to say, an essentially *cosmetic* difference, indicative already that the BICS/CALP hypothesis was being oversimplified and misapplied.[2] Whereas 'social' language was thought to be 'picked up naturally' through 'a process of osmosis', 'academic' language had to be 'actively taught'.

We have already considered some of the difficulties of the BICS/CALP hypothesis. Another of these lies in its internal logic and in the classroom translations that such a logic may seem to imply. Too easily, the BICS/CALP hypothesis can be summarized in the following oversimplified way:

> *These kids need a special kind of academic language in order to make sense of the academic curriculum, so our job is to teach it to them.*

Such a simplification can *either* (1) suggest that CALP comprises a *qualitatively* very different set of language skills from BICS, suggestive of a greater degree of complexity or sophistication (a suggestion which raises questions as to how the development of CALP fits in with the CUP hypothesis and how it is that monolingual students regularly and typically pass through phases in which BICS and CALP overlap before they become differentiated), *or* (2) present CALP unproblematically as, essentially, the teaching of specific vocabulary and linguistic conventions. Either interpretation suggests the necessity of 'giving bilingual kids the language first'[3] and presupposes the academic value of particular kinds of language related to 'standard' English and conventional English generic forms. Both interpretations imply the need to learn forms – and procedures – 'before' appropriate cognitive development can take place and, consequently, imply a language/cognition 'split' (Figure 7). In such a formulation, bilingual students are perceived to need a certain level of expertise in the dominant language (perceived, essentially, in terms of *signifiers*) before they can develop cognitively (by instruction *in and through* that dominant language). Two important effects of this are that (1) the cognitive–conceptual content of the second-language development is typically pitched at levels well below those that are appropriate to the students' age and experience; (2) cognitive development itself is 'held back' until such time as students are deemed to have the second-language skills that will enable such development to take place.

Once the decision to adopt a 'language-led' approach to teaching bilingual students is taken, any curriculum content – the development of concepts, the expansion of 'scientific' knowledge, cognitive–affective devel-

Figure 7 The language/cognition 'split'

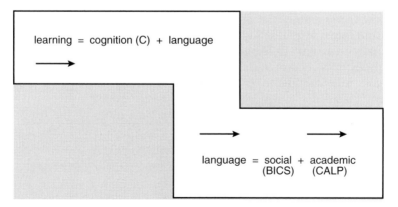

Note: *Figure 7 shows how, in the attempt to separate out language from cognition and social language from academic language, an artificial and unhelpful distance is produced between decontextualized academic language development (CALP) and the higher-order cognitive development (C) it is intended to support.*

opment, the development of abstract reasoning, hypothesizing, theorizing, developing creativity and so on – is, inevitably, very restricted in scope: if teachers believe that students cannot 'cope with' or benefit from the standard curriculum before they have the language to do so, then, clearly, without the language there is little point attempting to cover that standard curriculum. Decontextualized language-led work consequently either ignores the standard curriculum altogether, constructing its own micro-curriculum based upon 'everyday concepts' to do with the home, the family, 'living in the city' and so forth, or seeks to develop language skills through a modified version of the curriculum, setting cognitive levels according to measured L2 levels and following an incremental developmental model based on the hypothesis that little or no cognitive–affective development has already taken place through the medium of the student's existing language(s).

Examples of the latter approach – the attempt to develop second-language skills through the covering of a modified curriculum in withdrawal groups – were to be found in abundance at School B. It is important to note from the outset that the modified curriculum offered here provided not only the *context* for the development of the students' language skills, but also set the *language curriculum*: that is to say, language work focused on the 'academic language' – the vocabulary and structures – the students would need in order to follow a standard secondary-school curriculum, rather than on, for example, discussion and conversational skills or skills related to continuous writing activities such as storytelling. An illustration of how this approach impacted upon actual classroom practice is given in the extract from one teacher's medium-term lesson-plan notes (Figure 8). All EAL teachers at School B were required to record such plans in an open-access record-book in the EAL staffroom, showing how – to quote the head of department – 'progression was being planned for and monitored both academically and linguistically'. The class for which this particular set of notes had been compiled comprised a dozen Stage 1 students (see Chapter 1, Note 1), mostly aged twelve but also containing two fifteen-year-olds who had recently arrived in the UK with no English.

In these lesson-notes, we can see one of the logical developments of language-led pedagogy: not just the prioritization of language over cognition, but the prioritization of a very limited *range* of language. In mathematics, for example – where, as we have seen, the evidence suggests that initial L2 limitation is less problematic than it might be elsewhere in the curriculum (Collier 1987) – the *names* of shapes must be learned before any discussion of their *properties*,[4] while the ability to write, read and spell numbers 'orthographically' ('one', 'two', 'three' and so on) must precede arithmetical/computational work involving the numbers in combination. Initial work on shapes, meanwhile, is developed in terms of teaching students the linguistic order 'adjective + adjective + noun' (for example, 'large blue circle'),[5] while even in English itself, decontextualized 'language' (in the sense of vocabu-

Figure 8 Extract from medium-term lesson-notes

5th Jan.	T7	(English) Revision of all initial consonant phonemes taught last term and vocabulary – (m) (k) (t) (s) (b) (l) (n) (w) (r) (g).
11th Jan.	M1	(Maths) Learning shapes: 'Silent' way – adj. + adj. + noun.
	M3	(Maths) Drawing and labelling shapes.
12th Jan.	T6	(Maths) Continuing from yesterday. Introduce imperatives Fold, Divide, Number.

(i)   Listen and draw example.

(ii)   Label.

(iii)   Test on square/circle/rectangle. Adj. size 1 colour 1 noun.

18th Jan.	M1	(Music) Clapping to beats in time.
19th Jan.	T6	(English) Teach and learn initial phonemes (v) (j) (y) (e) (o) (z) and learn spellings for vocabulary.
1st Feb.	M1	(English) Listing of all spellings covered so far – making their vocabulary list.
	M3	(Music) Playing instruments in time.
2nd Feb.	T6	(Maths) Orthographic numbers 1–10.

Note: Column 2 indicates days of the week. Thus M and T refer to Monday and Tuesday, these being the only two days on which this teacher taught this class. Numbers after the letters refer to the location of lessons in a seven-period day.

lary, spelling and pronunciation) takes precedence over and controls the culture- and genre-driven inputs of language-in-use. One result of this is that the repetition of phonemes is not simply prioritized over but actually ousts any of the concept- or skills-based elements of the standard secondary-school English curriculum, such as storytelling or the expression of experience or opinion. The approach also, of course, entails a denial of any *existing* skills the students might have in these areas and an effective removal from the classroom of previous *experience* that might otherwise provide the material for reproducing and developing such skills.

The decision at Schools B and C was to teach language skills *through the medium of* a modified curriculum (as opposed, in bilingual education proper, to teaching the curriculum through the medium of, say, a first language). This entailed first making selections from the normal school curriculum on the basis that beginner-bilingual students could not be expected to cover the curriculum in the normal way, and second *simplifying* those selections, both linguistically and cognitively, in order to render them 'comprehensible' to the students. This decision, undertaken for apparently altruistic if misguided reasons, was based on the simplified distinction between everyday and academic language that we have already considered in Chapter 3. As one teacher at School B explained, echoing the views of all his EAL colleagues at the school:

> *If you go into a classroom and the teacher is nattering away teaching something and you don't understand his language, not only aren't you going to learn anything but you're going to come away demoralized and confused. You've got to get the language first; then you can understand what the teacher's teaching you.*

As Figure 7 suggests, such a linear, hierarchical, incremental model denies the possibility of a circular or dialectical relationship between *learning* and language, as well as of the inseparability of language and *thought*.

'Banished from the pool'

The language-led approach adopted at Schools B and C and elsewhere is essentially an 'immersion' approach to language development, but of a very special and limited kind and quite different from those described, for example, by Cummins and Swain (1986). In those models, immersion tends to imply total or near-total immersion in the everyday life and language of the school, with students attending most if not all of the standard lessons available to monolingual students. The view here is that students will best learn an additional language by spending most of the school-day 'immersed' in it. Such an approach works best – indeed, under certain circumstances may only work at all – when teachers use students' existing cognitive–linguistic development to support development of the additional language. In the absence of such a perspective, 'immersion' leads not to symbolic inclusion and repertoire extension but to the marginalizing, coercive, culturally geno-cidal pedagogies of eliminate-and-replace.

Sticking with the 'immersion' image, we might liken cognitive–linguistic instruction and development within such an approach to the teaching of youngsters of varying degrees of swimming ability attending lessons at their local pool. In the 'cognitive–linguistic pool' (Figure 9), monolingual and simultaneous bilingual students are viewed as progressing from a 'shallow end' of relatively simple cognitive–linguistic activity towards ever more complex levels, 'growing' in the cognitive–linguistic sense as they do so, so that they are never 'out of their depth'. Linguistic depth increases simultane-ously with cognitive progression. Thus, at the start of their school careers students are perceived as both linguistically and cognitively 'short'. As they grow and develop linguistically, so ever more complex concepts come within their reach: in chronological terms, they move progressively forward from the shallow end towards the deep end. The language-led philosophy suggests that secondary-age bilingual students, introduced to such a pool when they are still in the early stages of developing the additional language, will inevitably be 'out of their depth', since they will be entering the pool at the deeper end with insufficient linguistic 'height'. This view does not, however, take account of the fact that the students will not lack the skills or strength required to 'swim' in this pool or that, although the pool itself may be un-familiar and in some respects daunting and although they may feel the eyes of the world are upon them, they will have been used to swimming in not dissimilar cognitive–linguistic *mediums*.

Concerned at the possible negative effects of immersing their bilingual students in the cognitive–linguistic pool, teachers at School B sought to offer an alternative experience, based on a view that 'you can't just chuck them in at the deep end', on a proposed split between linguistic and cognitive devel-opment and on the basis that students do not already possess transferable skills. This approach perceived – and attempted to model – teaching as filling up a pool or series of pools with linguistic 'water', a little at a time (Figure 10). The view here was that with each increase in linguistic depth, ever more complex concepts could be brought within the linguistic swimmer's grasp, until a stage was reached when they could be released safely into the standard school pool. The role of the teacher in this model was to organize and control concept development according to an incre-mental notion of language learning. As the language became more complex, at a rate decided and controlled by the teacher, so the cognitive depth increased: that is to say, concepts of a corresponding complexity could be introduced.

This perceived need to control linguistic and cognitive depths, based on a perceived need to protect and nurture the bilingual student, has clear impli-cations for the way in which a child's learning is organized. To locate the

Figure 9 'Immersion': the swimming-pool view of cognitive–linguistic development for monolinguals and simultaneous bilinguals

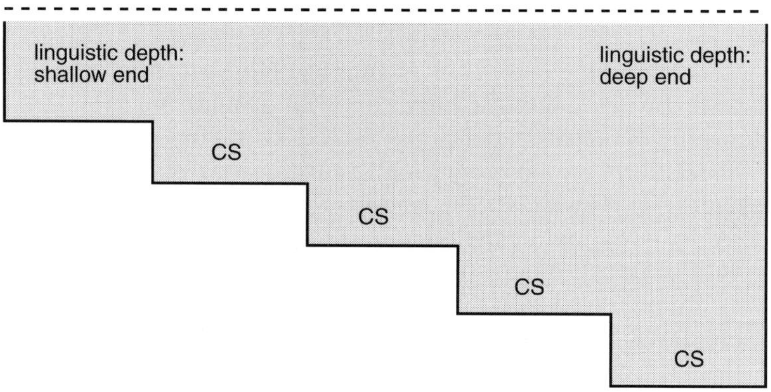

Note: CS = Cognitive 'step'

Figure 10 The 'you can't just chuck them in at the deep end' model

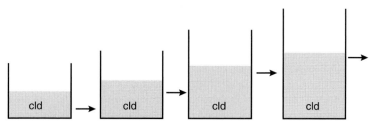

Note: cld= cognitive–linguistic depth

pedagogical approach implicit in the model within Bernstein's terminology, we could describe it in terms of 'strong framing', just as we could describe the restricted curriculum on offer in terms of 'strong classification'.[6] Here, the term 'frame' is used to refer to 'the degree of control teacher and student possesses over the selection, organization, pacing and timing of the knowledge transmitted and received in the pedagogical relationship', with 'strong framing' describing classroom relationships in which such control resides exclusively or almost exclusively with the teacher (Bernstein 1977, p.89). Endorsing this approach at School B, the Head of EAL thus described the work of the department as 'fairly traditional in relation to a lot of what goes on in the mainstream', arguing:

> *That means very carefully structured lessons, moving gradually from the basics to more complicated work, and it tends to involve a fair amount of whole-class teaching on the part of the teacher.*

In short, the language-led curriculum that characterized and promoted decontextualized work in withdrawal groups at this particular institution not only excluded students from the cognitive–linguistic 'pool' (as manifested in the normal classroom situation), it also promoted symbolic exclusion within the withdrawal group itself because of the particularly dominant, 'transmissive' role it inevitably thrust upon the teacher (see also Levine 1983, Wiles 1985a, Cummins 1996).

The Teacher as Pedagogic Missionary

If the language-led approach at School B inevitably marginalized its bilingual students in terms of ignoring their existing cognitive–linguistic skills and, as a direct consequence, arresting or decelerating their cognitive–linguistic development, it also suggested a particular kind of teaching *style*: a style, that is, which is not only transmissive and overly teacher-centred, but that is characterized by the teacher's use and encouragement of linguistic forms that often bear little relation to 'normal' language and that offer inappropriate support for the cognitive development they are claimed to promote. Although these strategies were particularly common in the withdrawal group, it must be said that they were also often in evidence in situations in which EAL teachers supported bilingual students in mainstream classes, or where class teachers, unsupported, attempted 'EAL teaching' using models drawn from the withdrawal classroom.

Underpinning these teaching strategies, which marginalize students even as they claim to include them, is a model of *the teacher as pedagogic missionary*. This model, which needs to be differentiated from that of *the teacher as transformative intellectual*, does not problematize the existing discourses of formal education, nor does it fix its aim 'towards social change and the common good' (Giroux and McLaren 1992, p.xiii). Rather, it seeks merely to impart to students those linguistic and para-linguistic skills already likely to be possessed by most monolingual students of comparable age,[7] on the basis that this will empower them by providing better – and faster – access to the school curriculum. I have called this the missionary approach partly because of its ethnocentricity and partly because it is constructed on humanist 'do-gooding' (and ultimately patronizing) principles, in the tradition of the Victorian missionary. Just as the (white) missionary seeks to convert the (black) subject from one set of cultural practices (seen as misguided or wrong) to another (seen as self-evidently and fundamentally right) through a simple process of gradual replacement, so the teacher as pedagogic missionary seeks to induct the bilingual student into dominant cultural practices and skills with little or no reference to existing histories, personalities or linguistic skills, as if working with a *tabula rasa* (Miller 1983). Furthermore, they do so without feeling the need to offer any explanation as to why such induction should take place, assuming that 'what's in it for the student' will be self-evident. In such a model, culture itself is treated – if not always recognized – as unproblematic, and such matters as the style and content of the school curriculum and the desirability of academic success as measured against standard assessment criteria is rendered neutral (Apple 1979).

Though the missionary model of pedagogy is generally unhelpful to students within the restrictive parameters of school 'achievement' and, in addition, does nothing in itself to challenge the discourses of empowerment and disempowerment in the wider society that operate continuously against bilingual students' best interests, it is (as in the case of the actual missionary) a model adopted by teachers often from the most understandable of motives. We have already considered some of the pros and cons of withdrawing bilingual students from the perspective of some schools and teachers, and it is fair to say that those same arguments are used with reference not just to organizational matters but to matters of pedagogy. The headteacher from one of the schools I have referred to, for example, made the following *organizational* arguments, which were clearly also *pedagogical* ones in that the form of organization being promoted and the educational philosophy underpinning it made certain pedagogical choices inevitable:

> (On the decision to withdraw students from mainstream classes) *It's hard enough when you can speak the language and know the customs; but when you don't, it can destroy you. I've seen it happen. I've watched these kids being destroyed.*

> (On equality of opportunity and access and the decision to teach a restricted curriculum) *Not that there ever is equality of access in the mainstream situation. You can send a bilingual child to the same lessons as a monolingual child and they can sit there listening to what to them is complete gibberish. But that isn't equal access. Actually, by covering the essentials of the curriculum here – a modified curriculum, yes – we give them far more equality, because we deliver it at a pace and in a language they can cope with.*

The decision here to opt for withdrawal goes hand-in-hand – and indeed is partly driven by – a pedagogical decision to provide 'early' bilingual students with a restricted curriculum geared not to their existing cognitive levels but to their proficiency in English: a key feature of the missionary approach.

The Language-led Curriculum: Exemplifications

The well-meaning restriction of students' cognitive development is not, of course, confined to bilingual students. Edwards and Mercer (1987), for example, have described how, in mainstream classrooms, teachers can – almost without realizing it themselves – persistently prioritize 'ritual' over 'principled' knowledge: the former being used to describe a student's knowledge of classroom *procedure*, including a practical understanding of classroom ritual (for example, how to get praise through giving the 'right response'),[8] the latter to describe genuine concept development. Part of the rationale of *teacher*-centred approaches to teaching and learning (implied by the prioritization of ritual knowledge), is precisely that existing student cultures *should* be marginalized: that there is neither the space nor the time, *given curricular constraints and demands*, to allow any deviations from the development of the 'ultimate' skills, knowledge and practice that students must endeavour to end up with by the time their compulsory schooling is done.

Edwards and Mercer's work is particularly useful in providing a taxonomy and a framework through which to deconstruct classroom activity generally, and for providing useful discussion material for teachers themselves. It also suggests, however, a critical tension for many teachers, which may help to explain apparent contradictions in their own and their school's behaviour – in particular, mismatches between publicly stated policy and actual practice (see also Keddie 1971, Sharp and Green 1975).[9] This mismatch, as has already been suggested, owes much to the moral, political and financial pressures that teachers are under to 'get students through exams' – that is, to 'empower' these students within the terms of existing, highly biased frameworks. It is hardly surprising, given such circumstances (for example, the need to get bilingual students to 'catch up' within an often inadequate timeframe), that teachers often feel particularly railroaded into pursuing inappropriate pedagogies with bilingual students, in an effort to cut corners that simply cannot be cut.

Such attempted corner-cutting can take many forms, as we shall see in the examples below. At its heart, however, is an attempt to provide bilingual students not with the cognitive–linguistic tools required if they are genuinely to develop cognitively and academically as claimed, but rather with 'ritualistic' expertise (basic forms of cultural or social literacy – 'communicative competence' – as recognized and practised within the dominant culture of the school) that will enable them to present an *impression* of understanding and knowledge that may well mask a hidden politics of cognitive–linguistic disempowerment.[10] That impression will include the students' use of the 'right' words and phrases – but it will also embrace their use of language in the wider symbolic sense of 'behaviour', including, centrally, a knowledge of procedure.[11] The particularly strong doses of such pedagogy to which bilingual students may be exposed in comparison with monolingual students (who are at least encouraged to participate orally in their learning, even if many of their contributions are subsequently rejected) must cause grave concern, not just for their cognitive–linguistic development but also for their social development, including the development of their social identities.

Some of the linguistic and procedural prioritizations incorporated in the language-led curriculum have been described elsewhere (for example, Moore 1995). The following examples, of six of the most common of these, are offered illustratively rather than exclusively:

- The primacy of procedure
- Boundary-fixing and linguistic rationing
- Inventing language
- Accepting wrong answers
- Excluding right answers
- Prioritizing ritual

All of the examples are drawn from observations carried out at School B during a period of one academic year. They are chosen for their typicality; that is to say, they are examples of practice regularly observed across a range of subject areas and with a range of teachers, and could in each case (as with the lesson-notes already cited) be linked to agreed policy (Moore 1995).

Example 1 The primacy of procedure

(a)   Teacher A: Okay, everybody. Now ... the first thing that we're
                   going to do. ... Look. *(Claps.)* The first thing that
                   we're going to do is ... we have to draw this table.
                   ... Now ... hold up your ruler ...

      N: Yes, Sir.

      Teacher: Hold up your ruler.

      A: Yes.

      K: Yes, Sir.

      Teacher: S, hold up your ruler. I want to see everybody with
                   a ruler in this classroom.

      N: Yes, Sir.

      Teacher: Hold up your ruler. Where is your ruler? R, that's
                   not a ruler.

      R: *(Holding up a set-square)* Yes ...

      Teacher: Hold up your ruler. Where is your ruler?

(b)   Teacher B: That's nice. Try to write at the end of the line or at
                   the bottom. ... Oh that's too untidy ... it's better to
                   draw on the line, see? ... Why have you started
                   drawing lines in ink? Why ink? I said do your
                   writing in ink and draw the line in pencil. All
                   drawing must be done in pencil.

(c)   Teacher A: I want to see good, neat tables. ... Tables never in pen.
                   ... Good ... well done, good table. ... Excellent,
                   that's good: you've spread it out very well.

Commentary

In each of these cases, drawn from a substantial number of similar accounts (Moore 1995), the EAL teachers, having carried out a series of reactivity experiments with their eleven- and twelve-year-old students, are getting the students to draw up a table in which to enter the results. The drawing up of the tables takes up the better part of half an hour in one case and nearly an hour in the other. One group of students are drawing up their tables for a second time, because the previous ones were (in the teacher's words) 'messy', with the students 'not seeming to have had a clear idea of what they were doing'. Consequently, the teacher has made a conscious decision to focus on matters of convention and procedure, arguing:

> *That's really got to be the main teaching aim at this point with these pupils. They can't even draw a table properly. Without that, they can't enter their results, and so it goes on. It's a matter of giving them skills in the right order, starting with the most basic – and that's really a matter of learning appropriate procedures.*

The procedure being given priority here is concerned with the manner of presenting information in an 'acceptable' way – a way which, to quote the teacher again, 'is expected in public examinations'. Unfortunately, subsequent interviews with the students suggest that this particular prioritizing was not *in addition to* but *at the expense of* students' appreciation and understanding of the experiments themselves, and of the names and properties of the substances involved (Moore 1995, pp.131–5). In these interviews, students showed a marked inability either to utilize the vocabulary that had been 'covered' in the lessons or to remember or describe the reactions that had occurred with any degree of accuracy.

We might suggest that in cases such as these teachers are effectively denying bilingual students the opportunity to develop what Selinker has called an *interlanguage*,[12] and to develop linguistically and cognitively *through* that interlanguage (Selinker 1974). They are doing this by promoting relatively unimportant matters of etiquette (Kress 1982) that can be learned fairly easily at a *later* stage in the student's development rather than as a prerequisite to concept development. In the process of doing this, all previous experience is denied. There is no attempt, for example, to ask the students if they have done this work before or whether, to their knowledge, results are presented in this particular kind of (tabular) form in the education systems of the countries they previously lived in. This exclusion of previous experience, which is, thus, also an exclusion of existing linguistic, cognitive and *cultural* skills, results in the students being treated as rookies on the linguistic parade-ground, whose only concern is to remember what has been drilled into them.

Example 2 Fixing the cognitive–linguistic boundaries: language 'rationing'

(a)   *Teacher C:*   How many experiments did we do with water?
       R: Half.
       Teacher: No, no. Not 'How much water was in the test-tube?'

- -

(b)   *Teacher D:*   What time is it now, C?

C:	Quarter ...
Teacher:	No. ... It's ten ... ?
P:	Fifteen!
Teacher:	Fifteen! It's ten-fifteen.

Commentary

Fixing the cognitive–linguistic boundaries is the process by which the teacher excludes from the classroom any manifestations of students' exhibiting cognitive or linguistic levels beyond those established by the teacher in terms of target-setting and progression. We have already seen one example of this in the lesson-notes, where in Music clapping in time preceded playing instruments in time, or in language-work the learning of phonemes was considered a necessary prerequisite to the pronunciation and recognition of whole words. Thus, when in one of Teacher A's lessons a bilingual student, R, called out the letters that spelt his name when asked to identify and sound out the letter 'r', the teacher's response was not to praise his student but to correct him: 'No, R: we don't want to know what begins with the letters; I want you to sound it for me.'

In Example 2(a), a not dissimilar event occurs. During the previous science lesson, the class had carried out twelve reactivity experiments: six using water on various substances, six using acid on the same substances. Thus, the answer to the teacher's question 'How many experiments did we do with water?' was 'Six'. Another way of putting this was 'Half' (that is, half the experiments were done with water, half with acid). Rather than accepting the possibility that the student's answer ('Half') was correct, however, the teacher assumed it must be incorrect because, as it transpired later, 'We haven't done complex fractions yet; *they don't know them.*' Because the teacher's assumption was that the students would possess 'only an everyday concept of fractions – like half a glass or half a test-tube' – the possibility of the student's possessing the 'scientific' concept was denied, and with it any opportunity to move beyond the cognitive level set (Moore 1995, pp.181–3). Furthermore, a possible right answer was dismissed as wrong, even though the eventual right answer provided a perfect match.

In Example 2(b), another teacher is working with the students on time-telling. Interestingly, in this case the teacher has thought about students' previous experience in this area, assuming that what he calls the 'digital' way of telling the time is likely to be more familiar to the students than the 'peculiarly English way' of using halves, quarters and so on. In this way, the teacher hopes to 'begin with something universal and transferable' and subsequently to move on to 'the more complex way of telling time that we still use a lot in the UK'. When one of his students does begin to use that 'more complex way', showing an unexpected if still rather tentative under-standing of the 'peculiarly English' system (that is, a developing grasp of common English *idiom*), he is instantly drawn back to the relative simplicity of the 'digital way' that prefers 'ten-fifteen' to 'a quarter past ten'.

Example 3 'Inventing' language

Teacher A:	OK. What was number four that we tested?
L:	Iron.
K:	Iron.
N:	Iron.
Teacher:	Very good. Number four was iron. *(Writes 'iron' on board.)*
	What was number five that we tested?

Commentary

Reference has been made elsewhere to the use of forced and unnatural language in the classroom (for example, Stubbs 1983) and especially to the use of such language with bilingual students (Wiles 1985a). Such language often *results from* the fixing of boundaries described in Example 2. In Example 3, for instance, the teacher uses an odd construction – 'What was number ... that we tested?' – on the basis that he has 'not yet taught the students the English cardinal numbers' (one, two, three) and that consequently the introduction of ordinals (first, second, third) would 'confuse them' (Moore 1995, pp.173–81). This particular bit of boundary-fixing forces the teacher into inventing the odd linguistic construction in order to say what needs to be said in language that is 'already familiar'. The construction itself is one that the students are unlikely to hear outside their classroom, but that – bearing in mind that they are in this lesson specifically to 'learn English' – they might be forgiven for mistaking as standard.

This is precisely the kind of boundary-fixing that parents often undertake in relation to much younger children: for example, 'Put it in the big cupboard in the bedroom, where we hang the clothes' (rather than 'Put it in the wardrobe'). There are significant differences, however, between very young children developing expertise in their own 'home language(s)' and much older children developing expertise in a second language *having already achieved fluency in their home language(s)*. It is likely, for example, that the kind of parent-talk quoted above is something that these bilingual children will already have experienced as young children and moved beyond. What is required now is not support for learning *language itself*, but help in applying existing cognitive–linguistic skills to the learning of a *new language. A reversion to parent-talk not only provides the students with false models of everyday English: it also forces them into the humiliating position of having to return to a discursive practice and role that they have long since outgrown and in which they were cast in a subordinate role.*

Example 4 The acceptance of incorrect answers in linguistically correct forms

Teacher C:	Is five centimetres longer than eight millimetres … ?
J:	Shorter.
Teacher:	Give me a whole sentence, please.

- -

Teacher C:	Is twenty centimetres longer or shorter than twenty-five millimetres?
B:	Twenty centimetres is shorter than twenty-five millimetres.
Teacher:	Good. Well done. Lovely sentence, B. Did everyone hear that?

Commentary

The above are examples of the teacher showing greater concern for a student's language than for the answer it expresses (Keddie 1971). In the EAL classrooms observed at all three secondary schools in the research projects, it was by no means uncommon for teachers to overlook – or to appear not to hear – substantively incorrect answers, either because of 'over-listening' to *incorrect* language forms *or* because the answer was expressed in the *correct* linguistic form (Moore 1995, pp.163–5). There was evidence through subsequent interviews with bilingual students that this often impeded concept development, or sent students away with misconceptions (which, however, they could express in spot-on academic language!). We might surmise that this prioritization of linguistic *forms* over cognitive–linguistic *development* also contributed to a larger message to the students, about what the school thought of their existing cognitive–linguistic skills and, by implication, about how they rated the students' 'home' languages and cultures in relation to the 'standard' language and cultures of the UK.

Example 5 The denial of correct answers in linguistically incorrect
forms

Teacher C:	L, tell us what happened next.
L:	Then fizzy.
Teacher:	We ... did we see fizzing?
	No. ... We could hear a fizzing noise.
J:	Water is coming.
Teacher:	Water came out. We did it yesterday, so it's finished.
Various:	Heating!
Teacher:	*(Ignoring this answer.)* Did it come out like a tap?
J:	No. 'Cause it was smoking.
Teacher:	What do we call smoking water? It's not really smoke; smoke is from a fire. But water that looks like smoke, we call it ... vapour.

Commentary

In this example, the teacher seems more concerned with getting the language 'correct' than with getting the answer itself right or extending cognitive development. Indeed, on each occasion that the students begin to show evidence of a developing understanding of reactivity experiments, the teacher interrupts with the 'correct form of words', emphasizing again the importance of expression over understanding or even over interest in the subject. Such prioritizations of language, which effectively devalue answers that may be substantively correct, may be seen as part of a wider process whereby ritual appears to be valued above intelligence.

Example 6 Prioritizing ritual

Teacher C:	We held it in the flame.
Students:	*(Unbidden.)* We-held-it-in-the-flame.
Teacher C:	We call it 'it' ... not 'the test-tube'. We don't want to say 'the test-tube', because it's too many words. So we say 'it'. 'It burned'. ... J said it was like on fire, so we say: 'It-burned-with-a-white-light.' *(Teacher writes 'it' on the board as she finishes speaking.)*

Commentary

As in Example 1, the teacher focuses on formulaic, ritualistic language structures ('It burned with a white light') rather than on more fundamental questions of purpose and process. Language as a formal system was allowed to dictate the entire content of this particular lesson, the teacher determined to give her students 'the kind of language they will need if they are going to understand what the teachers are saying to them'. This entailed introducing appropriate linguistic forms and getting the students to practise them by oral repetition. As time went on, the teacher would, she suggested, introduce 'more complex' linguistic conventions related to the subject area, such as 'A test-tube *was held* over the flame' instead of – as in this lesson – 'We held a test-tube over the flame.' By this time, students would 'understand words like "test-tube" and "flame" because we will have done them, they will have heard them a lot of times'. Consequently, it would be easier for them to put these terms into the passive form.

There is, of course, nothing intrinsically objectionable in 'giving students the scientific language they will need'. There can be a problem, however, if this notion of language is divorced from the notion of concepts and if it is prioritized *at the expense of* cognitive development: that is to say, if by the time students have acquired expertise in the appropriate signifiers and linguistic etiquette, they have fallen so far behind in their concept development as to experience genuine problems when they are, finally, allowed into the mainstream classroom (another reason, perhaps, for the kinds of under-achievement referred to by Cummins: not so much that students have only developed expertise in BICS, but that they have developed expertise in a *perverted* kind of CALP at the expense of developing abstract, decontextualized thinking and reasoning skills). A noticeable effect of the concentration on 'language' in the lesson from which Example 6 is taken was that, in the process, Science itself became a separate, almost incidental thing. Questions the teacher might have asked monolingual anglophones of the same age – such as 'Why do these changes occur?' or 'How might knowledge of reactivity be helpful outside the experimental situation?'[13] – were never asked of her bilingual students, despite the fact that she was the only teacher at the school capable of conversing with most of them in their strongest language.

Symbolic Exclusion in the Inclusive School

In the above examples of the language-led curriculum in practice, students have certainly not been ignored by their teachers and cannot be said to have been marginalized in that sense (indeed, we might say that the teachers have attended to their students' learning a bit too zealously as well as misguidedly). The students have, however, been treated as unsophisticated learners, with, as it were, no previous experience. Their own feelings about this, expressed forcefully, coherently and often very bitterly in interview,[14] suggest that the approach is often frustrating, patronizing and humiliating.

In the following chapters, I want to consider situations in which schools and teachers did make conscious attempts to include their bilingual students' existing experience, language skills, knowledge, cognition and expressive skills – that is to say, situations in which *symbolic inclusion* was attempted, often as a matter of official school or departmental policy. I shall explore how things can go wrong even in these situations of 'partial inclusion': specifically how, in such situations, cultural exclusion can occur, almost 'accidentally', partly as a result of the pressures and conditions under which teachers have to work. Overcoming this kind of 'back door' exclusion, I shall suggest, demands, on the teacher's part, a certain *distancing* from their own, habitually 'invisible', cultural preferences, in addition to a serious questioning of 'received wisdom' about such matters as what schooling is – and should be – for, and what represents 'good' or 'correct' student response. Such a questioning may, in some cases, include a radical reassessment of the kind of society in which the teacher and their students live, in which, often, 'the voices of the center appear either invisible or unimplicated in the historical and social construction of racism as an integral part of their own collective identity' (Giroux 1992, p.116).

In addition to considering examples of ineffective classroom practice in the would-be inclusive school, I have sought to present cases of what might be called fuller inclusion, suggesting techniques and tactics that teachers can adopt to achieve a partial countering of cultural–symbolic bias in the wider social structures in which they operate.

Notes

1   One-year teacher-training courses in particular devote, by their nature, increasingly little time to the teaching of bilingual students – a problem often exacerbated by a lack of continuing professional development in this area or of the funds and expertise to provide it.

2   It is not difficult to find the roots of this oversimplification of the BICS/CALP hypothesis in Cummins' own contrast between 'the manifestation of language proficiency in everyday contexts' and 'the manipulation of language in decontextualized academic situations'. The specific contrast here between 'manifestation' and 'manipulation' is particularly illuminating, appearing at first glance to support the argument that 'social' language is indeed 'picked up naturally' (that is, it 'just happens'), whereas 'academic' language needs to be deliberately learned.

3   See also Walkerdine's account of how Piaget's theories posit a language/cognition split in which the 'world of objects, the signified' are 'appropriated' first by the child and only then 'represented by signifiers' (language) (Walkerdine 1982, p.130) – a reversal, of course, of the model adopted at School A, where primacy is given to language within the perceived split.

4   Interviews with Mr P. indicated that such discussions occupied an unspecified place in his future plans, located at a time when the students 'had the language to talk about the shapes'.

5 Stubbs (1983, p.44) has described teachers' talk in general as often being characterized 'by discourse sequences which have few, if any, parallels outside teaching'. Wiles, describing EAL courses, has talked of a tendency to use English that bears 'only a distant relationship to English as it is regularly used. [Such courses] try, for example, to teach learners sentences they will rarely hear or be called on to use ("This is the green pencil. The boy in the blue coat is posting the letter."), require them to answer in "full sentences", and correct them for using dialect forms which go uncorrected when used by their peers' (Wiles 1985a, p.20).

6 'Classification' refers, among other things, to the separating out of 'subject areas' both within the overall curriculum and within 'subjects' themselves.

7 There are problems here, of course, because of the presupposition that a chronological age can be matched to a level of cognitive development or cognitive experience – itself a highly questionable hypothesis.

8 See also Plowden on how 'children's knowledge of the right words may conceal from teachers their lack of understanding' (Central Advisory Council for Education 1967, para.535).

9 Part of the problem, as has already been indicated, is the external pressure on teachers, recently exacerbated by the introduction of standardized age-related testing and league tables of academic achievement. Arguably, such pressures encourage teachers to teach in ways that, 'deep down', they feel very strongly to be wrong, and to rush into 'panic measures'.

10 This could suggest another reason for bilingual students' who have been judged to be doing relatively well linguistically 'falling behind grade norms' in mainstream classes (Cummins 1984, p.130). That is to say, the deficiency may lie not within students' language development as such, but rather in inappropriate pedagogies that have inadequately prepared them for the kind of cognitive development required of public curricula and syllabuses.

11 This emphasis on matters of procedure anticipates issues of generic knowledge and skills referred to in subsequent chapters.

12 The term 'interlanguage' refers to the 'imperfect' versions of an additional language that a developing bilingual uses *in the process of learning that language*. The learner may well, for example, incorporate elements of their first language(s) into their L2 performance – including generic or procedural elements – in the form of 'direct translations'. Selinker (1974) and Miller (1983) have argued that interlanguage may be an essential stage in L2 development, and that constant, consistent 'correction' of students' language could, in the long term, prove very damaging to the learner, resulting in a very stilted and restricted use of L2. Miller has suggested that additional-language teaching could incorporate early 'errors' as 'acceptable, provisional features of [the] target language' (Miller 1983, p.141).

13 I am aware that not all monolingual anglophone students will be asked these particular questions either. The two questions I have quoted, however, were asked of monolingual anglophone students at School A – significantly, during the course of a lesson from which the bilingual students had been withdrawn for decontextualized language work.

14 I have not included data from interviews with bilingual students, in line with an agreement made with students at Schools B and C during the period of research. This is purely and simply a matter of confidentiality.

5 Partial Inclusion

Pedagogy and the Notion of 'Cultural Visibility'

This is an ethnocentrism which transforms a division of classes into the negation that there can rightfully exist other tastes. One class affirms itself by denying to another its right to participate in the culture, declaring openly that another aesthetic or set of sensibilities has absolutely no value. Once the legitimate culture has affirmed distinction, it rejects, above all, any aesthetic that does not know how to distinguish the forms and current styles of art, especially the inability to distinguish art from real life.

(Martin-Barbero 1993, p.81, referring to the notion of ethnocentrism and class in Bourdieu 1968)

Multiculturalism is generally about Otherness, but it is written in ways in which the dominating aspects of white culture are not called into question ... the norm of whiteness [becomes] an ethnic category that secures its dominance by appearing to be invisible.

(Giroux 1992, p.117)

School A: The Inclusive Policy for Bilingual Students

The first case study in this section is drawn from data gathered at School A, referred to already in Chapters 2 and 3. The organizational issue at this school – where over 50 per cent of students were bilingual and over 50 different first languages were spoken – was well on the way to being settled in favour of a move away from withdrawal towards full mainstream support. It would, however, take the better part of two more years for this settlement to become part of the generally unquestioned culture of the school, and it was a development that still raised objections from many staff.

The shift of culture had enabled the school to debate much more fully than before pedagogical and theoretical issues to do with bilingualism, and to alter its practice accordingly under the joint leadership of a progressive, strongly anti-racist headteacher, a committed and very knowledgeable head of EAL, and a senior teacher given responsibility for overseeing developments in provision for multicultured students across the school curriculum. There was a growing acceptance at the school that students' bilingualism ought to be advantageous (both to the bilingual student and to the school community) and that it was the school's responsibility to do all that it could to ensure that this was so. It was also increasingly understood that, in the initial stages of sequential bilingualism, cognitive–linguistic development could – and should – take place in the students' strongest languages, and that such languages should be maintained and developed rather than forbidden or restricted. Thus it was that after-school classes in various languages – including Italian, Bengali, Chinese and Arabic – were held on the school premises, that Bengali, Arabic and Italian were offered as upper-school options, and that it was becoming increasingly common for students to be allowed and encouraged to use their first languages in class, both for discussion and for written tasks. Not only members of the EAL department, but many other teachers too, especially in the influential English and Languages departments, were attending courses on bilingualism-in-education and engaging in serious reading around the subject. Particularly influential were the early writings of Cummins (1979a, 1979b, 1984), Krashen (1982) and Levine (1983, 1990), and the support given by these researchers to, respectively, the potential advantages of being bilingual, the role and importance of social and emotional factors in language-development, and the case for including bilingual students in mainstream classes.

Nowhere was this shift of priorities and perspective more evident than in a grasp of and support for Cummins' notion of Common Underlying Proficiency (see Figure 6 in Chapter 3) that permeated many areas of the school's curriculum. One Head of Year, for instance, who was also a member of the school's Art department and who worked very closely with EAL teachers, spoke in the following terms of the developing bilingual students in his own classes:

> *What you have to remember is that these [bilingual] kids don't come to us 'cold': they already know a lot about Art ... like what it is, what it's for. ... They have an understanding that it's to do with looking at things in certain ways and then making symbolic or imaginative representations out of that, and they know that it's to do with making use of a whole range of materials and colours and textures. They've got skills, too. They may not all be exactly the same skills as they'll need, say, to pass a public examination in Art: but basically they're there. ... They know how to handle tools ... and colours. [Our job is to add] skills and approaches to the ones they already have while at the same time recognizing the value of existing skills and approaches. In fact, they've got a lot to teach the monolingual ... kids, and we often use their work to show the whole class that there are different approaches that* they *could adopt.*

This approach was underpinned by broader political and professional development agendas at the school, aimed at critiquing both curriculum content and teaching styles in a conscious break with colonial, ethnocentric perceptions and practices from the past: agendas implicit in a raft of whole-school policies promoting equality of opportunity, including one for the Arts, which argued:

> It is our responsibility [to provide] an arts education that gives positive recognition to the differences of culture and heritage, and that respects and affirms the identity of each individual child. ... The study of the arts in a multicultural curriculum ... necessitates a conscious break with our ethnocentric tendency to interpret and value art forms from the base line of our own cultural forms.

Such views as this suggest – in contrast, it must be said, with the enduring cynicism towards mainstream inclusion of some other teachers at the school – that classrooms are places of *opportunity* for teachers and students alike, and that some very significant ground can be made towards meeting the needs of bilingual students, even with relatively inexperienced teachers, provided the will is there. In doing this, they also draw attention to three further points that will be of use in considerations of the Art and English lessons described in this and the next chapter:

1   Though some skills may be transferable, there will always be others that are not, that cannot easily cross the 'cultural divide' (implied in the notion of students having to 'add skills and approaches to the ones they already have'): that is to say, the theory of Common Underlying Proficiency alone is not enough for an understanding of the developmental experiences and needs of bilingual students or how to approach those experiences and needs (see also Gonzalez 1993, on cognitive–linguistic forms that are *culture-specific*).

2   In teaching bilingual students the 'new' skills they will need – those skills which are not transferable – the teacher's job is not to *replace* existing skills, but rather to extend the students' symbolizing and representational repertoires (see also Levine 1993, p.192, on the notion of repertoire extension, and Bakhtin 1986, p.96, on the importance of commanding a 'repertoire of genres').

3   The logic of such views enables the teacher to embrace a teaching situation in which Common Underlying Proficiency and the need for students to gain expertise in a relatively narrow range of skills and approaches (those defined in examination and other school curricula) does not preclude the desirability or indeed the practicality of genuine pluralism in the classroom (as opposed, for example, to the pseudo-pluralism condemned by Sarup 1986, which merely marginalizes 'alternative' cultural forms and preferences by including them in a marginal way).

This logic was supported by many other teachers at the school including the Head of English, who explained the high presence of Stage 1 bilingual students in English classes as follows:

> *It's really all to do with how you perceive English and how you perceive language. Pupils are using language in every subject area – as the Bullock Report pointed out in 1975!*[1] *English is* about *language, but it's not, essentially, about teaching it* to *people. … It's about showing them how to use it effectively, and how to respond in certain ways to the language of others – in, for instance, the study of literature. An English lesson in England is not essentially different in that respect from a French lesson in France or a Bengali lesson in Bangladesh – though of course it's a lot different from, say, an English lesson in France or a French lesson in England. What we're about is developing reading, writing, speaking and listening skills that are, essentially, cross-cultural. For instance, if you have a Bangladeshi child in your English class who can write in Bengali but not in English, it seems to me to be perfectly valid to get them writing a letter or a story or whatever in Bengali. That way, they'll still be developing their letter-writing or story-writing skills, and as their English develops they'll simply be able to transfer these skills; they won't run so much danger of getting left behind.*[2]

Views such as this, as well as accepting the validity of Common Underlying Proficiency as one basis upon which to structure students' learning, would appear to support both Levine's and Cummins' models of language-in-context (referred to in Chapter 3), in which the proper contexts for bilingual students' second-language development are perceived as the mainstream classroom and the students' existing cognitive–linguistic (and indeed expressive–affective) skills. It was a view which had widespread though not unanimous support at School A, and which was supported through a number of structures. These included:

- the move to reduce language instruction through withdrawal;
- the organization of all classes in all subjects into unsetted groups that were also linguistically and culturally mixed;
- the provision of first-language development classes for as many students as resources allowed for.

The view was not, however, without problems in execution, as we shall see. The most obvious and significant of these were that the view itself was not shared by everyone at the school and, in particular, that it was not shared by key teachers in subject areas such as Science and History, who continued to argue, persuasively, that students could not possibly follow the respective curricula without sufficient English language skills, and that to attempt to force them to do so would be demoralizing for the students as well as potentially very damaging to public examination results.

One immediate result of this opposition was that the school found itself in a position of adopting a policy which divided subjects into those deemed 'language light' (essentially, the 'practical' subjects) and those deemed 'language heavy' (the 'academic' subjects). In 'language light' subjects, it was thought that Stage 1 bilingual students' lack of English would offer the least impediment to progress and understanding. In the case of Art, for example, which was perceived as an essentially 'visual' subject in which the teacher could communicate relatively easily through showing examples, using sign language, pointing to materials, 'getting the students started' and so on, it was felt that the bilingual students would be able to 'keep up' relatively easily. As we shall see, this was not necessarily the case, mainly because language itself is far more than the words we use, and because classrooms and curricula are cultural constructs which demand of the teacher some consideration of – and knowledge of how to deal with – differences in understanding, prioritization and performance between cultures. Nevertheless, the policy was implemented to ensure that, as far as possible, bilingual students were never withdrawn for decontextualized language work from practical subjects. The corollary was that they were very often withdrawn for such work from academic subjects.[3]

Two further problems relating to the school's understanding and implementation of Common Underlying Proficiency were first a widespread tendency at the school happily to accept the theory in relation to physical and creative subjects, but not in relation to 'academic' subjects, which were perceived as 'language heavy', and second a danger that, despite teachers recognizing that the theory does not necessarily apply to *all* skills, they would act as if this were the case and, in so doing, overlook *culture-specific* aspects of pupils' work that were *not* transferable. In the examples quoted above from the Head of English, for example, it might be argued that although some aspects of letter-writing and story-writing are indeed transcultural or transferable and that they consequently justify the pedagogic approach being suggested, there are others that might not be: that is to say, there might well be *generic* differences in matters of style, appropriateness and content between letters and stories that are acceptable within one cultural–linguistic context and letters and stories that are acceptable within another. If such possible differences are overlooked, there is a danger that the teacher will treat manifestations of such differences in a student's work simply – again – as 'errors': that is, 'This student does not know how to write *a* letter or *a* story (in *any* language [implied]).' Such a danger has implications for the development of genuine pluralism in, say, the Art or English classroom, since it implies that there is only one way or set of ways of going about things, even though those ways may be expressed through different languages. This essentially monocultural way of perceiving the various 'products' – which are, in essence, cultural artefacts – of bilingual students according to some kind of pseudo-universal quality control is not only another form of symbolic exclusion, but can result, as we shall see, in misdiagnoses of such students' attainment and potential.

Because of the general change of attitude towards bilingualism in School A (if not always towards bilingual *students*) and the shift to debates around more strictly pedagogic issues, many of the problems associated with withdrawal – for example, the restricted, language-led curriculum, or the social and linguistic isolation from monolingual peers – appeared to have been eliminated. As we shall see, however, other problems – associated with pedagogy – now emerged, as the debate moved on into the shadow of what would become the next paradigm: that of full inclusion and empowerment (see Figure 4 in Chapter 2). These problems concerned the way teachers continued to marginalize students' cultures – particularly the less 'visible' aspects of those cultures – even as they sought to demarginalize specific, highly visible linguistic aspects (for example, allowing students to talk to one another in Bengali, or even to write a story in Bengali, but insisting that the story should be written in a specific, very English *way* and treating that way as correct rather than arbitrary). A major danger here lay in teachers *assessing* bilingual students in such a way that the pedagogical question became closed and self-referential, restricting the possibility of moving on into the empowerment paradigm: that is, *this student is deficient and therefore [implied] simply beyond empowerment.*

Nozrul's Art Lesson: 'Defining the Situation'

By way of exploring these issues in more detail, I want to consider the case of one student, 'Nozrul', whose experiences were replicated in various forms and to various degrees across the curriculum at School A.

Nozrul is an eleven-year-old Stage 1 bilingual learner: one of those students in the eight to twelve age-range who, in the view of Cummins and others, should have 'the best prospects for developing proficient bilingual and biliterate abilities' (Cummins 1996, p.68). Six weeks have passed since Nozrul and his mother and two younger brothers arrived in England from the Sylhet region of Bangladesh. On his arrival, in October, Nozrul was offered an immediate place at School A. At his school in Bangladesh, which he had attended for four years, he had studied, according to his own testimony, Mathematics, Science, Bengali, Islam, Physical Education and elementary English, but no Art or Craft subjects and nothing of what his new school called History and Geography. Having been at his new school for a little under two weeks, Nozrul is about to experience his first Art lesson. His teacher, Mrs Green, an experienced classroom practitioner and a practising artist herself, suggests in interview that she takes 'a positive attitude towards bilingualism' and is very aware of her responsibility 'to make sure that all children do their best, regardless of their ethnic background or class'. In answer to the question 'Are some skills transferable between cultures?' her answer is an emphatic: 'Yes, definitely ... absolutely. And that's what we try to build on.' She is, however, less than enthusiastic about the large numbers of bilingual students entering her classrooms with, she feels, inadequate induction for the students and inadequate information for the teacher. She feels that the school and, subsequently, individual teachers within it have been 'progressively dumped on' as a direct result of central and local underfunding. She believes that this makes an already difficult teaching job almost intolerable, as well as failing to serve the best interests of bilingual families.

On the day that Nozrul joins them, Mrs Green's Art class are sitting in a circle around a central table on which are positioned three ornamental figures: two of kings dressed in the manner of the three Wise Men from the Nativity story, the other of a traditional Western European clown. Mrs Green has asked the class to choose one of the figures to draw and colour in, intending – though not actually stating – (1) that the students are not to move away from their desks unless given specific permission to do so (in order to change a rubber, sharpen a pencil and so on); (2) that the students' drawings are to be naturalistic/representational reproductions *drawn from a fixed viewpoint*. These constraints and expectations are not stated by Mrs Green because, as she explains later, it is unnecessary to state the obvious: 'I would have thought that, whatever your culture ... , when you are asked to copy something, that is what you do.'

While the other students in the class – several of them bilingual students who have been in the country for less than two years – get on quietly and in a generally stationary position with their task, Nozrul repeatedly leaves his chair to walk about the room, apparently examining his chosen figure – the clown – from a variety of different viewpoints. Each time he does this he is chastised (in English, with the support of voice-tone and gesture) for not staying in his place.

When Nozrul has completed the drawing to his satisfaction (Figure 11), he takes it to Mrs Green for her approval prior to colouring it in. It is a drawing that is unlike that of any other child in the class: the figure's arms emerge from its jaws, there is a gap between head and hat, its legs have no discernible feet and the decoration on the figure's back (not visible from where Nozrul has been sitting) appears on its front. As such, it is reminiscent of the drawings of much younger children, described by L.S. Vygotsky:

> Often children's drawings not only disregard but also directly contradict the actual perception of the object. We find what Buhler calls 'X-ray drawings'. A child will draw a clothed figure, but at the same time will include [its] legs, stomach, wallet in [its] pocket, and even the money in the wallet – that is, things [the child] knows about but which cannot be

seen in the case in question. In drawing a figure in profile, a child will add a second eye or will include a second leg on a horseman in profile. Finally, very important parts of the object will be omitted; for instance, a child will draw legs that grow out of the head, omitting the neck and torso, or will combine individual parts of a figure.

(Vygotsky 1962, p.112)

Vygotsky's account is both interesting and relevant here, if only because it demonstrates that Nozrul's drawing style is by no means unique or even unusual. What may be perceived by the teacher as unusual, however, is that though the style itself is familiar, its appearance in the work of a student of this age may not be. The question then becomes (or perhaps should become): 'Is this because the student has some deficiency in, say, motor coordination or hand–eye coordination skills, or even perception? Or is it rather that this student simply has not learned a particular style of representation yet (the naturalistic, fixed-viewpoint style, for example) and is still using a fundamentally symbolic representational style?' If this latter is the case, then the issue is clearly a cultural–social rather than a physical or psychological one, being concerned primarily with genre development: an interpretation which demands a very different approach from that taken by the teacher who interprets the representation as a sign of personal *inadequacy*.

Figure 11 Nozrul's clown

In the event, Vygotsky's non-judgemental description of certain aspects of children's drawing forms a stark contrast with Mrs Green's response to Nozrul's. Having quickly sent him back to his seat, Mrs Green resignedly shares her conclusions about what Nozrul has produced. For her, the simple line drawing, with its apparent anatomical errors and physical naivety, means only one thing: Nozrul has 'a learning difficulty'. Furthermore, it is a difficulty that he shares with 'many of these [bilingual] children'. Nozrul 'cannot even see the object properly'; he needs 'special [learning] help' as well as language support. Mrs Green, already anxious about the development and chances of other sequential bilingual students in the class, as well as of a small group of students diagnosed as having special educational needs, feels at a loss as to how to provide Nozrul with that kind of help. As she frustratedly argues: 'I'm not a special needs teacher: I'm just not trained for it. Any more than I'm a language specialist.'

What I do not want to call into question here is Mrs Green's commitment to her job (she has, for example, put in many 'additional hours' to her work, mounting wall displays and helping students complete projects), or her genuine feelings of frustration and concern. Nor would I want to question her common-sense observation of Nozrul's artistic product. His drawing was, undeniably, of the kind normally associated in Western European cultures with the efforts of a much younger child, and this invites all sorts of explanations as to why this should be so. It is, rather, in that area of explanation or interpretation that we have the most to gain from analysis, and in particular through a consideration of what Woods and others have called 'defining the situation' (for example, Woods 1992).

Woods uses the term 'defining the situation' with reference to effective and defective classroom interactions. Effective teaching and learning, Woods argues, is heavily dependent on the relationship between the teacher and the student, and in particular on both parties having a shared understanding of what is happening in order for 'joint activity to ensue' (Woods 1992, p.341). To clarify this point, Woods describes how meaning is often conveyed in the classroom situation through looks and gestures as well as through speech and writing. Arguing that teachers and students need to be able to 'take the role' of one another and 'interpret situations in the same way' in order for 'smooth interaction to occur', Woods points out, however, that '[j]ust as objects can be interpreted differently on different occasions or by different people … so situations must be interpreted' (Woods 1992, p.344). Where, for example, a teacher and a student interpret the same situation in different ways, the door is open not only for misdiagnosis on the teacher's part but also for correspondingly inappropriate pedagogy.

Despite Mrs Green's suggestion that the task she set was 'simple' and that 'whatever your culture … , when you are asked to copy something, that is what you do', there is clear evidence, I would suggest, of what we might call a *cultural mismatch* between her interpretation of this particular situation and that of her bilingual student, as a result of which effective interaction was rendered impossible. For Nozrul, the task set was not necessarily a simple one, nor one that was not open to interpretation. Here was a student who as yet understood hardly any English and who could not reasonably be expected to work out from his teacher's verbal instructions what, precisely, he was being asked to do. The best such a student could do to establish what the task actually might comprise was (1) observing what other students were doing, (2) using his previous experiences of drawing and classroom behaviour. If we take these possibilities into account, we may well come to the conclusion that his behaviour was not necessarily 'odd' at all. In attempting to make sense of Nozrul's behaviour in a way that does not marginalize him as 'defective', for example, we might not unreasonably consider the following possibilities:

1   Nozrul had no clear idea of what he was supposed to do: in particular, he had not had any previous experience either of figure-drawing or of drawing anything 'photographically' from a fixed viewpoint.
2   In order to complete what was an appropriate and finished picture within his own cultural terms, it was necessary for him to walk about the room to see the parts of the figure that he could not see from where he was sitting.
3   What Nozrul needed to learn from his teacher was how to develop the styles of representation he was already using, and to add to those – in the fullness of time – the different cultural styles and forms in which he would need expertise if he was to be able to do well in, for instance, a public examination in Art (as well, that is, as continuing to use art for his own purposes).

In the event, when Nozrul did take his picture to Mrs Green she was in no doubt that the pedagogic challenge was not a cultural one (which she could approach positively, drawing from her existing expertise) but a psychological one (which was beyond her). Based on what she had learned of child development *within a psychological rather than a cultural or discursive paradigm* (her references to her own teacher-training, for instance, were characterized by repeated mentions of the work of educational psychologists), her analysis of Nozrul's drawing, rightly or wrongly, was that it showed that Nozrul could not 'see properly' and that he had 'a severe learning problem'. Having decided that he is a child with learning difficulties – and increasingly frustrated that she can 'do nothing for him' because she is inappropriately trained and resourced – Mrs Green very soon sees Nozrul (and in contrast to the perception many other teachers have of him) as a 'difficult' student who must merely be controlled in order to minimize the disruption he can cause to the rest of the class. Thus, a successful lesson for both teacher and student in this situation becomes one in which direct conflict has been avoided: Nozrul quietly 'getting on' – with virtually anything he wishes to do as long as it disturbs no one else in the room – leaving Mrs Green free to help the children she can 'genuinely help'. Though Nozrul makes progress in other subjects – including 'good progress' in English and Mathematics – he achieves very little in the one subject in which his EAL teachers expected him to experience the least (language-induced) difficulty.

Diagnostic Issues

It is not difficult to understand the diagnosis made by Mrs Green, or her reasons for making it. It is a diagnosis prompted by a dominant psycholog-ical discourse of development, based on universals and patterns of conformity rather than on variability and idiosyncrasy: the discourse that Mrs Green would have been familiar with from her teacher-training days and which would have found support both in Art examination criteria and in the developing National Curriculum for Art (DFE 1995a). Within the terms of this discourse (see also Sully 1895, Burt 1921 and Lowenfeld and Brittain 1970), children proceed through various 'stages' of development, which are characterized by – and can be monitored against – specific outcomes ('naturalistic' or 'realistic' drawing comes after 'primitive' drawing, perspective follows flatness, and so on). Children who are still only drawing 'primitively' at an age when, according to the charts, they should be able to draw more 'naturalistically' are, by definition, 'backward'.

There are, of course, alternative ways of looking at development which can lead the teacher to alternative diagnoses of a student's work. Some of these are located within the socio-psychological paradigm (Vygotsky 1978), others within the paradigm of discourse analysis and psycho-semiotics (Walkerdine 1982; Atkinson 1991, 1998), and others within theories of culture (Moore 1995). Vygotsky has argued, for example:

> Children do not strive for representation; they are much more symbol-ists than naturalists and are in no way concerned with complete or exact similarity, desiring only the most superficial indications. We cannot assume that children know people no better than they depict them; rather they try to name and designate than to represent.
>
> (Vygotsky 1978, p.112)

For Vygotsky, children do not draw 'primitively' merely because they are incapable of drawing any other way, but because this is the method of repre-sentation best suited to their particular purposes. When a student aged *eleven* draws in this way, we might well ask ourselves the question: 'What are *this* student's purposes in the execution of this work of representation?'

In support of such a view, Atkinson has argued persuasively for an experiential model of drawing development, which 'does not assume a predictable hierarchical progression, involving related assumptions of an evolution from inferior or primitive to superior levels of ability', but which recognizes that children 'use drawing to represent a range of experiential orientations' (Atkinson 1991, p.58). This developmental model, unlike those which seek to locate development within the psyche of the individual child and against a universal map or chart, takes full account of cultural variations and idiosyncrasies. As Atkinson argues:

> Here [in the school situation], what constitutes ability ... is not some natural state but the valuing of the production of particular drawing forms within a cultural tradition above other, less valued kinds of production. The use of the term 'drawing ability' tends to produce a closure whereby certain drawing forms occupy a kind of dominance over others.
>
> (Atkinson 1994, pp.1–2)

Atkinson's observations are of particular relevance in considering the case in question, for two reasons. First, they transpose the issues of diagnosis from the realm of internal, individual, psychological development (a still dominant discourse that continues to promote culturist practices in schools) to that of essentially social *discourse*. In the *discursive* view, not only is education about initiating young people into various (culture-specific) discursive practices (see also Walkerdine 1982), but the very 'values' and criteria by which young people are assessed are themselves merely discourses, open to challenge and interpretation. A school student who does not produce the kind of drawing required (by the teacher, by the examination board, by the National Curriculum) may have failed to do so not out of some innate lack of 'ability', but through insufficient experience of a particular discursive practice or through a preference – perhaps a very passionately held preference – for producing an 'alternative' drawing. *In the case of Nozrul, for example, it is perfectly possible not only that Nozrul had never, for cultural and perhaps specifically religious reasons, been asked or instructed to draw something like a human figure before, but that he might have come to Mrs Green's class with a preconception that to render such a figure 'life-like' was actually wrong.* As Leary, among others, has commented on this issue:

> Much of Islamic art has ... been described as 'aniconic', and Muslim attitudes to figurative art may involve *rejection* of human imagery.
>
> (Leary 1984, p.15; my emphasis)[4]

The second point of relevance in Atkinson's observations is that discourse itself is located very firmly within the context of culture and within that which is, specifically, culturally variable (see also Landes 1965; Volosinov 1986, pp.28–9). From this perspective, the Art teacher seeks to eliminate value-judgements based on notions of 'civilized' and 'primitive' art, attempting to bring 'a global perspective to the studio [and] reflect that each work of art is an experiential response of its creator [that] can be understood only in [cultural–]contextual terms' (Bartle-Jenkins 1980, p.16; see also Read 1964). In particular, suggests Bartle-Jenkins, teachers need to acquire a certain *distancing* from cultural values acquired, as norms, from their own childhood. The misrecognition of such norms – that is, perceiving them as 'universals' rather than as 'arbitraries' – may, as Ann Taber has argued, lead the teacher incorrectly to assume that the use of certain artistic devices ('scale', 'perspective' and so on) 'is part of growing into artistic maturity, and separates the experienced painter from a beginner' (Taber 1981, p.61).

Pedagogical Implications: The Notion of 'Cultural Visibility'

Once a drawing such as Nozrul's is located within the discourse of cultural pluralism – including, that is, an understanding that certain forms of representation are not only favoured *within* cultures but also *between* them – alternative definitions of Nozrul's behaviour and of his drawing immediately appear more convincing than those implied by the 'universal development' discourse. Such a location also offers more help and encouragement to the *teacher*, suggesting immediate strategies rather than the inevitability of failure.

An illustration of how this alternative, inclusive approach to working with bilingual students can operate in practice is provided by the insights of another practising teacher, Ann Taber. Taber (1978, 1981) identifies a range of areas in which what is accepted as 'good' and 'normal' within one culture – let us say, within the privileged culture of a particular institution – may be considered strange and even 'bad' within another culture (for example, a marginalized culture in a particular institution), and vice versa. Taber not only questions the Western European's unquestioning acceptance of certain 'norms' of representation as 'correct' and 'real', but strives herself to attain that 'distancing' recommended by Bartle-Jenkins *that not only enables her to appreciate qualities in her Asian students' work that might otherwise remain hidden, but also makes visible to her the normally invisible processes and promulgated preconceptions by which the marginalization of such students' cultures is established and perpetuated.* In a passage that reminds us immediately of Nozrul's situation, Taber argues:

> One needs to think more carefully about what is taken to be a 'realistic' representation of a three-dimensional world. Our standard method of drawing objects from a fixed point of observation (more or less the procedure of photography) produces a picture that totally distorts

certain aspects of reality ... *I began to realize that I was judging [my students'] work by the standards of a procedure that they had not attempted to use.* Their drawings had an element of truth and power that projective representation cannot achieve as it involves technical problems that mar visual clarity. ... The projective method is only a 'realistic' style when defined by current 'Western' ideas.

(Taber 1981, pp.61–2; my emphasis)

Taber's view of the bilingual child's *artistic* development is broadly in line with Selinker's and Miller's view of the bilingual child's *linguistic* development, that begins by looking not at what the child is not doing but at what the child can and is doing, treating 'misses' at achieving the target representation not as errors but as a kind of 'interlanguage' that needs to be recognized and understood by the teacher if appropriate assistance is to be given (Selinker 1974, Miller 1983). Taber's recognition that drawing from a 'fixed point of observation' needs to be culture-referenced and that in Eastern cultures 'artists have experimented with different projective representations to produce more expressive compositions or to emphasize symbolic meanings' contrasts poignantly with Mrs Green's 'culture-free' assessment of Nozrul's drawing, as does Taber's account of her own bilingual students' responses to her request that they should draw a still-life composition. Taber was, she says, 'somewhat dismayed when they picked up the objects which I had taken such care to arrange, and replaced them in a way that would show an aspect they considered best suited for pictorial representation' (Taber 1981, p.61).

The parallel here with Nozrul's walking about the room in order to see parts of the figure that he had wanted to draw but could not see from the fixed viewpoint is an important one, as is the opposition between Taber's response to her students' actions – allowing them to deviate from her lesson plan and to challenge her assumptions – and that of Mrs Green, who viewed such attempted interference as naughtiness. This second opposition is partly explained by the following observations:

Although I was often delighted by qualities of richness, intricacy and patterning in the students' work, I was sometimes concerned by what seemed to me to be a lack of both powers of observation and imaginative originality. Most of the children did not seem to be very concerned with the kind of observation that is expected in the English schools when a 'realistic' picture is attempted. The children seemed unconcerned about overlapping the objects in a scene, the scale of objects against people, foreground and background size adjustments and 'correct' perspective.

(Taber 1981, p.61)

Taber's comments about 'powers of observation' are strikingly reminiscent of Mrs Green's observation that her student was 'not even seeing things properly' and of a subsequent observation that '[h]e can't even draw a straight line. ... How do you begin to teach basic techniques like that to a child of this age ... ?' While Mrs Green attributed this observational issue to an inability on her student's part, however, effectively marginalizing her student and his culture in the process, Taber is more inclined to treat it in terms of her students' preferences, which she is happy to welcome into her classroom: in her words, they 'seemed unconcerned'.

Taber's decision to treat her students' work as 'different' or 'unexpected' rather than merely 'wrong' leads both to different diagnoses of her students' behaviour and to the development of alternative pedagogies which include, at their heart, a focus on what we might call *cultural visibility*: that is to say, pedagogies based on attempted understandings of what cultural preferences *underpin* the students' cultural representations or artefacts, coupled with a recognition that the teacher's own customary ways of viewing and representing are themselves *no more than customary*. What Taber is, effectively, arguing for is what we might call a *Cultural Awareness Programme*. Such a programme is aimed at helping students and teachers to a proper understanding and appreciation of cultural difference, including the important concept that 'different' does not in any way imply 'better' or 'worse'. Consequently, it is committed to a pedagogy of *repertoire extension* ('additive biculturalism') rather than one of 'correct-and-replace': that is to say, to a pedagogy in which bilingual students are initiated into new discursive practices *but not at the expense of initially more familiar practices*, which are also simultaneously encouraged and celebrated.

To put this in more concrete terms, such a pedagogy results in new forms of representation, favoured within the English school system, being learned as important additions to forms of representation in which the bilingual student already has expertise and which are already valued outside that system. (Here, we can see the difference between partial inclusion, which operates within existing frameworks, and full inclusion, which demands a movement beyond those frameworks in order to change the frameworks.) In the terms of this inclusive pedagogy, a student like Nozrul would not be diagnosed – at least, not without a great deal more evidence – as defective: nor would he be taught – or, as in his particular case, symbolically excluded – on the basis of such a diagnosis. Rather, he would be shown alternative ways of drawing, including new techniques, that would widen his representational repertoire and at the same time help him to succeed within the English school system along with all its cultural biases. This would involve, centrally, showing him examples of the kind of drawing styles the teacher wanted him to add to his repertoire so that he had a clear idea of what was required, as well as offering plenty of praise and constructive criticism for every exhibition of his existing skills, *and introducing the rest of the class to examples of artistic representations from within the student's initially strongest culture.* (For an example of such strategies at work within the same school as Nozrul's and Mrs Green's, see Moore 1995.)

Common Underlying Proficiency: The Need for a Cultural Dimension

All of the ideas discussed so far in this chapter – the argument for broadening our concept of language towards one of culture-differentiated styles and forms; the potential 'invisibility' of those representational styles and forms to native practitioners, that brings with it assumptions about their status and 'correctness'; the need for teachers to stand back and examine their own and their students' existing cultural practices in relation to one another; and the notion of common underlying proficiency as a useful diagnostic and pedagogic tool – are brought neatly together in the work of Martin Lewis (1987), who also moves us on a step further in the quest for more developed forms and models of partial inclusion.

Drawing a parallel with Saussure's description of language in terms of 'langue' (that is, the normatively identical forms and processes from which individual 'speech acts' are constructed) and 'paroles' (the individual speech acts themselves), Lewis talks of the 'language' of art and of its acts of 'speech' (Saussure 1983). 'Speech' in this sense refers to individual artistic or representational creations and 'language' to the accepted patterns, possibilities and available techniques from which those speech acts derive and in whose terms they exist and are valued. One problem confronting Art teachers working with newly arrived sequential bilingual students is that in order to diagnose such students' representational 'performance' (their 'paroles') they must first know something of the representational 'language' (the 'langue') within which the students are *already* working. 'If we are insufficiently familiar with the "language"', Lewis argues, 'we are unlikely to understand its "speech": and if we do not understand someone's speech we run the risk of labelling it second-rate' (Lewis 1987, p.31).

Lewis's analysis of the task facing the Art teacher offers – like Taber's – a very manageable illustration of the task facing all teachers of Stage 1 bilingual students, who must get to understand[5] their students' language (here, I use language in the broader sense to incorporate most of what we know as *culture*) if they are to have any real chance of understanding what their students do, write and make in the classroom situation and what pedagogy is appropriate to the development and extension of such activity. If this sounds daunting, it is not meant to. Certainly, if what was being required of teachers was that they actually 'learn' the vocabulary, syntax and calligraphy of any number of other languages' symbolic systems, the job would be an impossible one: however, what is really required – and what teachers might reasonably expect to achieve – is a familiarization, within one's own subject area, with the relevant *general* styles and forms of language and knowledge favoured and prioritized within those symbolic systems, along the lines recommended and practised by Ann Taber. This 'getting to know' another person's preferred ways of communicating and doing things necessitates, of course, a prior but ever-developing *awareness* of one's own taken-for-granted ways of operating. As Lewis says, in words reminiscent of those of Martin-Barbero with which this chapter opened,

> If we are unaware of the construction of our personal reality, it is virtually inevitable that we will view the construction of the reality of others as an appendage of our own. Although we may enter the worlds of others with sensitivity and enjoy qualities we find there, we may perhaps see only decoration and surface. ... The messages that do get through can remain peripheral to our own deep truths. In such an event, our own world view remains untouched.
>
> (Lewis 1987, p.31)[6]

'Reality' for Lewis is clearly not a constant: it varies from culture to culture, both in its perception and in its representation through sign systems that will include not only words and groups of words but visual representations, gestures, movements, notions of social etiquette and so on. Teachers must, suggests Lewis, make themselves aware of this variability, and learn to perceive the world as

> a universe of sign systems if they are to encourage their pupils in explorations of seemingly familiar culture, be able to communicate about it to those who know it less well, and wish to promote intelligent entry to patterns of culture that are unknown, distant or alien.
>
> (Lewis 1987, p.31)

The two interrelated strands of this approach – to see one's own culture as a set of arbitraries and simultaneously to see one's students' cultures in the same way – have in common the notion of making 'visible' or problematic things which are, in the normal course of our lives, 'invisible' or taken-for-granted (for instance, the taken-for-granted notion that there is only one set of criteria by which to evaluate the drawing of an object, regardless of the drawer's cultural background). In this respect, they call to mind Cummins' notion of Common Underlying Proficiency, examined in Chapter 3, in which there are 'invisible' skills that are common across languages and cultures, underpinning 'visible' differences. What we might argue with reference to Mrs Green's diagnosis of Nozrul's work and behaviour is that, far from being unaware of this notion, she assumed *too much* for it – acting, in effect, as if (to use Lewis's terminology) Nozrul's 'langue' was identical to her own – and that she simultaneously took *too little account* of the invisible differences between cultures that would have helped her to explain the visible differences.

Fully to appreciate how this works, we might do worse than consider the slightly modified version of Cummins' 'Dual Iceberg' representation of Common Underlying Proficiency, shown as Figure 12.

The representation in Figure 12 is identical to that shown in Chapter 3, except that two 'hidden' areas have been shaded in on either side of the larger triangle. It is precisely these shaded areas that proved problematic in Mrs Green's diagnosis and that need clarification if the Common Underlying Proficiency theory is to stand up to serious interrogation and to be used in support of both the inclusive and the emancipatory paradigms. These areas are 'below the surface' and consequently 'hidden': but they are *not* common. They are, in fact, that part of a person's 'langue' that is culture-specific, that lies only just below the surface of the 'visible'[7] manifestations of their language and culture. They are the very areas that teachers need to explore if they are to understand and respond appropriately to the traps that Common Underlying Proficiency can lay, and if, in particular, they are to appreciate that though some skills and forms are common between cultures, others need very specifically to be learned. These areas I have called, provisionally, Variable Underlying Proficiency, in order to suggest both their distinction from and their kinship to Common Underlying Proficiency.

It is the central purpose of the following chapter to illustrate and to elaborate the notion of Variable Underlying Proficiency in greater detail and in a different pedagogical context, arguing that an understanding and appreciation of the notion is an essential prerequisite both to genuine ('developed') partial inclusion and to militations for truly emancipatory schooling. While the current chapter has devoted itself to the ways in which cultural marginal-

Figure 12 The 'Dual Iceberg' representation of bilingual proficiency: modified

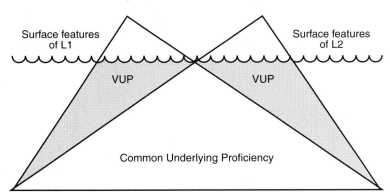

Source: Adapted from Cummins 1984, p.143
Note: VUP = Variable Underlying Proficiency

ization can occur in mainstream Art classrooms, it is intended that readers will make their own 'translations' by considering the ways in which such marginalizations can occur, in different forms, within any identified subject-area. In doing this, it may be useful to keep in mind Dunn's ever-pertinent question: 'Do students from different cultures have different learning styles?' (Dunn 1987, p.3).

Notes

1   Bullock, A. et al. (1975) *A Language for Life,* London, HMSO.
2   For interesting examples of writing development in which scripts in L1 gradually incorporate L2 elements and characteristics, see also the National Writing Project 1990, pp.54, 65–9.
3   This strategy might be seen to support the notion of Common Underlying Proficiency elaborated in Chapter 3: that is to say, the theory that certain skills acquired within one cultural–linguistic context can be put to ready use in another cultural–linguistic context with relation to a new set of cultural practices – skills that are, so to speak, 'transferable' through not being culture-specific. However, it also suggests, interestingly, that certain skills may *not* be readily transferable: hence the reluctance to include bilingual students in mainstream classes that were deemed to be 'language heavy'.
4   See also Bartle-Jenkins' observation that Muslim students might be 'very unlikely to identify with a norm regarding figurative representation' (Bartle-Jenkins 1980, p.16).
5   I have used 'understand' here on the basis that understanding is not the same as learning. The suggestion is not that teachers should, literally, 'learn' other languages and cultures in order to become multilingual themselves, but that they should put aside easy assumptions about bilingual students' performance and representations, and seek to find out and appreciate differences between the dominant school culture's and their students' own favoured ways of seeing and doing.
6   See also Martin-Barbero's reference to the way in which ethnocentrism hegemonically considers 'a manner of perceiving the world to be obvious and rooted in nature when that perception is no more than one among many possibilities' (Martin-Barbero 1993, p.81).
7   'Visible' is metaphoric, suggestive of that which is readily apprehensible because it lies, as it were, on the surface. Thus, 'visible' would include (for example) that which is 'audible'.

6   Partial Inclusion

Issues of Genre and Ethnocentricity

In April 1988, the St Lucian-born linguist Morgan Dalphinis described his own UK classroom experiences on arriving in an English school. Very early on, one of Morgan's teachers asked the class to write compositions based on their personal experiences. Morgan's response was to write a story which included everyday scenes of his life in St Lucia, which included the line 'a man fell off the [banana] truck and his head was bleeding'. Morgan's teacher, resisting the temptation to alter the non-standard 'his head was bleeding', chose, instead, to pick Morgan up on the actual content of his writing. 'Did this,' she asked, in a tone clearly indicating profound scepticism, 'really happen?' The answer to this was yes, it really did happen. However, Morgan's teacher remained unconvinced. 'I got the feeling,' Dalphinis said, looking back on the incident later in life, 'that she was questioning my normal reality. ... The semantic *content* [of my work] was not within her particular frame of reference.'

Abdul's Love Story: Matters of Style, Etiquette and 'Reality'

In the same school as Nozrul is Abdul, a fourteen-year-old Bangladeshi boy who has been living in the UK for eighteen months and who had virtually no written or spoken English on arrival. Much of his time at the school has been spent in small withdrawal groups, but now he spends the vast majority of his time in mainstream classes, sometimes with the support of a member of the school's EAL department. Perceived by his English teacher as a 'polite, hardworking student', he is following, among other subjects, a public examination course in English, in an unsetted class in which he is one of ten Sylheti-speakers and in which all but two students are bilingual.

Abdul's English teacher, Ms Montgomery, has set the class a project for their examination folders, first reading them a short story about a teenage boy's secret and unrequited love for a girl in his class, then inviting the students to write love stories of their own with the instruction that they should be based as far as possible on their 'own experience' and that they should be 'true to life'. After one hour-long lesson and a homework, Abdul, working alone, has produced the first draft of the first chapter of his story (Figure 13).

In addition to Ms Montgomery, a support-teacher, Mr Geddes, works with the class. Mr Geddes is a full-time member of the school's substantial

Figure 13 Start of first draft of Abdul's 'Love Story'

Love Story

by Abdul

one aponar time I fund a grill and I ask har exquiseme. wher you going she said?

I went to go some way wher you ask me for.' I said No I ~~y~~ Just Ask you you going I am sorry about that have you dont mind   she . said thats OK and anther I fund har on the bus~~y~~ and I ~~y~~ was set on the Front and she was set on the back about I Five Minuts ago two bay was come And ther set back of the set then this two bay said to hiair hellow ~~y~~wher you going ~~y~~ And she was ~~sket~~ skate.

and bays ~~ge am a-treyn~~g wha trey to do some bad think,

And O go ~~everthe~~ overth and ask hiar ther ~~go~~ gona ~~table~~. tabale with you she said yes

Can you half me plase. then I take ~~hai~~ hire and ~~we goin~~

EAL department. He is very committed to working with mainstream teachers and has been in the vanguard of the move away from the large-scale physical withdrawal of bilingual students. He describes himself as convinced of the value of 'recognizing bilingual pupils' existing language and learning skills' and of 'allowing them to produce work in [their first language] or English or a combination of the two'. It is Mr Geddes who sits down with Abdul to work with him on the preliminary draft of his story and his initial 'corrections' of Abdul's work are of two kinds. First, he focuses on

- The reproduction of acceptable standard English sentences, spellings, punctuation and paragraphing
- Presenting the story so that it makes immediate sense to any reader
- Helping Abdul with some of his more obvious linguistic confusions (between, for example, 'sit', 'set' and 'seat')
- The presentation and general layout of direct speech

Mr Geddes' initial corrections, which could be described in terms of 'formal linguistic knowledge' (Loveday 1982, p.61) rather than, say, style or register, are written by the teacher on to Abdul's draft. They are made with little explanation as to what was wrong with the original, on the basis that 'Abdul does not yet have the language to make sense of such explanations and it would just confuse him.' Mr Geddes' second set of corrections, made simultaneously with the first, relates to Abdul's storytelling *style*. Again – and for similar reasons – there is little explanation given to the student as to why these are necessary (for example, 'Let's get rid of some of these "ands"' or 'That sounds a bit more grown-up'). Indeed, there appears to be little differentiation in Mr Geddes' own mind between these corrections and the others. In answer to the question 'Are you not changing the style here?' for example, Mr Geddes replies: 'No, I don't think so. It's the same basic story. I've just made it hang together a bit better.'

It is evident from Mr Geddes' remarks (evidenced by the use of the word 'better') that he himself has perceived a certain *neutrality* in his corrections of Abdul's work: a neutrality that enables him to perceive corrections of style in the same way as corrections of grammar, spelling and punctuation. From this perception – which has to be opposed in the strongest terms – just as there is a 'correct grammar', so there is a 'correct' way of constructing and presenting a story: something that is neither negotiable nor culture-specific. The fact that, almost by sleight of hand, Mr Geddes may have begun transforming Abdul's story (through his elimination of simple connectors) from an essentially *additive* style, that we might associate with cultures with a strong oral bias, to a more subordinative one that we might expect to find in a more literacy-oriented culture, is an issue he does not feel obliged to address.[1] Whatever the impact of all this on the student, after two further sessions Abdul presents the second draft of the first part of his story, shown in its entirety (Figure 14). His handwriting still bears the influence of the Bengali script, but his spelling, punctuation and grammar are now very much 'standard English'.

Figure 14 Second draft of Abdul's 'Love Story'

Love Story

Once upon a time I saw a girl and I asked her, 'Where are you going?'

She said 'I'm just going somewhere. What are you asking for? Do you want to know for some special reason?'

I said 'No. I was just asking where you are going, I'm sorry. I hope you don't mind.'

She said 'That's okay.'

Afterwards, I saw her on the bus. I was sitting at the front and she was at the back. After about five minutes, two boys got on. They sat at the back near the girl and one of them said to her 'Hello. Where are you going?'

She was scared, and the boys tried to do something bad to her.

I went over and asked her, 'Are these boys troubling you?'

She said, 'Yes. Can you help me, please?'

I took her and we got off the bus.

Then I said, ' Can you get home all right?'

She said, 'No, I can't go home. I'm too scared.'

I said 'O.K. I'll take you.'

After half an hour, she said, 'I want to say something.'

I said, 'What is it?'

'How do I tell you? I can't tell you.'

I said, 'Go on. Tell me what it is.'

Then she said, 'I love you.'

Then I said, 'I love you too.'

Another day she and I went to the park. I said to her, 'Do you have any brothers?'

She said, 'Yes. I have one brother.'

I said, 'How old is he?'

She said, 'He's fifteen or sixteen. I'm not sure.'

Then I said, 'Have you got a sister?'

She said, 'No I haven't.'

Then she asked me, 'Do you have any brothers or sisters?'

I said, 'Yes. I have one brother and three sisters.'

She said, 'How old are they?'

I said, 'My brother is twenty-five years old and one of my sisters is twenty. Another sister is twenty-one years old, and the other one is eighteen.'

Then she said, 'Are they married?'

Then I said, 'Yes, two are married and one is not married.'

Then she said 'What about your brother?'

I said, 'My brother is married. He had two daughters and one son. Now he's only got two daughters because his son died.'

She said, 'Oh'.

I said, 'Have you got a father?'

She said, 'Yes, I have.'

We went home. Now we go out every day.

End of part one.

Nowadays, when I show the two drafts of Abdul's work to student-teachers or teachers attending professional development sessions, the reaction is invariably the same: Abdul's first draft shows life, interest, enthusiasm – his personality shines through; there may be an abundance of surface errors, some – perhaps a very small number – of which need to be followed up by the teacher in a sympathetic, explanatory way, but these do not in any way destroy the immediacy and appeal of a piece of writing that is very impressive for a student who has been in the country for so short a time. The second draft, by contrast, though technically correct, has lost its vitality: it is no longer Abdul's essay but the work of Mr Geddes, who has effectively appropriated it. Mr Geddes' initial approach of wholesale technical correction followed by Abdul's effectively copying out a 'technically correct' version of his original story is universally condemned, not only as an act of theft on the teacher's part but because it provides opportunity for no real learning to occur, merely (Vygotsky 1962) a 'parrot-like repetition' of the teacher's own legitimated version.

These criticisms of Mr Geddes' approach are all perfectly valid. Why, then, we may ask, should an experienced teacher, whose professed philosophy suggests a total commitment to anti-racist practice, undertake such horrendous acts of pedagogy with his multicultured student? The answer is not hard to find, and indeed we have already touched upon it in previous chapters. *It lies, in essence, in Mr Geddes' own assessment of the impossible*

*situation in which students like Abdul – and, by implication, their teachers –
find themselves.* Thus, in interview, Mr Geddes makes the following observations about Stage 1 bilinguals of Abdul's age:

> *With students like Abdul – yes, I'd have to admit that you sometimes have
> to cut corners. The main reason for that being that if you don't, they won't
> ever catch up. I don't know if you've got any idea how long it takes a pupil
> of this age to catch up in English, but according to current theory it can be
> several years – by which time, of course, it's too late. At this stage of the
> game, you sometimes just have to do a lot of the work for these kids, and
> just hope that they learn from being shown. It's a risky business, of course
> … you don't want to take over completely, and make them think it's not
> their work any more. … But what's the alternative? I mean, kids like
> Abdul have got to be ready to get through a public examination system in
> less than two years time. If they're not up to it, they don't get entered, and
> if they don't get entered that's it – they're on the scrap-heap. Getting kids
> like these through exams in such a short space of time is no mean feat, I
> can tell you.*

Unlike Mrs Green, who simply felt she was not equipped to cope with a
student she had diagnosed as beyond help, Mr Geddes occupies an opposing
position but ultimately, as we shall see, with little difference to the end result.
His humanitarian desperation to get his students through a public examination – knowing that they will be empowered by doing so and disempowered
by not doing so – is not, perhaps, one that many would condemn. Mr
Geddes knows that certain technical standards are required to do well in the
exam, he adjudges that if he proceeds at his normal pace insufficient technical progress will be made in the time available, and out of a sense of duty
and near-panic he seeks to 'put everything right' with Abdul's essay in one
fell swoop. Unfortunately, such a strategy, when carried to these extremes, is
doomed to failure, simply because it attempts the impossible: not only does
the teacher effectively end up writing all of the students' essays for them –
which, apart from anything else, is unlikely to do a great deal for those
students' sense of worth and self-esteem – but the students learn very little in
the process, since they are not actually being taught but merely 'corrected'.

For Abdul and Mr Geddes, however, the problem does not stop here –
because Mr Geddes knows that it is not only sound 'technique' that will be
required in the examination: *his student will also need to demonstrate that he
knows how to write a story in the 'approved' style, against pre-established
assessment criteria enshrined (1) in the National Curriculum for English, and
(2) (more critically at this stage) in the public examination syllabus.* It is this
knowledge that informs a *second* set of corrections made by Mr Geddes to
Abdul's work, illustrated in Dialogue 1.

Dialogue 1

Mr G: (*Reading through Abdul's revised draft with him.*) 'After half an hour she said, "I want to say something." I said, "What is it?" "How do I tell you? I can't tell you." I said, "Go on, tell me what it is." Then she said, "I love you." Then I said, "I love you too." ' Yes ... I'm a little worried about this bit. Would she say 'I love you', just like that? It seems a bit sudden. ... Would they really say that? Maybe they should say it another time, when they've got to know each other better? What do you think about that?

Abdul: (*Shrugs.*)
         [...]

Mr G: All this stuff about relations. ... This isn't really necessary, is it? ... For the reader. ... What do you think?

Abdul: (*Silence.*)

Mr G: I mean, I think you could really cut a lot of this out, couldn't you. Cut most of this out. (*Puts lines in the margin against this section.*) Just put here (*writing in the margin*): 'We talked about our families. She said she had a brother. I told her my brother was married ... '. You see, that's the other thing ... I don't know ... I mean, do people talk that way? In real life? Do they talk about how old their brothers and sisters are?

Abdul: Yes, Sir.
         [...]

Mr G: And this here: you suddenly say, 'Now he's only got two daughters because his son died.' And she (*Mr Geddes smiles*) ... she just says 'Oh'.

Abdul: (*Smiles with Mr Geddes.*)

Mr G: I mean, don't you think. ... Do you think they'd just talk about it like that, as if it didn't matter?

Abdul: (*Silence.*)

Mr G: Would they say that?

Abdul: Yes.

Despite his stated reluctance to explain too much to Abdul for fear of confusing him, in this dialogue Mr Geddes clearly does go further than in his previous technical corrections, in giving some indication to Abdul as to what is 'wrong' with his story from a stylistic, 'generic' point of view. What he does *not do* is explain to Abdul *why* these stylistic/generic alterations need to be made (for example, not to make the story intrinsically better, but to give it a better chance of gaining high marks in the public examination). The three stylistic points homed in on by Mr Geddes – all to do with issues of 'realism' – are:

- The girl's and boy's professions of love
- The boy's announcement of his nephew's death
- The long, detailed conversation about relatives

With regard to each of these, Mr Geddes asks: 'Would they say this?', 'Is this how people talk?' – clearly assuming the answer 'No'.

Abdul's reactions to Mr Geddes' criticisms are not, however, the same in each case, and not one of them is 'No'. Thus, Mr Geddes receives a shrug in answer to the first question, and a clear yes ('This *is* true to life') in answer to the other two. This difference in response (however insignificant it may appear in transcript) is, in fact, very important and tells us something about Abdul's *own* reality, the reality that is born of experience, that he carries with him in his own head. When he says 'Yes, it is true to life for the girl and boy to enter into such lengthy conversation about their relatives, or for the boy to announce so bluntly (to Western ears) that his young nephew is dead', Abdul may have meant two things:

> Yes, it is the kind of conversation that Bangladeshi youngsters (such as he) might engage in in real life,

or

> Yes, it is the kind of conversation that might be found in that other reality – or rather, those other realities – of Bangladeshi *storytelling*.[2]

When Mr Geddes questions these two episodes, he is, likewise, not merely saying

> Western children do not actually talk to each other like this and therefore no children living *in* the West talk to each other like this,

but also

> One of the essences of good storytelling is to make your story as close to reality, that is, to one particular reality, as possible (just as he has implied earlier that another is to make your story *elliptical* or *subordinative* – the favoured style in privileged Western European societies – rather than *linear* or *additive*).

In other words, Mr Geddes' assumption, in the time-saving exercise he feels himself pushed into, is that there is *a* way or set of ways of talking to one another and *a* way or set of ways of telling a story: in both cases, the ways favoured and promulgated by privileged cultural groups in British society. Within the realms of this particular field of *etiquette*[3] – for such it is – you do not formally discuss relatives with a potential lover on your first meeting – either in real-life situations or in fictional ones – and if someone in the family dies, you are not so cold-hearted as to talk about it as if it were just another aspect of living. These are the ways, the conventions, the discourses that Mr Geddes – like most of his colleagues at the school – has been brought up with and successfully initiated into, and, in the heat of the classroom situation, there is no question in his mind that these are the right ways, the right conventions, the right discourses – an assumption borne out and supported by the very values and criteria enshrined in the English exam-ination towards which Abdul is being taught. The possibility of multiple realities, leading to linguistic diversity in the broadest sense that embraces genre, perception and form,[4] remains *invisible* in the pedagogic act, as does the possibility – we might say, the likelihood – that Abdul has previously learned (and even been praised for his expertise in replicating) ways of telling stories that do *not* conform to the culture-specific criteria enshrined in the English National Curriculum or public examination system: ways that may, for example, give a very low priority to such matters as 'convincing dialogue', 'well-rounded characters', 'social realism' and all the other criteria against which Abdul's story is likely to be judged. For the teacher's purposes on this occasion, the student's previous learning experiences and expertise in the replication of cultural–linguistic forms might as well not exist: the teacher's task is not a matter of extending an already rich and varied language repertoire to embrace new forms and styles, but to introduce quasi-universal 'correctness' into a consciousness that has been previously empty in this department. In short, for all Mr Geddes' multicultural convictions, Abdul's alternative[5] way of telling a story has been perceived as a *deficient* way: cultural pluralism has not been embraced and the teacher's pedagogy is fashioned accordingly.[6]

It would be rash to impute aspects of students' linguistic–academic development solely to pedagogy or even to their school-based experiences. Such a claim would overstate the impact that any one teacher or school could have on a child's thinking and behaviour, and would deny other factors to do with the students' perceptions and experiences of life inside and outside the institution, *including how they are encouraged to think about themselves as learners*. It still needs to be said, however, that despite Mr Geddes' suggestion to Abdul to 'take [the story] home … see if you can make Chapter 1 any better [and] start work on Chapter 2', and despite Abdul's remaining a friendly, courteous member of the class, this particular student undertook no further work on his love story, nor, for the remainder of the school year, did he produce any writing that was not directly copied from a magazine or a book. It also needs to be said that when students are told by influential adults whose views they have been brought up to respect 'What you have done is not true to life', the implication clearly is:

1   This is not true to *my* life.
2   My reality and my way of representing reality are correct, therefore yours is incorrect.

The poor self-image that such discourses can create in students is one that may never be shaken off. There is a very real danger that such students, when they have also only recently arrived from another country, will grow up thinking not, in terms of academic discourse, 'They do and see things differently here' but 'They do and see things *properly* here' – a misunderstanding that will inevitably make an already difficult school situation significantly (and unreasonably) more difficult; for it is surely easier to learn new ways that are set into existing frameworks, where they can coexist with ways already learned, than it is to learn new ways that must *replace* old ones.

Variable Underlying Proficiency: Mr Geddes, Mrs Green and Ms Montgomery

Although Mrs Green and Mr Geddes both perceived and approached difficulties with their bilingual students in different ways, both teachers expressed a support for the notion of the transferability of skills between languages, if not between cultures: that is to say, both supported, in theory, Cummins' notion of Common Underlying Proficiency (CUP) described in Chapter 3.

Logically, such a view ought to militate against old-fashioned remove-and-replace strategies in the teaching of bilingual students, whose rationale is that it is necessary to 'abandon' a first language (or culture) in order to develop high-level skills in an additional one: that is to say, a belief in the transferability of skills ought to suggest a broad 'repertoire extension' model of pedagogy based on a belief in 'additive bilingualism' (Lambert 1967) and 'additive multiculturalism' (Triandis 1980) rather than one of cultural–linguistic genocide founded upon a belief in 'subtractive' biculturalism.

That support for the theory did not lead to such outcomes in these two cases may be attributable partly to circumstances (such as lack of time and resources) but partly, also, to a deficiency in the teachers' understandings of the CUP theory. As was suggested in Chapter 3, this may, in turn, be attributable to a certain weakness in the theory itself. What both teachers failed to recognize was that although large numbers of cultural and linguistic skills are indeed transferable and that good teaching seeks to take full advantage of this fact, *there will always be some skills that are not transferable because they are culture-specific*. Thus, Mrs Green assumed the transferability of (all) skills, but had a very clear and ethnocentric idea of what those skills looked like, appearing to see them as *universals*. When she encountered work in which those skills were missing, she assumed this signified 'no skills at all' and treated her student as deficient. Mr Geddes did not think his student deficient, but failed to appreciate that the criteria for a good story within one culture might in some respects be fundamentally different from those in another. To use Hammersley and Atkinson's formulation, we might say that Mr Geddes, despite his good intentions, failed to perceive his 'own' culture (also that prioritized within the mainstream curriculum) as anything but a reflection of ' "how the world is" … not conscious of the fundamental assumptions, many of which are distinctive to that culture, that shape [his] vision' (Hammersley and Atkinson 1983, p.8)[7]. Thus, although Mr Geddes ascribed equal value to different languages in the *formal* linguistic domain (Loveday 1982), this took place, arguably, *at the expense of* ascribing equal value in the domain of genre and style (the *functional* domain). To use Lewis's 'langue–parole' metaphor, this is the equivalent of teachers valuing what they perceive as their students' 'langues' (in this case, quite literally, their first *languages*, perceived in the superficial terms of basic syntax and vocabulary) but not necessarily their 'paroles'. It is for this reason, perhaps, that Abdul may have been given space in school to study his own strongest language (Bengali) for three periods a week as one of his optional subjects, but that there was no room outside the Bengali classroom for him to use the styles and forms of that language where these differed significantly from the styles and forms of standard English. Put bluntly, in Bengali lessons Abdul's storytelling style *could* win the approval of his teacher; in the English classroom, where things were done differently, it did not. In this way, the marginalization of the Bengali language itself was confirmed, even through the very act of its inclusion as a *bona fide* curriculum subject.

Given what has been said about the habitual invisibility of one's own cultural preferences and practices, and the role this invisibility played in the marginalizations that took place within Mrs Green's and Mr Geddes' classrooms, we might legitimately ask: *are teachers condemned to living with this situation and, if not, what steps might they take to make visible to themselves that which is characteristically invisible?* The answers to these questions have already been partly answered in Ann Taber's writings about her deliberately 'open-minded' practice with bilingual students in her Art teaching, described in the previous chapter. Such practice, however, need not confine itself to the Art classroom, and indeed was present in other subject areas at the school attended by Nozrul and Abdul. The following example illustrates similarly orientated pedagogy in another English class at Nozrul's and Abdul's school.

Mashud and Ms Montgomery

Another fourteen-year-old bilingual student, Mashud, also had Ms Montgomery as his principal English teacher at School A. Like Abdul, Mashud was in his second year of living in England. He had come from the same region of Bangladesh as Abdul and the boys had experienced similar educations before coming to the UK. During his time at School A, Mashud had, like Abdul, made steady progress in English, his second-language competence being described by the EAL department as 'average for his age and experience'. Orally quite reticent in his second language (though not in his first), his attempts at replicating standard English grammatical structures in his speech and writing were, like Abdul's, developing slowly but surely. He wrote copiously and with great enthusiasm – if not yet with a developed command of register and genre – and in this respect his written work was impressive.

Ms Montgomery had noticed very early on in her work with Mashud that this student had a habit of responding to every written task – whether it was the writing of a story, a description, a set of views, or even a letter – by producing a very formulaic, fairy-story-like piece of work, usually with a moral in its tail. This was by no means uncommon in the work of her Bangladeshi students: however, the fact that Mashud was a very prolific writer had brought the issue into particularly sharp focus for her.

Rather than approaching this aspect of Mashud's work in terms of 'deficiency', Ms Montgomery had adopted, from the very start, what might be called a cultural – and *anti-culturist* – approach to his written assignments, employing precisely the kind of 'cultural distancing' that was not demonstrated by Mr Geddes. Thus, a first attempt to account for Mashud's idiosyncrasy was formulated by Ms Montgomery in the following terms, shortly after taking over as Mashud's English teacher, at one of her weekly planning meetings with the support-teacher with whom she co-taught this class:

> *Mashud seems to have a background where making up stories is not so highly valued … not nearly as much as learning moral tales. I suppose that must have something to do with his culture … if it's more strongly oral-based than our own … or even with the sorts of dangers in Bangladesh, which are maybe more predictable, and located more in the natural environment than they are here … I don't know … I don't know enough about it, really. … Here, on the other hand, making up your own stories and writing them down is a very highly valued activity.*

Ms Montgomery's reaction to Mashud's writing immediately sets itself apart from that of Mrs Green (who consciously dismissed her student's output as evidence of irremediable inadequacy) and Mr Geddes (who appeared to feel he could allow himself no time to explore and build upon *difference* in the face of the urgent need to produce conformity). Though her commitment was in one important respect the same as Mr Geddes' – to help her student achieve well in the public examination in English – her orientation to his existing skills and preferences was very different and, as we shall see, would lead her to a correspondingly different orientation in terms of pedagogy. In order to understand this alternative orientation, we need to keep in mind that, despite her admission 'not to know enough' about her student's existing cultural skills and preferences, Ms Montgomery plainly did know enough not to dismiss Mashud's idiosyncrasy as a problem of cognitive–linguistic origin, preferring to *ask herself* questions about her student's cultural–linguistic background. Those questions led to a tenable hypothesis – on the basis of which she could structure future pedagogy – that Mashud might be used, in a social world 'outside' his current school, to different sets of priorities and to different generic forms in spoken and written language from those demanded by the English public examination system. We might say that, as an educated professional, this teacher had (1) recognized that her student had a *history*, and (2) understood that however little she might be able to discover of the *detail* of that history, she could not ignore it if she wanted to help her student to progress.

These understandings on the teacher's part had the immediate effect of opening up a questioning, sympathetic discourse which, at future planning meetings, enabled other issues to be recognized, discussed and tackled in a far more informed and productive manner than might otherwise have been the case. At a subsequent planning meeting, for example, the question of Mashud's 'essentially oral' culture was to resurface, this time finding its focus in the structure of his narratives.

Dialogue 2

Support-teacher:	I wonder, you know, if you're remembering stories for repetition, if you're likely to order them in a particular way: also, to cut out ... not adjectives as such; they could have an important function ... but a lot of what we would call 'background detail'.
Ms M:	All that description and 'characterization' stuff. ... Yes ... I suppose you could be right. It would in a sense be irrelevant, wouldn't it. I mean, the moral would be the important thing ... not what kind of day it was, less still what mood people were in. ... None of that so-called realism or naturalism that we're so into ... that could all just be so much clutter. ... When you think about it, there could be the most enormous gap between what Mashud has been brought up to value in narratives and what we're telling him he should be valuing.

By Ms Montgomery's own admission, she did not know enough about Bangladeshi or Sylheti storytelling traditions to be able to expound with any degree of confidence on the cause of Mashud's particular way of going about things;[8] nor did she have immediate access to anyone she could ask. The key to her future pedagogy, however, lay in her very wise recognition that 'there could be the most enormous gap between what Mashud has been brought up to value in narratives and what we're telling him he should be valuing' – a recognition that clearly had implications not only for assessing and developing Mashud's own writing but also for assessing and developing his response to the writing of others (that is, the study of *literature*). It is this recognition – reminiscent of Ann Taber's understanding of her bilingual students' work and in direct contrast to the apparent lack of understanding of Mrs Green and Mr Geddes – that effectively marks the point at which Ms Montgomery was able to distance herself from the normally hidden assumptions she had been bringing to the classroom with her, in such a way as to make visible and open to criticism the cultural preferences and procedures underpinning those assumptions.

An example of how these perspectives affected her future pedagogy *vis-à-vis* Mashud (and, indeed, *vis-à-vis* other Bangladeshi students within her classes) can be traced through her work with Mashud's class on an autobiography project – a project which had been selected very much with Mashud and the other bilingual students in mind, on the basis that it would provide opportunities for these students to elaborate and build upon existing strengths and preferences (for example, through the inclusion of elements of the moral tale) while at the same time inviting key extension skills such as 'creative redrafting',[9] 'describing unique events', 'reporting conversations' and 'introducing and elaborating characters' feelings and motives'. Prior to setting this project up with the whole class, Ms Montgomery had taken pains to express privately to Mashud her very genuine appreciation of the 'moral tales' that he had previously written. She had supported this private appreciation with a more public recognition of the stories' worth, by mounting four of them on the classroom wall. Immediately before getting Mashud started on the autobiography project – which invited students to write their own life-stories to date – Ms Montgomery had also taken him and some other students aside, to explain to them that she wanted something very specific from this piece of writing: 'something completely different, that you may have never been asked to do before – writing about things that actually happened, that you saw or that happened to you and your friends and families, using your own memories and trying to make it as real as possible for your reader'.

In the event, the autobiography project proved very successful in terms of the objectives Ms Montgomery had established. While Mashud's first draft contained distinguishable elements from the moral-tales genre (stories of being attacked by an angered cow, being 'caught cold' and injured in a wrestling match, having a grandparent killed by the military when anxiety for his family drew him away from a safe haven), these elements were all, simultaneously, real-life events, personalized for the reader through the selection of specific details: that is to say, a particular generic preference may have contributed to the *selection* of the events, but their actual description was rooted in an alternative genre that prioritized 'verisimilitude' and the need to engage the reader sympathetically (Figure 15).

Figure 15 First 'corrected' draft of Mashud's autobiography

Sometimes I think I can remember things I did, things I saw from the age of eleven, but I don't think I can remember things before that. My mum and dad told me they had a small house in a small village between the jungles. When the war began, everybody went to the jungle to save their lives. People took food with them and a lamp and a torch for light, because in those days we didn't have electricity in Bangladesh.

People who used to live at the top of a hill or between the fields had to dig a hole that they could hide inside and save their own and their children's lives. My parents said they used to live on the hillside and they dug a hole and hid in it, covering it over with some branches and leaves. My grandfather heard that we were in trouble. He used to live in another village, quite far away. He was so worried that he came looking for my parents, but he never saw anybody. He was shouting and looking for them. The Military were not far away. They heard him calling, and they came and one of them shot him. After about an hour my parents came out and someone told my dad that his dad was dead. He was shocked. It was that night that I was born.

My dad told me they had gone to look for a doctor. Also, I was lucky to be born that night because the Military had gone on to another village.

When I was about ten years old we had some farms, and every family who had a farm if they couldn't look after it by themselves they got another person as a paid help, usually someone very poor.

We had four cows. One day school was closed and I was looking after the cows. Suddenly, someone came up behind me and showed a piece of red cloth to the cow. The cow started chasing me. I was running. The cow pushed me with its horns and I went rolling down the hill. I was shocked and hurt in my chest. It took me months to get well.

But in Bangladesh it's lots of fun with your friends. Every morning, we go to the swimming pool with a lot of friends. Then we go to school. School starts at ten o'clock and we have a half-hour break at eleven o'clock and finish at four. Also we have a half day every Friday because all Muslim people go to the Mosque to pray.

Sometimes after school everyone goes home for dinner, and after that, when the sun goes down, all the boys come out into the fields to play football and other games. It's nice fun every afternoon, except Saturdays – because every Saturday we have a market just beside our house. It's our own market, and we also have our own chemist and a small sweet-shop.

I have two uncles, one in Bangladesh and one in England, and I also have two brothers and a sister in Bangladesh.

Once, in my primary school, we held a competition like a wrestling match, and I was in it. I had a big guy against me. I couldn't handle him at all. He was too strong for me, and so big. There were a lot of people around and I didn't know what to do, I was so shy and scared. Suddenly he jumped on my ankle and broke it! I was at home about three months. I can still remember how my ankle hurt.

In the winter time we had a big fruit garden. We grew bananas and mangoes and jackfruit, apples and lemons. Some seasons we sold them if we had a lot, or else we'd eat them.

At Ramadan my parents used to fast until 2.30p.m. to 9.00a.m. I used to fast some time if I could, but I couldn't very much. I got too hungry. My parents slept most of the time to use the time up. I used to get some mangoes and jackfruit for them and wash it for them. Ramadan lasts one month. After Ramadan we celebrate. The day we celebrate is called EID. On that day we get new clothes and extra food and we go to our cousins' and friends' houses and have nice fun. On that day we can do anything we want to do.

Also every year we have a big market and we call it 'Mala'. Everybody goes. They have nice toys and music and a magic show. We enjoyed Mala a lot.

Another day, before the summer holiday, we had a sports day. We played badminton, volleyball, cricket and throwing heavy stones. There was so many people in the field. I was playing badminton. We had great fun.

As intended by the teacher, the bulk of Mashud's essay comprised actual life-events and details (Mashud's traumatic birth during the Bangladesh War, descriptions of games with friends, family activities and a passage on Ramadan and EID) whose interest was, as it were, 'intrinsic' rather than supportive (see also Moore 1990, 1995). When two specific difficulties did arise with the essay – the first (raised by Mashud himself) that it was 'too short', the second (noticed by Ms Montgomery) that the essay followed too linear, chronological a pattern for the genre – these difficulties were not subjected to instant 'correction' by the teacher, but became opportunities for further developmental work in which the onus for elaboration was placed clearly with the student. Thus, over the length issue Ms Montgomery engaged Mashud in the following way:

Dialogue 3	
Ms Montgomery:	Well, what else could you say?
Mashud:	*(Shrugs.)*
Ms M:	How about something more about the things that you did with your friends? The wrestling match was interesting. What other things did you do?
M:	Yes, Miss.
Ms M:	Also, you haven't yet said anything about your life in England. You could write a bit about that; what it's like here for you.
M:	Cold, Miss.
Ms M:	*(Laughs.)* Yes ... cold. ... Well, you could say that. What else could you say?
M:	*(Shrugs.)*
Ms M:	Well, you think about it. Write down more bits on a separate sheet of paper and then show it to me.

When Mashud had, as suggested, produced two further pieces of writing – one on going hunting and fishing with friends, one on his family's first days in England – these, in turn, were used strategically by Ms Montgomery to address her second concern – that of the overly chronological (and therefore, to Western European eyes, 'messy') structure of the essay. Dialogue 4 gives a taste of how this matter was approached by the teacher.

Dialogue 4

Ms Montgomery:	That's really excellent, Mashud. Very good. Do you think this is long enough now?
M:	Miss ... *(Tone implies 'yes'.)*
Ms M:	So all you've got to do now is add these bits. ... But ... don't just put them on the end. In this kind of writing, it's best to put things together ...
M:	Miss?
Ms M:	Mmm. ... It's hard to explain ... look ... *(Points to Mashud's work.)* Here ... the War. ... Here ... your home. ... Here, you and your friends playing. ... Here, Ramadan. ... Now ... these new bits. ... You and your friends playing. ... Put that in here.
M:	*(Pointing to the second new piece of writing.)* This, Miss?
Ms M:	Er ...
M:	Here, Miss!
Ms M:	Yes. Good. Put that bit at the end. It actually goes there quite nicely, doesn't it? Good. Well done.

In addition to effecting these two insertions into his original draft, Mashud voluntarily made two other organizational changes to his essay, first removing a piece about two uncles from its original location (surrounded by paragraphs dealing with recreational activities with his peers) to a new location in which he describes other matters related to his immediate family, then moving a short paragraph, about a sports day in Bangladesh, to create a new paragraph dealing with games and recreation.

Subsequent analysis of Mashud's drafting and redrafting of his autobiography essay indicated the use of new techniques not previously seen in his writing (Moore 1995). These included:

*   The evaluation of personal experience
*   The adoption of a conversational narrative voice
*   The use of redrafting skills of a far more complex nature than he had previously deployed

These redrafting skills provided some evidence that Mashud had begun to think more flexibly about the *organization* of his work, recognizing that in addition to the linear approach to narrative writing adopted (quite appropriately) in his moral tales, in which events were always presented strictly in accordance with when they happened, there existed alternative ways of presentation, involving (in this instance) the 'collection' of information and events into 'sets'. This 'collection approach' may be seen as a useful additional tool in an activity such as the autobiography project, suggesting that Mashud had successfully accomplished some of the generic–linguistic repertoire extension that his teachers had hoped for.

As to the teachers' other intention, to achieve repertoire extension without devaluing or denying the continued development of Mashud's *existing* language skills, this had already been partly achieved through the avoidance of words or demeanours that labelled such skills as 'wrong'. It would be underlined in future lessons, however, through a range of related activities. These would include:

* Following up the autobiography assignment with an assignment inviting all the students in the class to write moral tales
* Involving Mashud in the introduction to this activity, through asking him to orate two of his own tales to the class and to offer general advice on how the tales should be presented as well as what kinds of story were appropriate
* Devoting time to discussing with the class the notion of 'genre', explaining that different kinds of writing are linked with different kinds of assignment not only within but between cultures – another activity in which Mashud and other students would have opportunities to describe to their monolingual and bilingual peers the kinds of writing and speech that were linked to particular representational activities within their own 'first cultures'

While recognizing the dangers of basing too sweeping a set of claims on Ms Montgomery's lessons with Mashud, it has to be said that, just as Abdul's interactions with Mr Geddes coincided with the end of his writing career at school, so Mashud's interactions with Ms Montgomery coincided with some notable developments in his. In subsequent assignments, for example, Mashud made regular attempts to replicate new forms or genres, showing a growing awareness of the different language styles expected of different tasks. Increasingly, he broke out of his previous reticence, to invite monolingual English peers to read and comment on drafts of his work, and he began to make substantial alterations to early drafts by reshaping the text and making significant additions and deletions – an activity encouraged by his introduction to the English Department's word-processors. If Ms Montgomery had not been entirely responsible for these developments, her approach had certainly helped to create an environment in which their development was permitted and encouraged. While Mashud had, like Nozrul and Abdul, been set an unfamiliar task within the context of an unfamiliar language and culture, he had responded positively and constructively to the task under his teachers' guidance, and would continue to value himself as a writer, going on to achieve a good grade in the public examination for this subject.

Beyond Partial Inclusion: Ms Montgomery's Evaluation

Where do we locate Ms Montgomery's work with Mashud in terms of inclusive/exclusive education and, particularly, within the categories 'undeveloped partial inclusion' and 'developed partial inclusion' (Chapter 2)?

Of all the differences between Ms Montgomery's approach to Mashud's learning and those of Mrs Green and Mr Geddes to their bilingual students, there are two that stand out. The first is that, for different reasons, Mrs Green's and Mr Geddes' pedagogies were characterized by a sense of impatience, in either case linked to stresses experienced as incoming forces from the world outside the immediate classroom situation. In Mrs Green's case, this led to a dismissal of her student on the grounds that she lacked the skills and training to make any impact on the perceived enormity of 'his' problem; in Mr Geddes' case, it resulted in an ultimately unhelpful overlooking of the complexity of the task his student had been set and of the ways in which genuine learning occurs. Ms Montgomery, by contrast, managed to remain both patient and, to a degree, untouched by those external tensions.

The second difference is that although Ms Montgomery gave instructions to her student that seemed to leave little room for debate or manoeuvre (for example, 'put that in here') and although much of her work focused on the surface quality of Mashud's work, she always actively encouraged him to make decisions of his own, implying, through this action, a recognition of the cognitive–linguistic skills and indeed (to use Bourdieu's expression) the 'cultural capital'[10] that he already possessed. In doing this, she never lost sight of the fundamentally social nature of learning, or of the central role played *by* language in *developing* language.

Bearing in mind the apparent success of Ms Montgomery's pedagogy, it may come as a surprise that her own evaluation of this pedagogy proved to be very self-critical. This criticism related, principally, to the fact that she had offered 'no real explanation' to Mashud as to *why* his original piece might benefit from rejigging in the way she had proposed.

Much has been made in this and the previous chapter of the dangers of devaluing students' existing cultural forms and preferences while one is helping those students to acquire and develop expertise in the new cultural forms they will need if they are to enjoy a full range of options and opportunities in the wider society in which they live. What I have tried to argue is that this challenge is best met by adopting a policy of extending cultural–linguistic repertoires (Bakhtin 1986) rather than by treating certain cultural–linguistic forms as intrinsically 'correct' and attempting to substitute these for other cultural–linguistic forms perceived and treated as 'incorrect'. With hindsight, Ms Montgomery found it impossible to say whether the changes to Mashud's work, effective though they were in terms of actual and possible academic success, were evidence of an extension of his cultural–linguistic repertoire, or whether they were simply the manifestation of the sort of substitution process she had sought to avoid, resulting from a not unreasonable misunderstanding on Mashud's part that his earlier efforts had indeed been 'wrong' and that his subsequent efforts were 'correct'. These doubts were to lead Ms Montgomery to think very carefully about broader issues related to cultural reproduction, and in particular to relate her anxieties to emergent issues of culture and pedagogy that were relevant to all her students, whether they were bilingual or not:

> *I see now that we really need to explain things more … to all our bilingual kids. Showing them the right way – if you can call it the right way – is step number one. You can make some headway in that, even when the language gap is fairly wide. Step number two is to explain to them – and to explain to all children – why certain ways of doing things have come to be accepted as right and proper. For that, you actually need to be able to communicate on a far more sophisticated level because you're getting into the area of politics and sociology. If we can't be provided with bilingual teachers who have been trained in this sort of pedagogical approach, who can explain to these pupils the complicated nature of language, culture and class, there will always be a danger that we [monolingual English] teachers will end up doing things we're trying not to do.*

While Ms Montgomery's observations might be considered somewhat harsh,[11] it is hard to question her wisdom in continuing to challenge her practice rather than resting on past achievements, or in linking her experiences with Mashud to wider issues, including those of educational funding. This last point emphasizes again the importance of contextualizing teaching strategies within the wider education system and in particular within considerations of the complex issues surrounding the positionings and developing identities of practitioners which take place at the intersections of forces, ideologies and desires that may often be contradictory. Such considerations have already been touched on through reference to *symbolic violence* (Bourdieu and Passeron 1977): that is to say, the assertion, chiefly through educational systems, of one set of cultural forms and preferences by the powerful groups of people who own and practise them, over other sets which they perceive – and encourage *their* owners to perceive – as inferior forms. One understanding of the story of Abdul and Mr Geddes is as a graphic example of symbolic violence at work. That is to say, Abdul's existing, *actively learned* ways of telling stories are perceived by the teacher – acting as unknowing agent of a dominant cultural group – as incorrect, unlearned ways, and are responded to accordingly through a strategy of eliminate-and-replace. (This, anyway, is how Mr Geddes' response may appear to his student.) It could be argued, however – and Ms Montgomery very bravely appears to be suggesting just such a case – that Mashud, despite his 'success', was just as much a victim of symbolic violence himself: that is to say, that he perceived his 'initial' ways of organizing his work as incorrect and the school's ways, mediated through his respected teacher, as correct. If he did not 'give in' in the way that Abdul appeared to, this was because the symbolic violence perpetrated against him was simply carried out with greater subtlety. Certainly, Ms Montgomery's pedagogy did not actively, at any point, invite a shared opposition between teacher and student to that wider, less easily threatened symbolic violence that resides within the formal, public criteria by which Mashud's work (and, we might suggest, Mashud himself) would, ultimately, be assessed.

What we can say about Ms Montgomery's pedagogy is that, like Ann Taber, it pushed much more closely up against the boundaries of what can be achieved within the partial inclusion paradigm than, say, that of Mr Geddes. While all three teachers may be said to have been operating within a liberal, humanist tradition of teaching, Ms Montgomery and Ann Taber were apparently able to achieve a greater degree of cultural distancing than Mr Geddes, and were consequently better equipped to support their students' development within the existing constraints of a marginalizing system. Theirs was thus a more fully developed form of inclusion, involving not just the physical inclusion of the marginalized student in their class-rooms but a genuine attempt at symbolic inclusion. We might say that Ms Montgomery's pedagogy stands at the boundary between partial inclusion and full inclusion – a boundary which she could either attempt to cross (an ambition implied in her recognition of the need to 'explain things more') or at which – with no criticism intended – she could opt to remain.

The road to full inclusion is, as has already been indicated, a road that has to travel outside the school (physically and/or symbolically) in order to effect the hegemonic changes necessary for its successful conclusion. As Ms Montgomery seems to suggest, however, there are things that can be done within the classroom situation – and in spite of prevailing ideologies and their imposed constraints – that go beyond the forms of pedagogy she has practised. Meanwhile, her suggestion that one can only go so far with students for whom the teacher's language-of-instruction is relatively new and unfamiliar moves us beyond considerations of bilingual students – where the visibility of marginalization is generally quite high – to considerations of other students who are symbolically excluded. Inevitably, this leads to considerations of the experiences of *bidialectal* students, who continue to suffer from irrational prejudices about their preferred cultural–linguistic forms and styles, underpinned by a view – often very strongly held even within the teaching profession – that these forms and styles, too, are not just different (from 'standard English' forms and styles) but essentially defective. It is to some of these experiences that I now want to turn and, in examining them, to consider how teachers might begin to push yet closer against the boundaries of symbolically inclusive education, in ways that engage critically with the dominant cultures and criteria by which their students are judged.

Notes

1   For an elaboration of these differences in relation to oracy- and literacy-based cultures, see Ong 1982. If we accept the hypothesis that the additive form of storytelling is favoured within certain cultures, any criticism of it is shifted from the notion of 'universal correctness' and becomes no more than a matter of taste – rather like criticizing someone for wearing 'loud' clothes or enjoying pop music, simply because one prefers sober clothes or would rather listen to jazz.

2   Asian students have often pointed out to me that there are strong echoes in Abdul's story of the Indian love-story film genre.

3   Differentiating between grammatical and stylistic corrections, Kress describes the latter as 'paradigm cases of the notion of error arising out of conventionality'. The function of such correction 'lies in coercing the one who is corrected into adherence to convention. In essence the question is one of etiquette and manners, like opening your egg at the blunt or pointed end' (Kress 1982, pp.188–9).

4   In an interesting but undeveloped remark during the course of interview, one of the EAL teachers at the school observed: 'Multiculturalism has never got as far as valuing the plurality of genres.'

5   The word 'alternative' is somewhat problematic. In using it, I do not intend to reinforce the erroneous notion of the inherent 'correctness' of so-called standard forms from which 'alternatives' are deviations. As I hope will be clear from the body of my text, the alternatives I speak of are to be perceived as *different* but in no way subordinate to the forms favoured by the dominant cultural groups. Interestingly, some schools now speak of 'English as an Alternative Language' rather than 'English as an Additional Language', going some way towards addressing the power imbalance implicit in the latter term.

6   It is worth drawing attention to Mr Geddes' third criticism, related to the young lovers' mutual profession of affection, and Abdul's responsive shrug which suggests an uncertainty on his part. On the one hand, he has been asked to make his story true to life. On the other, when he does just that – or thinks he has done just that – he finds his work criticized for its *not* being true to life. It is a shrug that suggests: 'I do not know' – which may not be surprising given the task Abdul has been set. Abdul has been asked not simply to write a piece of *fiction* (an activity that, like Nozrul's being asked to produce a figurative drawing, he may have been relatively unused to), but to write a very particular *kind* of fiction, with its own very particular conventions and norms. Within that piece of writing, he faces the additional task of having to introduce direct speech, a notoriously difficult and variable subgenre (see, for example, Volosinov 1986, pp.109–59). He has been advised that this direct speech must be 'naturalistic', 'true to life'; but he has also been aware that he is writing a story and that stories are *not* 'life' but have their own particular conventions and 'realities'. The task is made yet more difficult by the fact that he is not merely being asked to write a story *in* a partic-

ular style, but that he is also being asked to write a story *about* a style: that is, a style – also culturally variable – of *courtship*.

The above should give some indication of the extreme difficulty and complexity of Abdul's task. In a task such as this, the differentiation of content from style is virtually impossible., since the content in a very important sense *is* the style: when Mr Geddes criticizes what Abdul's characters are saying to one another, for example, he is simultaneously criticizing the manner of their discourse. Whether Abdul has responded by attempting to write according to the rules of a genre of storytelling – perhaps an essentially oral genre – learned in his native Bangladesh; whether he has attempted to represent a new kind of 'realism'; or whether he has sought some kind of middle course is not immediately inferable from the story itself.

7 See also Schutz 1964.

8 Nor, indeed, could she be expected to without appropriate professional development and the time to devote to such development.

9 Previously, Mashud had produced second drafts of stories at his teachers' request, but these had amounted to neat copyings-up of teacher-corrected originals, with virtually no structural or expressive modifications.

10 'Cultural capital' refers to the cultural skills acquired by a human being – not necessarily within the school setting – that can, as it were, be 'cashed in' for privilege and success, often in the form of academic success which can, in turn, be used to acquire high-status, well-paid jobs (Bourdieu and Passeron 1977). Much has been written elsewhere about the necessity for children to achieve expertise in the various genres, forms and behaviour-patterns valued by their schools if they are to have any chance of being perceived there as successful, and of the fact that some children, notably indigenous middle-class children in whose homes tastes, values and social and learning conventions are most likely to match those of the schools they attend, come to school initially better equipped in this respect than others (see especially Kress 1982, Brice Heath 1983, Tizard and Hughes 1984). In the case of children arriving in school *in a new country*, it is not unreasonable to suppose that the gap between the values and conventions of home and school may be particularly wide, regardless of social class, and may indeed appear wider for older than for younger children. At one end of this particular spectrum, younger natives will bring with them 'home' values and experiences of social and learning conventions which may reflect or contradict those they will encounter in the school environment; at the other end, older non-natives are likely to bring not only 'home' values and conventions, but, crucially, considerable experience of social and learning conventions *in a school situation* – that is to say, in the school or schools they attended before migrating. One possible effect of this is that such children may already think they know how to succeed in school and may bring with them clear but mistaken notions of their new school's expectations and values, assuming that these will be the same as those they have encountered in schools elsewhere. These expectations and values must confront their new teachers' own visible and invisible notions of what appropriate school behaviour comprises. Such students may have brought with them 'cultural capital' that was of value in the country of their birth, only to find that in the absence of any exchange rate mechanism it is quite worthless in the country to which they have moved. See also Levine's observation that bilingual students may be 'bemused by their lack of success in English schools, coming as they might have done from successful school careers elsewhere' (Levine 1981, p.27).

11 As her comments imply, for instance, if she had attempted much more with Mashud this might only, given his current levels of L2 proficiency, have resulted in confusion and demoralization.

7 Working with Bidialectal Students

'Standard English', Power and the Pathologization of Difference

It is very important that children in our primary schools learn ... to read and spell, and to write in *proper English*.

(Thatcher 1987, emphasis in original)

It would be perverse for schools to acknowledge and value the language of Punjabi or Italian children, while criticising and rejecting non-standard British dialects.

(Edwards 1987)

By bidialectal students, I mean students who may habitually operate in one dialect of a specific language (for example, 'standard English') in one set of situations (such as the school classroom) and in another dialect of the same language in other situations (such as the school playground or the home).

In terms of school experience, there are clearly likely to be significant areas of difference between bilingual and bidialectal students just as there are likely to be key similarities. The bidialectal students whose experiences I shall be describing were, for example, all 'simultaneous bidialectals' (as is typically though not inevitably the case), while the bilingual students I have written about were all 'sequential bilinguals'.[1] They were also able to make immediate 'surface sense' of the vast majority of their teachers' instructions, because – in the receptive sense – they were already fluent in the forms of English used by their teachers. Similarly, it was not difficult for them to gain extra guidance if needed from other English-speaking students in the classroom. In common with bilingual students, however, these bidialectal students were, as we shall see, systematically marginalized by a culturally biased school curriculum, imposed by central government, that was outcome-monitored through public tests and examinations and that typically pressed teachers into the service of reproducing and validating dominant cultural forms and values whether they wanted to or not. As with the bilingual students, this essentially *curricular* marginalization was typically carried out – from a very early age – within the caring, Arnoldean discourse of emancipation-through-education. It did not confine its marginalizations of such students to matters of the mere mechanics of language (whether, for example, it is preferable to say 'she and I' or 'me and her') but, as in the case of bilingual students, dealt both with matters of *genre* (that is to say, one's manner of presenting and representing the world, whether this be in a work of art or in the writing up of a science experiment) and – even more worryingly – with matters of *perception and experience* ('How do I, *in the first place*, see and experience the world I am [re]presenting?'). It is hardly surprising that young people in these circumstances will often develop poor self-image, including (as we shall see in the first case study) very negative perceptions of themselves as learners and language-users – in the worst cases leading to what Trudgill has referred to as 'linguistic self-hatred' (Trudgill 1983, p.209; see also Coard 1971).

Such marginalizations – which first label certain cultural practices as 'non-standard' and then (supported and tacitly validated by this initial labelling) dismiss non-standard forms as inferior or wrong – have often led, logically, to the kind of eliminate-and-replace pedagogies that we have already considered in relation to bilingual students, rather than to pedagogies that favour notions of repertoire extension. They are underpinned by certain misconceptions about so-called standard and non-standard cultural practices, among which those shown in Figure 16 – presented in terms of one particular form of dominant cultural preference ('standard English') – are key.

These misconceptions are lent some support in the UK by the National Curriculum for English (1995), through such affirmations as 'standard English is distinguished from other forms of English by its vocabulary, and by rules and conventions of grammar, spelling and punctuation' and 'the grammatical features that distinguish standard English include how pronouns, adverbs and adjectives should be used and how negatives, questions and verb tenses should be formed' (DFE 1995b, p.3). Common sense, however, should tell us that they are indeed misconceptions rather than timeless truths. The English of Chaucer and Shakespeare, both of which pre-date standard English, bear as much (and arguably rather less) similarity to standard English as, say, some Caribbean dialects of English[2] – a circumstance

Figure 16 Misconceptions related to 'standard' and 'non-standard' English

- Standard English is the basic, primordial English from which all other Englishes are variants
- Standard English uses rules; non-standard English breaks them
- Standard English is: 'grammatically correct English spoken in any accent'; non-standard English is 'sloppy'[3]

which suggests that 'correctness' has been conferred upon standard English retrospectively (by those who use it as their main or only dialect) rather than being intrinsic to it.[4] Similarly false, as Figure 17 indicates, is the notion that only standard English makes systematic, rule-governed use of 'parts of speech' and can be 'proved to do so' through analysis. As Trudgill (1983), Stubbs (1976) and others have demonstrated, standard English is no more than a *regional* dialect in essence, which has become a (arguably, *the*) dialect of power in English-speaking nations, and has, in the process, had its status transformed to that of a *social* dialect. Arguments in favour of *learning* standard English constitute, of course, a separate, if related issue: the suggestion that, as long as current standard English *is* a language of power, all students need to be able to develop advanced levels of expertise in its various forms and manifestations is not, for example, an unreasonable one. The point is, however, that such development needs to be seen as a matter of expediency rather than as evidence of – or support for – standard English's *superiority* (indeed, but for quirks of history what we now know as cockney English might currently be spoken as 'standard').[5] *One implication of this is that although teachers may have a duty to help their students become expert users of standard English forms, this does not need to be – and indeed ought not to be – at the cost of devaluing or seeking to eradicate other dialects.*

Figure 17 *Parsing 'standard' and 'non-standard' sentences*

'My friend and I went to the shops.'

My	Possessive adjective (first-person singular)
friend	Common noun (singular)
and	Conjunction
I	Personal pronoun (first-person singular, nominative case)
went	Verb (intransitive, past tense)
to	Preposition
the	Definite article
shops	Common noun (plural)

'Me and me mate goes down the shops.'

Me	Personal pronoun (first-person singular, nominative case)
and	Conjunction
me	Possessive adjective (first-person singular)
mate	Common noun (singular)
goes	Verb (intransitive, present tense used to describe past events)
down	Preposition (also used as adverb)
the	Definite article
shops	Common noun (plural)

Both sentences are rule-bound and can be described through use of the same rule-related taxonomy. In the latter case, for example, 'me' is a correct (that is, customary) form of the possessive adjective first-person singular, as well as being the correct form of the personal pronoun, first-person singular, in the nominative case. 'Went' is not 'wrong' within the rules of this dialect; however, in this instance 'goes' is used to add liveliness and immediacy, and to signal the telling of an anecdote.

The notion that non-standard forms of a language may be just as valid intrinsically as standard forms, in that non-standard forms enable their users the full range of expression offered by standard ones, has been convincingly and famously elaborated by William Labov in relation to language studies undertaken with young black Americans. Arguing that non-standard dialects of English do not represent a 'restricted code' and that neither they nor students who habitually use them should be marginalized as deficient, Labov suggests:

Our work in the speech community makes it painfully obvious that in many ways working-class speakers are *more effective* narrators, reasoners and debaters than many middle-class speakers who temporize, qualify and lose their argument in a mass of irrelevant detail.

(Labov 1972, pp.192–3)

Labov's assertion of the richness and validity of so-called non-standard dialects, which suggests, again, that standard dialects are *invested* with correctness and superiority rather than being correct and superior *in themselves*, is echoed by Terry Eagleton's observation about similar investments in the identification of curricularized *Literature*, itself suggesting that just as no single dialect of a language is inherently superior to another, so no single body (or, for that matter, single piece) of writing can be said to be superior other than as a matter of fashion and transitory opinion:

There is no such thing as a literary work or tradition which is valuable in itself, regardless of what anyone might have said or come to say about it. 'Value' is a transitive term: it means whatever is valued by certain people in specific situations, according to particular criteria and in the light of given purposes.

(Eagleton 1983, p.10)

Both Labov and Eagleton root their understanding of 'standard English', whether approached from the point of view of students' language-use or from the point of view of curricularized literature, very firmly within issues of genre and – through genre – within issues of cultural preference and cultural reproduction. The notion of genre is central to our understanding of the performance of bilingual students already considered in Chapters 5 and 6, and will, as we shall see, be equally significant in our considerations of classroom experiences and practice involving marginalized bidialectal students.

Kress, whose *Learning to Write* still provides one of the most accessible and complete accounts of how cultural reproduction works in actual classroom situations, uses Bakhtin's concept of the 'utterance' to explain not only the phenomenon of genre (specific *ways* of telling stories, writing up science experiments, expressing an answer in mathematics and so on) but, more importantly, the role played by genre in validating and non-validating cultural–linguistic *preferences* in ways that disguise those preferences as norms. At the heart of this analysis is Kress's assertion that:

> Learning language can ... be regarded as the learning of cliché. Learning genres is no exception to this rule – it represents the child's socialization into appropriate and accepted modes of organizing knowledge, of knowing, and the modes of representing perceptions and knowledge to others. ... This represents a vast convenience to society and no doubt to individuals. ... However, it is important to recognize [that genres] *are* conventions. Other conventions can be imagined: indeed ... children constantly invent their own modes of organizing and knowing, which do not, however, become recognized as such but rather are categorized as errors.
>
> (Kress 1982, pp.123–4)

The suggestion that forms and styles of expression validated by formal schooling and related examination syllabuses and criteria are conventions rather than universals does not, as has already been pointed out, mean that we should not be teaching our students these conventions. We might strive to *change* the conventions, or to persuade society as a whole that these *are* conventions (that is, to move beyond what is immediately achievable in the classroom, towards influencing curriculum change), but until such strivings result in the desired hegemonic change we are somewhat compelled to continue to teach them for the limited empowerment they might bring our students within a fundamentally disempowering system (a system whose disempowering effectiveness, of course, relies quite heavily on the creation of genres and their presentation as 'normality'). Why, then, should we bother to consider genre at all, other than as a passing reference? The answer is that only through an understanding of genre (along with understandings of various other aspects of education) will we be able to make sense of what our students are doing when they do something 'different' or 'unexpected' and, specifically, only through an understanding of genre will we be able to arrive at accurate assessments of our students' skills, areas of expertise and knowledge, and, ultimately, their *needs*. In other words, we need to understand that there are 'non-standard' as well as 'standard' genres, and that when students' work fails to conform to the legitimized genre of the school curriculum, it may be conforming quite expertly to some other genre whose legitimization takes place somewhere else.

The practical significance of all this will become immediately apparent in the case studies that follow. Before proceeding to those studies, however, it may be useful to consider, briefly, another aspect of genre theory as described by Kress, and that is the notion of 'error' which we have already considered in relation to bilingual students. Describing formal education as 'a system which is largely arbitrary' but which 'is presented as basically logical', Kress argues that:

> The gap between the adult's value-system – which is ultimately society's – and the child's, is covered by the concept of 'error'. It enshrines a view which accepts the naturalness of sets of value-systems (be they table-manners, duelling-codes, or spelling conventions) and thereby labels behaviour which falls outside the system as unnatural, incorrect, unacceptable, etc., without inquiring into the bases of that behaviour.
>
> (Kress 1982, p.180; see also Atkinson 1998)

Such an analysis, which acknowledges that 'a child's action may be unconventional and yet highly logical' (Kress 1982, p.181), will be particularly useful in two of the case studies that follow: that concerning the assessment of young readers, who apply easily observable logic and reasoning skills in arriving at answers deemed by their adult judges to be 'wrong', and that of a teenage writer, Winston, whose logical selection of an appropriate form for one of his essays again falls foul of the overriding preferential generic rules of the larger social and education systems.

Marginalizing Experience: Jason's and Steven's Reading Assessments

It follows from what has so far been argued that in a perfect world expertise in more than one dialect – increasing dramatically the user's options in terms of voice, register and adaptability to audience – would be an advantage rather than, as is so often the current perception, a disadvantage. For monodialectal standard-English users, the difference inherent in other dialects would not be pathologized (as it currently is, for the purposes of personal gain and reproduction of the socio-economic status quo) but, rather, would be embraced by such users and creatively utilized. We live, however, in a very far from perfect world in which, from a very early age, bidialectalism is often actively *dis*couraged in favour of monodialectalism. Inevitably, such a policy leads both to 'successful' outcomes (the student develops full expertise in the use of the 'standard' dialect and is deemed personally successful) and to 'unsuccessful' outcomes (the student fails to develop sufficient expertise in the 'standard' dialect and is considered to have failed).

To illustrate how the promotion of monodialectalism operates in and through actual classroom practice, I want to begin by looking at some eight-year-old students at an inner-city primary school.[6] The school in question had a multiethnic intake and took its anti-racist, equal-opportunities policies very seriously. A series of staff meetings, for example, had been devoted to the issue of how to raise achievement of all students, with particular reference to issues of genre, class and ethnicity, while the school's recently acquired motto was: 'Working towards excellence for all pupils'. The class teacher, Ms Ainsley, was particularly supportive of the school's policy in these areas and complemented in-school work with voluntary extra-curricular activity, working with students across the school to put on plays and other performances with a strong multicultural emphasis. Hard-working and dedicated, she gave her young students a great deal of time at weekends and evenings, and ensured that they explored the city's many museums and art galleries through a series of organized trips. She had attended numerous professional development courses since achieving her initial teaching qualification and was an ardent supporter of the Vygotskyan view that education should be aimed 'not so much at the ripe as at the ripening functions' (Vygotsky 1962, p.104) – a view which, she suggested, involves 'stretching all pupils so that they can achieve their full potential'.

I had spent several months working closely with these students and Ms Ainsley, and in particular watching them at work with the computer reading-program *Developing Tray* (ILEA/ILECC 1986)[7] – a kind of refined, flexible, computer-run cloze program which encourages students' reading development (and, inferentially, their writing development) through prioritizing the hypothesizing, predictive, contextualizing aspects of engagement with texts. *Developing Tray* allows the teacher or student operator to feed text on to a computer screen a bit at a time, with preselected letters – in some cases, whole words – removed and presented as dashes or asterisks. Students, normally working with their teacher in groups of two to twenty-five, are able to recreate the text unfolding before them through a process of joint oral activity, constantly checking and rechecking their developing hypotheses against fresh information as it appears on screen. When, after however long it takes, they have arrived at a group reading with which they are happy, the original text is revealed to them so that they can see how close a match it provides to the text they have produced.

Observing these students at work on the computer program had provided a helpful window on their reading strategies and development (Moore 1996c), showing how young readers bring their own 'extra-textual' experiences to bear on their reading of texts and how developing, idiosyncratic under-standings of their world(s) are combined in this exercise with developing understandings of the rules of *language*. Thus, on one occasion, two boys, Jason and Steven, had randomly called up an extract (given the title 'Fishing') from the very complex D.H. Lawrence poem, 'Fish' (Figure 18) – a text aimed at a much older readership.

Figure 18 Extract from 'Fish' (Developing Tray) – *complete skeleton text*

```
                    F******
     _ h _ v _  w _ _ _ _ d  w _ _ h   _   l _ _ g   _ _ d
                  _ _ d  _ udd _ _ ly  pull _ d
                    _  gold-and-greenish,
            lucent  ****  f _ _ m  b _ l _ w
                  _ _ d  h _ d  h _ m  fly
            l _ k _  _  h _ l_   round  my  h _ _ d,
            lunging  in  the  air  on  _ h _  l _ _ _

            h _ v _  u _ h _ _ k _ d  h _ _  gorping,
                    water–horny mouth
                and seen his horror tilted ***
                (his red-gold, water-precious,
                  mirror-flat bright ***)
       _ _ d  f _ l _   h _ m  b _ _ _ _  _ _  my  h _ _ d
                  w _ _ h  h _ _  mucous,
               l _ _ p _ _ g  l _ f _  _ h _ _ b ...
```

Note: The text is shown in its entirety, as drip-fed on to the screen by the students' teacher over a period of nearly one hour.

In their attempted reading of the D.H. Lawrence poem, the boys had got as far, with their teacher, as:

> I have waited with a long God
> and [something] pulled
> a gold-and-greenish,
> lucent [something] from …

At this point, the teacher entered the next word, 'b_l_w', whereupon the following animated discussion ensued:

Dialogue 5

Jason:	Bellow.
Teacher:	Bellow?
Steven:	Portobello!
J:	Framed bellow. ... No!
	[...]
S:	Years ago ...
J:	*(In a deep, giant's voice.)* Fee-fi-fo-fum.
T:	*(Looks surprised.)*
S:	*(Explaining.)* That's what's bellow.
T:	Oh, I see. Bellowing – like shouting out.
S:	Yeah. You can't say Portobello, 'cos Portobello is B-E-L-L-O.
T:	You go there, do you? Portobello?
S:	Yep.
J:	Bellow, bellow, bellow, bellow ...
T:	*(Enters more text: '_ _d h_d h_m fly'.)*
J and S:	And had him for ... fly ...
T:	Mm. Let's go through it, shall we, see what we've got?
T, S and J:	I have waited with a long God and [something] pulled a gold-and-greenish lucent with ...
J:	It can't be 'with'.
T:	Why not?
J:	It could be 'what'.
T:	Well, let's ...
J and S:	What ... from ...
J:	Bello(w)!
S:	Or ...
J:	Wood from 'bello!
S:	What's from Portobello! Yeah, he could have bought it from Portobello!

In this extract, we see something of the way in which reading 'works' and something of what makes for an efficient – and indeed a happy – reader. Much of this involves the reader having to make sense of a text through processes of accommodation and *negotiation*: that is to say, the reader considers the extent (1) to which their reading matches their experience of the world (fictive and non-fictive), and (2) to which it matches their understanding of such linguistic matters as punctuation, how words are spelled and basic rules of grammar. Always the reader is trying to find a reading which – to their satisfaction – provides an acceptable match both experientially and linguistically. Such a process involves, inevitably, elements of provisionality as well as of creativity. Thus, in the above example we find one student, Steven, coming up with the reading 'Portobello', almost as an involuntary response to another student's suggestion of 'bellow', which had reminded him of a local street market he had visited. Steven quickly realized that the spelling of Portobello made it an unsuitable hypothesis, however, and was anxious to drop it. The other student, Jason, was more reluctant to reject the hypothesis. Remembering, as it later transpired, an incident earlier in his childhood when he had gone with his father to collect wood from a place near the same market, he was quick to read the starred word as 'wood' and to develop the 'Portobello' hypothesis along the lines 'wood from 'bello', ingeniously recycling Steven's earlier reference and readily adopting the poetic device of a place-name abbreviation. This provisional reading was subsequently laid to rest, along with several others, once the students had guessed 'rod' and 'fish'.

Observations of students' reading together in this way, articulating their strategies as they go along, can prove very illuminating. The evidence provided by Steven's and Jason's articulations, for instance, suggested that these two students had all the skills they required to be competent as well as recreational readers, and that in this area of their work there was little need for concern – a view supported by the facts that after an hour's highly excited engagement with the text, Jason and Steven ended up with a reading of the poem that precisely matched Lawrence's original and that they continued to talk animatedly about the poem for some weeks after.

Less illuminating were the results of a standardized reading test that these same students and their classmates were obliged to take, at yearly intervals, as a result of local government policy. Such tests – designed to provide the teacher with 'reading ages' for each student which could then be measured, diagnostically, against chronological ages and fed into appropriate pedagogies – often appeared to highlight problems which did not, on the basis of other evidence (such as their work on *Developing Tray*), appear to exist. In the case of Steven and Jason, for example, I was dismayed to learn that on the basis of the standardized tests both students had been identified by their class teacher as 'causes for concern'. Further investigation revealed that a year previously, when Jason and Steven had last completed the test, Jason had scored a reading age of 7.3 (7 years and 3 months) against his then chronological age of 7.7, while Steven had scored a reading age of 8.6 against a chronological age of 7.11. More interesting, perhaps, were the results of the latest test, carried out at much the same time as the students' reading of 'Fish'. According to this assessment, Jason now had a reading age of 7.9 against a chronological age of 8.7, while Steven also had a reading age of 7.9 against a chronological age of 8.11. In other words, according to the results of the latest standardized test both boys' reading had slipped back in the intervening year. Jason's reading age had gone up but not to the same extent as his chronological age (a gap of 4 months had increased to a gap of 8 months), while Steven's reading age had actually gone down quite significantly. According to this data, which starkly contradicted the richer evidence provided by careful observation of the students' reading strategies and reading interests, the two boys were now, somehow, worse readers than they had been a year before – an apparently nonsensical judgement. This assessment had, in turn, led the class teacher to describe the current reading skills of the two boys as 'just about average' (in the case of Steven) and 'below average' (in the case of Jason) – a view shared, interestingly, by the boys themselves, who described themselves as 'about average' (Steven) and 'not all that good' (Jason).

Precisely how, we might ask, can students who appear to show themselves to be very effective readers in one situation come to be perceived as very ordinary – or even somewhat deficient – readers in another? To answer this question, it is necessary to look at the reading test itself and at the responses that some of the students made to it.

In brief, the test sat by Jason and Steven and their classmates comprised a series of sentences, in each of which a word had been left out and replaced with a blank. At the end of each sentence there were five different words. The student taking the test had, in each case, to select one of the five offered words to insert into the blank, so that the sentence 'made sense'. In such a test, the students' reading skills are not, ostensibly, assessed on the basis of their recognition of individual, decontextualized words, but on their ability to make use of context-clues to read whole sentences: that is to say, on the face of it the test sits not uncomfortably with 'progressive', 'multicultural' approaches to reading and the teaching of reading that resist overemphasis on phonics or individual word-recognition in favour of encouraging hypothesizing and contextual evidence (Britton 1975, Goodman 1967). Does such a test really provide appropriate context, however? And to what extent can it genuinely claim to be culturally unbiased?

A few days after the students in Ms Ainsley's class of eight-year-olds had taken the reading test and had had their revised reading-ages duly recorded in their teacher's mark-book, it was agreed that a colleague who was undertaking research at the school should carry out a number of conversations about the test with various students from the class, with the intention of finding out *why* the students had got wrong answers: whether, for instance, they had simply not been able to read some of the words and had just made wild guesses, or whether, in making deliberate selections of words, they had applied some kind of 'alternative' logic that had been at odds with the internal logic of the test itself.[8] The initial purpose of these conversations was to arrive at a richer diagnosis of the students' reading performance, that would target weakness and pedagogy in a way that the naked reading-age scores could not.

Here is one student, Lynette:

Dialogue 6

R: Lynette, I noticed in your test the other day that one of the sentences was 'They ****** it is time to go home'. And the choices you had were 'walk', 'give' 'think', 'draw' and 'gone'. *(Shows student a transcript of this.)* Do you remember what word you picked?

Lynette: *(Hesitates.)* Gone?

R: That's right. Do you remember why you chose 'gone'?

L: They gone.

R: I see. ... Who's gone?

L: All the people.

R: The people? Which people are they, then?

L: The people at the party. ... They gone because it time to go home.

There are two very significant features of Lynette's commentary. The first is that, when asked to undertake the exercise this second time around, she chose the same word she had picked out in the test itself. This could have been coincidental, of course, but in the light of her subsequent comments we might reasonably assume that she had not simply picked out a word at random. *The second is that Lynette had clearly chosen the 'wrong' word in the test not because she could not read, but because of the interplay between her own readings of the world and her developing uses of standard and – in this case – non-standard English* (see also Dillon 1985, Freire and Macedo 1987). In seeking an answer to the question, Lynette – quite used to such activity through her use of *Developing Tray* – had done what all good readers do with this kind of 'readerly' text:[9] as in the case of Jason and Steven reading D.H. Lawrence's poem, she had sought to make sense of the text through seeking some kind of match between the internal, grammatical relations of the text itself and her own narrative, based on her experience of what life and the world are actually like – or could be like – 'outside' the text.[10] The trouble was, she had brought to her reading of the text a particular 'non-standard' grammatical usage (the abbreviated 'gone' for 'have gone' – a construction widely used in the Caribbean dialect of English regularly practised in Lynette's home and among many of her friends) – which enabled the 'wrong' kind of story or narrative to fit. In terms of sense-making, Lynette's 'They gone: it is time to go home' makes perfect sense. It just isn't the 'right' sense; in fact it apparently does not make *any* sense in the experience of the test's designers: the whole point of the standardized test, after all, is that there can *only be* one answer – an implication of which is, in this case, that there can only be one world, one perception of that world, and one form of English through which to experience and to describe that world.

Such cases as Lynette's were to prove not at all uncommon with this particular class. Steven, for example, whose reading skills have already been described, fell foul over the words 'rain' and 'bucket':

Dialogue 7

R: *(Showing test paper to Steven.)* Now, it said in the test: 'It began to "something", so we put our coats on.' The choice was 'rain', 'bucket', 'collar', 'dance' and 'spare'. And you put ... ?

Steven: Bucket, probably.

R: Bucket, that's right. You did. ... Now, why would you think it was 'bucket'?

S: Because it bucketed, didn't it. ...

R: You wouldn't think it could just be 'rain', then?

S: No. ... Well, it could be.

R: But you don't think so?

S: No, 'cos. ... If it was just raining, you probably wouldn't bother to put your coat on.

In this example, Steven had, just like Lynette, clearly thought very carefully about his choice of word, seeking to select not just any word that would fit but *the word that would fit best* – the word that, in the narrative constructed by the student, 'made most sense'. (It is worth recounting at this point an exchange made at the time of the test between Steven and Ms Ainsley. Steven had asked his teacher, 'Miss, what if you think more than one word fits?', to which Ms Ainsley had responded, first to Steven then to the whole class, 'You can only choose one. ... You can only circle *one* word. If you think more than one word fits, *just choose what you think is the best word, the one that makes most sense.'*)

Reasoning that people would not necessarily bother to put their coats on if it was 'just raining' (it might, after all, have been only very light rain), Steven had chosen the colloquial 'to bucket', meaning 'to rain heavily', knowing that this would *necessitate* the putting on of coats and therefore must be the right word in this instance – a little creative reasoning that made use both of the context of the sentence itself and of Steven's own extra-textual experience of life, but that scored no points in the test and indeed contributed to condemning Steven to a reading age significantly below his chronological age.

This last point raises a number of other issues. Two that I particularly want to consider here are (1) the selection and status of the verb 'bucket', and (2) the question of what is 'context'. The word 'bucket' in this situation is interesting for at least two reasons. First, it is a word that in standard English exists only in noun form – a sad impoverishment, perhaps, although defenders of monodialectalism might not see it that way. The *verb* bucket only exists in non-standard, 'colloquial' forms of English: it is for this reason that in the terms of the test it is unacceptable, the 'wrong' answer. What, however, was the logic behind the appearance of the word 'bucket' in the list of choices? Was it just randomly selected by the test's designers? Or was there some other purpose in its inclusion? Examples drawn from else-where in the test suggest no consistency – no overriding logic, that is – in the selection of the five choice-words. Thus, in many instances five similar-looking, similar-sounding or similar-meaning words (or combinations thereof) had been nominated: for example, 'unrest', 'arrest', 'rest', 'steal' and 'test', or 'better', 'rather', 'mother', 'other' and 'tether'. In other cases, such as those we have looked at, the words seemed on the surface to bear little resemblance to one another – certainly from a child's point of view. In Lynette's case, the words were 'walk', 'give', 'think', 'draw', 'gone'; in Steven's they were 'rain', 'bucket', 'collar', 'dance', 'spare'. I leave it to readers to speculate as to what, if any, motive underpinned these choices. It is worth noting in passing, however, that in either case there were:

- Three words that were very unlikely choices (no student in the class, for example, opted for 'walk', 'give' or 'draw', although cases could be made out for each of these)
- One word that provided the most obvious choice for (adult) speakers of standard English
- One word that made equal or even better sense to (child) speakers of non-standard English

In either case, the attractive-sounding non-standard option was deemed to be wrong.

The two examples we have looked at so far can be read to suggest a certain cultural bias in the test – a bias away, that is, from non-standard forms and usages towards standard ones – that resulted in judgements not so much of the students' *reading skills per se* as of their preferred cultural forms. The second point I want to develop, however, is to do with the notion of 'context' and whether this also is something that can be described as 'standard'.[11] I have already suggested that young readers like Lynette and Steven use contexts beyond that immediately provided by the text in their efforts to make sense of – to *interpret* – the text. Implicitly, the designers of tests such as this reading test must also be located within particular contexts: the contexts, for example, not only of their view of what represents (good) reading and how reading skills can best be assessed, but the context, too, of their own common-sense, 'habitual' perceptions and understandings of the world that they bring with them, willy-nilly, into the construction and design of such tests. *One result of this is that, almost invisibly, children taking the test have their own eyes, ears and voices marginalized as an intrinsic requirement of the test they are given*: that is to say, they do not only suffer if – or because – they regularly operate within non-standard 'language dialects', or because they do not understand the particular 'genre' of the standardized test, *but because they have a culturally driven view and perception of the world, which is very different from the dominant culturally driven view and perception of the test's designers or of many of the young people who (with rather more success than Lynette or Steven) are required to take the test.*

As a further example of what I am driving at, here are two more sets of responses to the test, involving Carrie, John and Steven's friend Jason:

Dialogue 8

R: It said 'If nothing happens, ring the "something" bell'. Right, now you had five words to choose from, which were 'better', 'rather', 'mother', 'other' and 'tether'.

Jason: Yeah.

R: And you went for …

J: Better.

R: Better. … Can you tell me, Jason, why did you choose 'better'?

J: 'Cos, right, there must of been two bells, yeah, and one worked better than the other one. So if you try one and it doesn't work, you try the other one.

R: And that …

J: That will work. … Well, you hope it will.

R: I see. So what sort of bells do you suppose these are?

J: Like … those bells the teachers use, you know, when it's time to come back in from play.

R: Right. … And if you have two bells …

J: And one doesn't work, 'cos it's not that good …

R: You try the –

J: The better one.

Dialogue 9

R: It said: 'The policeman tried to "something" the thief.' Your choices were 'unrest', 'arrest', 'rest', 'steal', 'test'. And you thought it was …

Carrie: Test.

R: Test. Why did you think it was 'test'?

C: *(Shrugs.)*

R: I mean, why couldn't it, for example, have been … 'arrest'?

C: *(Amused.)* You wouldn't try to arrest somebody, would you … if you was a policeman …

R: How do you mean, you wouldn't try … ?

C: Because you would do it. … You would just arrest them. … It's like …

John: *(Overhearing and laughing.)* I tried to eat my dinner!

R: I see. But why would the policeman want to test the thief?

J: To try and find out if he really was a thief … to trick him … trick him into giving himself away.

R: Oh, right. … So it's that kind of test. I thought it meant a test like this reading one.

C: *(Laughs.)*

In each of these instances, the children appear to have been approaching their task in the manner of 'a psycholinguistic guessing *game*' (Goodman 1967). Given very limited textual contexts, they adopted similar strategies to those they employed regularly when using *Developing Tray* and indeed when engaged in much of their other learning. This involved constructing, as with Jason and Lynette, narratives that would provide more elaborate contexts for them to be able to arrive at what seemed to them to be quite sensible readings. In this particular instance, they clearly perceived their task as interpreting what little text they had been given in ways that would incorporate one of the words or concepts they had been asked to choose from. The problem with the test, however, was that in this case there was a clear mismatch between the children's known world and that of the test's designers: indeed, the rejection of apparently perfectly valid answers (ones, that is, which produced an acceptable match between the internal grammatical logic of the text and the students' existing experience and language development) suggests that the known worlds of many of these children were actually 'invisible' to the test's designers.[12] Jason, for example, lived at the top of an open-access block of flats in the heart of a nearby council estate. Each flat had its own front-door bell or no bell at all: there were no entryphones here or in the other blocks on the estate where most of Jason's immediate friends and family lived. Other than these bells, the only bell Jason had any regular familiarity with was the old-fashioned hand-bell still used by his teachers to denote the end of playtime. This, it transpired, was Jason's principal, very limited, day-to-day experience of bells. The nomination of 'other' as the 'correct answer' suggests, however, that the test's designers' experience of bells was somewhat different: bells for upstairs and downstairs flats in converted houses, perhaps; bells on hotel reception desks; bells at the front entrances of office complexes. If this is true, we could argue with some justification that it was not merely Jason's reading skills that were being tested here (indeed, not Jason's reading skills *at all*), but that he was being downgraded because his lived experience was different from that of the test's designers and because it had no validation in their eyes: to all intents and purposes, it was either the 'wrong' experience or it simply did not exist.[13] *In short, the test made no allowance for such experiential diversity.*

None of this might matter too much if it were not for the fact that, as at Jason's and Steven's school, so much store is placed on standardized tests (which are really designed as only one assessment tool among many) or if the 'getting wrong' of a relatively small number of answers did not have so great an impact on a student's final score.[14] As it is, the potential dangers of such assessments can be very far-reaching. For example, students who may in practice be assessed as deficient in their use of standard English – or even in some notional view of 'standard experience and perception' – can clearly end up being labelled simultaneously poor readers, regardless of how good they actually are. That is to say, a lack of expertise in standard English or 'standard experience' gets equated with a learning 'difficulty' of quite a different order – a classic example of what Ryan (1972) has called 'blaming the victim' and what Cummins (1996), Walkerdine (1990) and others have referred to as *the pathologization of the individual*. This, I believe, is what happened to Steven and Jason. It explains the significant discrepancy between their 'official' status as readers and the alternative picture drawn not just from observing them at work on the poem 'Fish' but also, two weeks after the test, witnessing them read with no difficulty at all the sentences 'It began to rain, so we put our coats on' and 'If nothing happens, ring the other bell.' Impressive readers as these children were – able to tackle, enjoy and understand a very complex and demanding poem – they were still perceived as poor readers in the classroom on the basis of the reading ages ascribed to them in the standard test – as if somehow all other evidence of their ability was rendered inadmissible by this 'master signifier'. What is perhaps worse is that this perception was subsequently prioritized in their teacher's choice of pedagogy toward the two boys, including her choice of appropriate reading material for them. Thus, when I entered Steven's and Jason's classroom a few days after their reading of the D.H. Lawrence poem, I found them jointly labouring through a very undemanding text aimed, as the cover rightly indicated, at a readership significantly younger than their chronological ages, while a handful of 'good' readers in the class were reading and apparently enjoying far more complex texts aimed at a much older readership. Neither Jason nor Steven liked the book they had been given and, in stark contrast with their work on 'Fish', their concentration continually wavered as if to confirm the official view their teacher had of them.

Only time would tell whether Jason and Steven would develop into the involved, adventurous readers suggested by their work on *Developing Tray*, or whether they would become the poor, uninterested readers suggested by their performance in the standardized test. One thing does seem to be clear, however: as long as teachers lack the confidence in themselves to challenge the results and underpinning philosophies of standardized testing in favour of their own informed, professional, criterion-referenced classroom observations, minoritized students such as Steven and Jason will continue to be undervalued, not just as readers but in all other aspects of language and learning, simply because their worlds, like their words, may be different in some small but significant way from the validated, legalized worlds and words of their unseen assessors. As Cummins has observed:

> In the past, assessment had played a central role in legitimating the instructional disabling of culturally diverse students. Biased standardized tests have located the 'problem' within the student, thereby screening from critical scrutiny the subtractive nature of the school program, the exclusionary orientation of teachers towards subordinated communities, and 'banking' models of teaching that suppress students' experience and inhibit them from active participation in learning.
>
> (Cummins 1996, p.161)

A logical development of Cummins' argument is that student liberation can, in the end, only be achieved through and in conjunction with *teacher* liberation – that is, through an effective, sustained challenge to the discourses of ignorance and prejudice that keep afloat unequal, coercive power relations in our schools as well as in our larger societies.

Legitimation and Advocacy: Winston's 'Nuclear War' Essay

Cummins' concerns about the role of standardized assessment procedures are predicated on a more general view that, despite many surface changes to the ways in which teaching and learning are organized in schools (in the UK we might point, for example, to the development of mixed-ability groupings, to the limited validation of 'non-standard' literary texts, to an increase in assessment by ongoing coursework and so on), the 'bottom line' of education – what Cummins has called 'the underlying structure' – has remained intact (Cummins 1996, p.161). Another way of putting this is to say that the 'how' of assessment may in some instances have changed to suit the practices and experiences of a wider range of students, but the culturally biased, culturally reproductive 'what' has not (see also Moore 1998): students are still assessed primarily on their ability at regurgitating a very narrow canon of 'knowledge', much of which may be irrelevant to their own out-of-school lives and of precious little interest to them (Kress 1982, p.33), and at demonstrating that they can reproduce a very narrow ('standard') range of expressive styles and genres, mainly in the written form of a dialect over which they may feel, justifiably, they have little or no ownership.

It is precisely through a recognition of this critical fact that teachers begin to move away from the exclusively school-based inclusion of minoritized students (containing, as it invariably must, some element of legitimation on their part of the status quo of curriculum and assessment), towards forms of social action that look outward from the institution and that militate for changes to the structures themselves: what Cummins has described as a pedagogic move from a 'legitimating' function to one of 'advocacy' (Cummins 1996, p.162). While it is not within the scope of this book to describe the precise forms that this outward-facing teacher advocacy might take,[15] it *is* within its brief to consider forms of *outward-oriented action* that can be taken inside the classroom through cooperative learning ventures between teachers and their students: ventures, that is, which seek to inform students about the culturally biased nature of the curricula and assessment procedures to which they are subjected in and outside the school setting in order that they may, when they leave school, be better positioned themselves to militate for change in the deep structures and to resist coercive, reproductive, exclusionary forces that continue to operate against the best interests of multicultured people. Such ventures – aimed at developing students' *critical literacy* (McLaren 1988, Moore 1998) – are not about teaching bidialectal students to eschew expertise in the 'standard' forms and genres that may help them to success in public examinations and afterwards, but about helping such students to recognize and understand the discriminatory practices that operate against them, in order that they may be better able to oppose them (see also Kress 1982, pp.188–9, Shor and Freire 1987, pp.168–74). At the heart of these ventures is, as with bilingual students, a pedagogic agenda of repertoire extension rather than one of linguistic correction. Needless to say, this does not offer the teacher an easy ride: how, for example, does a teacher explain to their students how it is that the examination system, the national curriculum, even 'the school' itself appear to consider many of their favoured cultural–linguistic preferences to be wrong while at the same time encouraging those students to develop expertise in and to value these non-validated preferences? As we have already seen, however, the teacher's position may not, in practice, be quite as contradictory as it seems in theory.

In her seminal work *Ways With Words*, Shirley Brice Heath begins to explore what happens when children from communities with one set of language traditions (including traditions of telling stories) go into schools which espouse another. The children she describes, from the white, working-class community of 'Roadville' and the black working-class community of 'Trackton', have particular difficulty in adjusting to the demands of different-stories-for-different-situations imposed by the alternative cultural orientations of their middle-class schools and teachers who, in turn, must operate within the parameters of a dominant class's ideologies and cultural traditions. For Trackton children (whose experiences and preferences immediately call to mind Mashud's situation regarding his 'moral tales'),

> [t]he request for a story which simply recounts facts accurately has no parallel in their community. Their fictive stories in response to assignments which ask them to make up a story often fail to set the scene or introduce characters, and often the point of their stories is not clear to either teachers or other students.
>
> (Brice Heath 1983, pp.296–7)

What happens in time, Brice Heath argues, is that for some children the 'story' forms favoured by the dominant culture (and *legitimized* by classroom teachers as mediators of that culture's imposed curriculum) are gradually learned and incorporated into forms favoured at home, to a certain extent replacing them in the development of a new hierarchy of values. By the time they are ready to enter third grade, these children have already begun to incorporate into their oral stories several features of the written stories they have read in schoolbooks or had read to them by their teacher:

> They usually introduced characters, began and ended the story with a formula, and followed a right chronological order. Exaggeration of detail was far less common than it had been in the early school months, and sentences were often much shorter than those of their non-story-telling discourse. They also recognized and explained details which might not be familiar to the listener, using flashbacks and parenthetical-like comments.
>
> (p.300)

One girl in particular, Nellie, is described as having by this time

> acquired a number of story-telling strategies highly valued by the school. She abstracted her story and adhered to the temporal order and details of the actual experience being recounted. She provided enough validation through adjectives to help the listeners visualize the events of the story. She also structured her story according to those features of stories usually called for in school: she provided an opening, oriented the listener

to the setting and characters, gave the necessary details for understanding the set-up of the conflict, and moved to a climax or point in
her story. She used either or both formulaic openings and closings.

(Brice Heath 1983, p.300)

There are, as we have already seen, potential dangers in drawing too close
a parallel between the cultural experiences of young people in one part of
one continent and those of other young people elsewhere in the world.
Cultural exclusion and coercion, however, has certain key characteristics
wherever it is found. Notably, it seeks to promote the cultural interests of
the dominant over the dominated, through deliberate, systematized processes
of validation and legalization of some cultural forms, practices and norms,
and the invalidation and effective outlawing of others. (The UK National
Curriculum, with its repeated references to 'standard' English, to canons of
literature and knowledge, and to a very narrow range of approved genres, is
an example *par excellence* of how this works in practice). We might add,
however, that Brice Heath's reference to the 'fictive/non-fictive' issue also
highlights a common problem experienced by multicultured students, which
is again to do with *genre*. The failure of students in the UK to produce what
to their examiners and teachers represents an appropriate *discursive* essay,
for example, is particularly common among minoritized students, and it is
one for which schools themselves are consistently berated. It is not, of
course, that these students have nothing to say (indeed, it is arguable that
many of them possess much stronger, more thoroughly worked out and
more *genuine* views than some students who have achieved success in this
kind of writing). Nor is it that they 'don't know how to say (write) it'. It is,
rather, that they haven't learned – or, often, haven't *chosen* to learn – what, in
educated-dominant-class terms, is the appropriate form and style.

An example of this kind of 'inappropriateness' can be seen in the
following piece of work by a sixteen-year-old examination student, Winston,
attending the same UK school as Abdul and Mashud. Winston had been
asked by his English teacher to write an essay for his examination folder,
expressing his views on any subject that he felt strongly about. Examples of
essays successfully completed by previous students were shown to the class
and the teacher made much of the necessity of writing up the piece of work
in a particular way, urging the students to

*Write with feeling – show you care about this thing – but remember to
structure your essay and not to get carried away. You need an introduction, points for and against, and a conclusion. The way we've talked about
it before. If in doubt, think back to Linda's essay [one of the examples
shown to the class]. That's a very good example of how the essay should
be put together, and what the tone should be like: forcefully argued, but
not over the top.*

Winston chose to write on the topic of nuclear weapons, a subject he felt very strongly about, having taken part the previous year in a school debate on whether or not such weapons should be universally banned. When he had finished the first (and only) draft of his essay, he proudly showed it off to his classmates, telling them that he felt it was the best piece of work he had ever produced (see Figure 19).

Figure 19 Winston's 'Nuclear War' essay

Nuclear War

It has its dangers.

In the beginning there was peace on earth and no one knew of bombs, guns and missiles, It was just nice and peace loving.

But then hate struck the land like a swarm of locusts eating the mind from its God draining love and affection from the mind. When that was gone man started to experiment, wanted to fly, He wanted to go under water without holding his breath and go out of the living world that God gave him to explore other planets and the solar system and the future without even thinking what the after effects would be like. Man became a living time bomb.

Later on man became very greedy. He wanted to rule the world but time stood in his way, he needed time to think and time to plan and eventually time to die.

He tried to overcome this by building supersonic planes which can go faster than the speed of sound, made films in which they made a machine that could go back and forward in time. But in the real world they never did beat time itself.

As my description goes on, then people started to disagree and started to fall out with each other, so they had to think of a way to settle this, if I can't have it you can't have it either.

They built the Nuclear Bomb!

A bomb which can wipe out an entire life form in seconds which would have after effects which can prove devastating, all they had to do was sit back and wait for someone to move the queen. They made a film where someone did just that. It was called The Day After.

If I had three wishes one would be to get rid of all nuclear weapons and make sure that no man or woman ever interfered with Nature again.

When reading this essay to student teachers, as I often do, their reaction is similar to that of Winston's classmates at the time he wrote it. They are, almost without exception, full of praise and affection for the piece, suggesting, when asked to hypothesize a grade, anything from an A to a C (the three 'pass grades' in the English examination to which such a piece would be submitted). This widespread commendation is not hard to understand. If we wanted to be positive about Winston's essay, we might say that he responded to his task with great feeling and sincerity, that he successfully conveyed this feeling and sincerity to his reader, and that he adopted a form which, though not what was expected, seemed totally appropriate to him (Kress 1982, p.181). What Winston produced, we might argue, is a kind of religious sermon – one that seeks to go far beyond the sort of data-supported, point-by-point discursive essay that would achieve a good grade in the examination; one that takes on a cosmic scope, relating the advent of nuclear weapons to the spiritual evolution of humanity's obsession with Time, drawing, eclectically, on military–technological 'progress' (the development of submarines, supersonic flight, space travel) as well as on the arts (films which sublimate the desire to defeat Time by travelling through it, or which portray the after-effects of nuclear war). It is a piece rich in biblical imagery ('hate struck the land like a plague of locusts') as well as in metaphor (the major world powers involved in a chess game to be decided by a crucial move of the queen). It swings back and forth, the way sermons often do, between the voiceless assertion of biblical truths ('He wanted to rule the World, but time stood in his way ... ') to the directly personal ('If I had three wishes ... '). It is a powerful piece of writing with an apocalyptic perspective, whose sermon-form is totally in keeping with the nature of its message. We should find it not at all surprising that a young man for whom religion has always been a great explainer of the world should choose such a discourse for so important a topic.

Despite all this, Winston's essay was not favourably received by his teacher-examiners when the English Department at his school came to grade the students' folders of work. At their examination meeting, they were, variously, to describe Winston's essay as 'too short', 'disorganized', 'not really a discursive essay at all', 'lacking in data' and 'too close to speech'. They felt that it had 'not explored the issues', had 'nothing about the arguments for and against nuclear deterrence', contained 'no information on the nature of the build-up of these arms', was characterized by 'too much emotion and not enough rationality' and was generally 'too woolly', 'more like a poem', 'lacking in conviction' and 'scattered with surface-errors'. The particular piece of work was awarded a grade E, which was in line with the overall grade given to Winston and later confirmed by the examination board.

The judgements made by Winston's teachers – greeted with appalled disbelief by my own student teachers[16] – need to be contextualized within the rules and constraints within which teachers work. While acknowledging that the teachers were necessarily operating, as internal examiners, at the level of legitimation (of the *existing* system, with its culturally biased criteria) – that is to say, as policers of the system – this does not necessarily mean that the system and its assessment criteria were unproblematic to them, or that they could not see an 'advocating' alternative. That their judgements may have been pragmatic rather than complicit is, indeed, borne out by their comments upon having their judgements challenged by Winston's English teacher. As one teacher was to say, summarizing the views of the group as a whole:

> *Of course it's a shame [that Winston's essay can't be given a pass grade], but you just can't play fast and loose with the criteria. Whatever we may think personally about the regulations, if you let something like this through you risk having everyone else's grades dragged down.*

The observation that a high mark for Winston might jeopardize the existing high marks of other students was a valid one, showing an accurate understanding of how the system of moderated internal examining operated. When the internal examiners had awarded marks to all their students' work, a sample of students' work would be sent off to external examiners for 'checking'. If scripts were found to be marked too generously, perhaps outside the criteria guidelines, all scripts – including those which had not been seen by the external examiners – were in danger of being downgraded accordingly. Such a system is no doubt cheaper to run and more practicable than other possible systems. It also, however, has the 'advantage' of making teachers part of the judgement process and therefore of working with the criteria in a way that (if they are not to 'let their students down') ensures the reproduction of those criteria. To draw on Foucauldian analysis (for example, Foucault 1977), this is a step towards making the system – including its reproductive element(s) – self-regulating: the penalty for teachers not teaching the 'right' knowledge or genres is not a *physical* one directed against the teachers, but a *symbolic* one suffered both by the teachers (the burden of failing their students – not to mention the potentially dangerous government publication of inevitably poor results) and by their students (the withholding of cultural capital in its transactional form). The system becomes fully self-regulating when the students themselves see the selections of knowledge and genre that comprise the curriculum as universal or 'right' rather than arbitrary, interpreting their own given grades as signs of personal failure and stupidity.

Challenging the System: Cultural Reproduction and the Transformative Intellectual

The systemic context in which teachers operate when assessing work explains why they were able in this instance – indeed, why they were obliged – to grade Winston's essay in terms of 'an honourable failure' (to quote one teacher) rather than a pass. Questions need to be raised, however, as to (1) the extent to which teachers can or should challenge the imposed criteria (and the possible locus for mounting such a challenge), and (2) *the extent to which students – including this particular student – can or should challenge those criteria themselves.*

As has already been suggested, there are two possible arenas in which teachers can mount challenges to the culturally biased, coercive systems within which they operate, rather than merely seeking to do the best they can (Willis 1977) within a system which remains largely unchallenged and therefore 'legitimated'. In their dialogic work *A Pedagogy for Liberation*, Ira Shor and Paolo Freire identify a central task for schools and teachers as 'demystifying the dominant ideology' (Shor and Freire 1987, p.168) – that is, as helping students to understand and 'make visible' the kinds of cultural–ideological coercions to which they are typically subjected through pedagogies and school curricula. (This would include, for instance, helping students to appreciate that the 'standard forms' in which they are expected to acquire and demonstrate expertise are the cultural and ideological preferences of the powerful social groups who initiated and continue to control and monitor public education.) This task, suggest Shor and Freire,

> cannot be accomplished by the system. It cannot be accomplished by those who agree with the system. This [demystifying process] is the task for educators in favor of a liberating process. They have to do this through different kinds of educational action; for example, through teaching music or mathematics, teaching biology or physics or drawing, no matter.
>
> (Shor and Freire 1987, p.168)

Whether or not teachers can do anything to change the system through 'externally oriented' action is another matter, and one that I have not made the subject of this book. Shor and Freire certainly seem to suggest that this is currently problematic – that 'the system' is powerful and monolithic, and that only local subversions of it are practicable. Their 'critical pedagogy' 'invites people to know what is hidden from us and to know how we cooperate in denying our own freedom' (Shor and Freire 1987, pp.173–4) – but it does not necessarily involve revolutionary attempts at dismantling the system that denies that freedom. What it does attempt to achieve is the empowering of students, through 'illuminating reality', not, perhaps, to overthrow a coercive system but to recognize its manipulations and to be better able to 'confront' them (op. cit.).

It will be the main purpose of the next chapter to consider examples of how such cooperations might look in practice and what levels of success they might reasonably expect to achieve. In doing this, we will be moving beyond the boundaries of *developed partial inclusion* towards what might be referred to as *full partial inclusion*. We will also, however, be touching on that other question about resistance: that is to say, not teacher resistance *per se* but forms of student resistance and how those may or may not be supported *by* teachers.

Notes

1   *Sequential* bidialectal or bilingual students are those who have acquired high levels of competence in one dialect or language before adding to their linguistic repertoire any additional dialect(s) or language(s). Examples would be students moving to the UK at secondary-school age with high levels of proficiency in a non-standard dialect or in a language other than English, and needing to add the standard dialect of English to their repertoire. *Simultaneous* bidialectal or bilingual students are those who have acquired high levels of competence in more than one language or dialect from an early age: for example, students born in the UK of parents from non-standard-English-speaking backgrounds, where standard English was not the 'home language'.
2   Interestingly, the UK National Curriculum makes compulsory the teaching of Shakespeare texts – which are, effectively, texts written in non-standard English. It is less enthusiastic, however, about other 'non-standard' texts such as 'dialect poetry'. Non-standard dialects, it seems, can achieve posthumous respectability with the Establishment once they are safely embedded in the past and can be described in terms of 'heritage' or 'tradition'.
3   Stubbs provides a useful debunking of some of the myths surrounding standard and non-standard dialects, through a summary of issues related to dialect, accent and style. See, in particular, Stubbs 1976, p.33.
4   The same, of course, may be said of so-called standard *genres*.
5   In these days of globalization, we hear few serious arguments for one international language to replace individual languages, or that one language is the only 'true' language from which all others are deviants. Nor do people seem to believe that business or international political relations are incapable of being conducted by people who habitually operate in more than one language and who, more often than not, do not share the same level of fluency in the same languages – in the light of which, the 'convenience' argument itself might be considered spurious. An interesting role-play activity with student-teachers, aimed at effecting a detached consideration of these issues, involves setting up situations in a 'parallel universe' in which, say, Cockney or Glaswegian or a Caribbean dialect of English has become 'standard English' while what is now known as standard English is considered an inferior dialect, indicative of low social standing.
6   Primary schools in the UK usually cater for students up to the age of eleven, whereupon they transfer to secondary schools. Primary schools are typically divided themselves into infant schools or sections, catering for students up to the age of seven, and junior schools or sections, taking students through to eleven.

7   The computer program *Developing Tray*, which I have inevitably oversimplified, was designed by an English teacher, Bob Moy, working with the Inner London Educational Computing Centre located within the old Inner London Education Authority. The best account of the program's rationale is still to be found in the *Teaching Documents*, produced with the program and edited by J. Stephens. Particularly interesting is Moy's own account, *Thinking Under the Influence*.

8   The logic, that is, of the test's designers.

9   I use Barthes' distinction here, where readerly texts are designed to resist interpretation and writerly texts invite interpretation (Barthes 1975).

10 See also Cummins 1996, p.75, and Freire and Macedo (1987) on 'readers of the word' needing also to be 'readers of world'.

11 My argument is that tests such as this seek to *reify* context, stripping it of its essentially contingent, idiosyncratic nature.

12 Nor was this simply a matter of the differences between *any* adult's and *any* child's experience of the world. If that had been so, the problem would, arguably, have been not so serious, since all students would, at least, have been equally disadvantaged by the test.

13 The same case could be made for Carrie's and John's policeman, who was clearly someone who was out to trap people, and the policeman of the test's designers, viewed as a disinterested professional with a function to perform.

14 Jason, for example, would have achieved a reading age of 8.3 instead of 7.9 had his logical but incorrect answers been accepted – still misleadingly low, but at least a step in the right direction.

15 These might include, however, establishing and linking up with pressure groups, writing letters to relevant newspapers and journals, and seeking to vote on to union executives teachers with something to say about teaching and learning and not *just* about teacher salaries or conditions of employment, important though these matters are.

16 A different story emerges, of course, with experienced teachers, who are more familiar with the criteria and with this particular form of criterion-referencing.

8   Exercises in Illumination
Empowerment via Shared Criteria

[The teaching of literature in schools] operates within that English tradition which penetrates all aspects of cultural life in the country: namely, a firm separation of creation from criticism, of practice from theory.

(Exton 1984, p.70)

Revisiting Young Readers

Previous chapters have considered issues of repertoire extension within a generic perspective: in particular, 'What does this piece of work tell me about this productive human being?'; 'How might I extend this person's expressive–productive repertoire in order that they might be further empowered?'; 'How can I ensure that such an extension does not, in the process, threaten, devalue or destroy the person's existing skills and interests, or undermine their self-confidence and self-belief?' In this chapter, I shall suggest that in order to achieve genuine repertoire extension – for example, in order to help students successfully to incorporate 'standard' approaches and skills (even 'standard' *responses*) into a durable body of non-standard ones, we need first to accomplish two things: first, to clarify to our students exactly what the 'standard' forms and practices are (what the *genres* look like, but also by what criteria their successful reproduction is evaluated); second, to help our students to understand why – and by what processes – these 'standard' forms have achieved the status they have, and why it might be in the students' best interests to acquire and develop expertise in any of these forms and practices which are missing or underdeveloped in their current repertoires.[1] I want to suggest that the achievement of both these targets is facilitated by sharing with one's students – whatever their age may be and in whatever form may seem appropriate – the criteria, typically held in secrecy from them, by which they are being and will continue to be *assessed*: indeed, this may be seen as an indispensable prerequisite to such achievement.

To illustrate what I mean by this, we could do worse that return to the young readers, Jason and Steven, referred to in the previous chapter. Jason and Steven, it will be remembered, were awarded relatively low reading ages on the basis of a test which allowed for only one very specific set of word *meanings*. Their often highly logical yet 'non-standard' answers when given sentences with missing words and asked to fill in the gaps were regularly at odds with the answers expected and required of them by the test's designers, resulting in their existing reading skills being marginalized and effectively overlooked as part and parcel of a broader marginalization of their out-of-school cultural preferences and experience. An awareness that such processes may be at work in the assessment of students is plainly useful to the class teacher, as are such activities as those subsequently deployed in this case study, when students were invited to discuss their 'wrong' answers with an interested adult. *To what extent, however, can – or should – these lessons be built upon in ways that not only inform pedagogy and therefore provide indirect help to the marginalized students, but that help students themselves become independent navigators and negotiators within the value-laden cultural market-place in which they will have to operate?*

It was precisely this latter question that led Jason's and Steven's support-teacher, with the agreement of their regular class teacher, to undertake an additional activity that we have not yet examined: the activity of contextualizing the students' scores *with the students*. For this activity, the teacher spent some time talking to the same small group of students whose test responses we have already considered: that is to say, Jason, Steven, John, Carrie and Lynette. What follow are two significant extracts from these conversations.

Dialogue 10: Discussion of test with young readers (1)

Teacher:	You know, some people in the class put 'bucket' for this one. (*Shows students sentence: 'It began to ****** so we put our coats on.'*)
Jason:	Not me ... I put 'rain'.
Steven:	That's ...
Teacher:	What, Steve?
Steven:	That's not wrong. ... You could put 'rain' or 'bucket'.
Teacher:	Well, maybe. ... But the thing is, what you might probably not have known, although I know Ms Ainsley did mention it, is that only one answer is counted as right here. ... And unfortunately it's not 'bucket'.
Carrie:	Rain?
John:	That's what I was gonna say. ... And I did put 'bucket'.
Steven:	Oh, man. ... So 'bucket' [is] wrong?
Teacher:	Well, according to this test, yes. But what would you think if I said I didn't agree with the test? ... I mean, I've

---

often heard people say it 'bucketed' with rain, and I'm pretty sure – well, I know, actually – that I've said that myself on many occasions. *(Waits for response, which fails to come.)* I mean, how can it be that 'bucket' is a word that we can use here, that a lot of us would use here, but it counts as wrong and only 'rain' counts as being right in the test?

John:	I know.
Teacher:	John?
John:	Can I say this? It's 'cos – right – 'bucket' isn't proper English. 'Rain' is proper. 'Bucket' is ...
Carrie:	Why? ... Why isn't 'bucket' proper?
John:	It just ain't proper English. I mean. ... All right – do you think you would ever hear the Queen say 'I'd better put my coat on because it's starting to bucket?' *(Students all laugh.)*
Jason:	She would have someone come round in a taxi or something.
Steven:	One of them big gold carriages with horses pulling it ...
Teacher:	So, can I get this straight: are you saying, then, John that the Queen speaks proper English and Steve doesn't? Or we have to speak like her ...
Steven:	She does! *(Pause.)* She *thinks* she does!
Lynette:	What?
Steven:	Speak proper English.
John:	If she *thinks* she does, that's all that matters guy.
Teacher:	But isn't your English just as good as hers?
John:	Yeah.
Carrie:	Yes.
Steven:	Better!
Teacher:	So how come you have to use – like – 'her English' to do well in this test? That doesn't sound very fair to me, if your English is just as good.
John:	'Cos that's the way it is. ... That's just the way it is. You speak like the Queen and everyone thinks you're smart. ...
Teacher:	And you don't think it's unfair?
Jason:	Yeah.
Steven:	Yeah.
Teacher:	So – John – the big question. You said the Queen wouldn't say 'bucket', and it's not proper English: so why did you put 'bucket' in the test?

John:	*(Shrugs.)*
Teacher:	I think what I'm getting at is. ... It seems that if you want to do well in the test, you've got to put down what someone like the Queen might say. ... Even though it's not what you would say ... and even though what she says isn't really any more right or any better than what you would say ...
Jason:	That's right.
Steven:	*(Half under his breath.)* She's a snob.
Carrie:	She is, Sir.

Dialogue 11: Discussion of test with young readers (2)

Teacher:	Jason, and Steve, I got the impression from watching you working on that 'Fishing' poem that you were really very good readers. I mean, I'm still amazed how you read that whole poem –
Steven:	And got it right.
Teacher:	Well, yes. ... And you can still remember a lot of it, can't you? But I get that feeling about all of you. I mean, I've seen you, Carrie, and you, Lynette, and John – I've watched you all do really well on your *Developing Tray* sessions – and I was wondering if you also see yourselves as pretty good readers, or if you think there are things in your reading that you could do better at ... ?
John:	Well, I think that I'm a pretty good reader actually.
Teacher:	You do? Why do you think that?
John:	*(Shrugs.)*
Steven:	I'm a bad reader, me.
Teacher:	Why ... ?
John:	It's just, like, the books you can read. I've been on real books since I was about six.
Carrie:	John is a good reader.
Teacher:	Yes, I'm sure he is. ... But what I'm saying is that I think you're all good readers.
John:	We are – but I'm just the best.
Jason:	I'm not a really good reader.
Teacher:	I disagree! tell me why you think you're not a really good reader, Jason.

Jason:	Because – probably – no one ever really taught me to read good ...
Teacher:	Well, I see. ... That isn't exactly what I meant. I mean, you've given a reason why –
Carrie:	I know what you mean, Sir.
Teacher:	Yes, Carrie?
Carrie:	You mean, like, how do you *know* you're not a good reader.
John:	Or how do you know you *are* a good reader!
Teacher:	Well, how do *you* know, Carrie?
Carrie:	'Cos Miss puts us on the right books.
Steven:	The reading scheme.
Jason:	I've been on the same level for about three years, man.
John:	Three years? You can't have been. They didn't even use the reading scheme. ... How old were you three years ago? Five!
Teacher:	Well ... I don't like to mention it again, but what about the reading test, and the scores you got on that?
Steven:	Scores?
Jason:	We never –
John:	You don't get scores on the reading test.
Teacher:	Oh, I'm sorry: I thought you did. So ... if you don't get scores, it doesn't really matter then?
Steven:	No. ... Not really.

There is much that is interesting in these discussions and much light shed on the attitudes of the young people not just to language but to culture and class too, and to issues of compliance and resistance. Thus, from the students' point of view we see the term 'proper English' used, but it is not linked to issues of inferiority and superiority and is seen as 'right' only because a very powerful person (representing, perhaps, all powerful people) *thinks* it is right. Similarly, there is evidence of students recognizing the unfairness of the test they have taken and of the devaluation of their own language, but this is not linked to any obvious feelings of *victimization*. The question as to whether or to what extent these students feel they should 'play the game' (that is, give answers which they know other people will think are 'right', rather than answers which best suit themselves) remains unresolved because it is largely unasked – and it remains unasked largely because, through the withholding of critical information, the students do not know that the test is being used as the chief indicator of their reading expertise and development.[2]

From the pedagogical point of view, the support-teacher working with these students aims at achieving the two ends described above – i.e. sharing the assessment *criteria* and giving some indication as to where those criteria have come from – in a way that is wholly appropriate for students of this age and at this stage in their school careers. Avoiding overt political engagement, he chooses, rather, to establish a discourse that carefully avoids the binary opposition of 'right' and 'wrong', and then to exploit this discourse to introduce ideas related to repertoire extension and cultural bias: in short, to 'illuminate' ways of looking at language and learning that build on the students' existing awareness of cultural difference and social inequality. In doing this, he makes clear his own sense of injustice, indicating that to do well students may need to operate in certain ways, but that those ways are not necessarily *superior*.

Working with Bidialectal Examination Students: Defining the Genre

The critical sharing of assessment criteria is particularly important with students taking public examinations, chiefly because the stakes are so high. While one might anticipate that such an activity would be commonplace (after all, it would seem perverse to enter anyone for a test without first telling them what they had to do to succeed – unless, of course, one wanted them to fail), my own colleagues in schools complain endlessly that such sharings far too often are overlooked or – in the worst cases – viewed as a form of 'cheating'.[3]

The potential value of a prolonged and systematic sharing of assessment criteria with students in this category is well illustrated in the following study of a high-school teacher, Mr Browning, working with a class of fifteen- and sixteen-year-olds towards an English examination assessed completely by coursework. Having first provided his students with a simplified version of the examination criteria, including information related to the desired length and organization of assignments, to their content, to technical standards (such as spelling, punctuation and grammar) and to appropriate uses of language, the teacher sought to help his students *make their own sense* of these rather abstract, 'disembodied' notions through getting them to assess scripts previously submitted to and assessed by the examining board – some by students who had also attended this school, some by students from other schools. They were then given opportunities to compare their assessments with those awarded by the board, as a way of comparing their own interpretations of the criteria with those of their future judges. This also provided them with an opportunity to compare their *own* criteria for evaluating various pieces of writing with the examining board's criteria, and to highlight and discuss any significant discrepancies.

The class with whom Mr Browning worked at this criteria-sharing activity was interesting and slightly unusual in that it was made up of students all of whom had been identified by the school as having behavioural problems and being unlikely to achieve pass grades in any examination subject: indeed, they had not even been entered for examinations in several subject areas. The students were also, with only two exceptions (neither of whom are referred to in the following examples), black and habitually operated in non-standard dialects of English.

Mr Browning had already involved the class in one criteria-sharing activity, and by now they were quite used to – and confident about – taking the examiner's role. This initial exercise had involved the students in selecting favourite pieces from their own and one another's writing, and sharing these with the rest of the class. Out of discussions about why they had made their selections, it became clear that specific criteria were being regularly cited by the students in deciding and articulating what was 'good' about writing and what was not. These sessions revealed, for example, that the use of unusual or unfamiliar vocabulary (words like 'jaundiced' and 'zeitgeist') was particularly highly valued by the students (many of whom randomly scoured the class dictionaries for 'new words' they liked the sound of, even, in some cases, structuring whole narratives around individual words), while matters to do with spelling and punctuation were, generally, considered less important. Mr Browning's subsequent exercise with these students took the form of a full-scale moderation of previous students' work. These previously assessed scripts, some written by students at the same school, some by students at other schools, covered a range of grades from 1 to 'unclassified' (for scripts below 5). The students in Mr Browning's class studied the scripts carefully, initially working on their own, and were invited to suggest examination grades for each script. These grades were then compared with the actual grades that had been given and Mr Browning was able to discuss any discrepancies with the students, referring back to the examination criteria and to the particular ways in which these had been interpreted. The first example of writing offered to these students – a story entitled 'Marrige' – is shown, in part, as Figure 20.

Figure 20 Start of Student A's 'Marrige' story

Mr and Mrs Butch lived together for four years Mr Butch's name is fred and his wife is called helen, they both own a Butcher shop called 'Butch's Butcher Shop.'
fred never liked his wife much she was always nagging and nagging at him.
'Helen come and help in shop please
'I'm fixing my hair'
'So what your only working in shop'
'So what, people come in you know I want to look Good'

'one of these days I'm gonna kill you'
'What was that'
'nothing, nothing at all'
'I'm coming now anyway'
'Hello Mr Brown'
'Hello Mr Butch, how are you?
'oh! fine thanks and you.'
'Not too bad'
'Hello Mrs Butch'
Hello Brown hows Mrs Brown?
'Not to bad just a bit ill'
'Oh well I'll give you some chops to give her'
'thanks, thanks alot, bye'
'Bye'
'Bye, helen why did you give her that meat'
'well shes sick'
'Yeah and whos ganna have to pay for it Me'
'oh it's just money'
'well if its just money you Pay for it'.
'And we need some shopping will you go and do it please, I'll look after the shop'.
'yea and you'll give out more meat'.
Helen was a lazy woman, so while her husband went shopping she closed the shop.
She was combing her hair again, her husband come back from shopping and saw a sign saying closed, when he got in he didnt open shop he went downstairs and got a large chopping knife, and walked in the bedroom to kill her as he opened the door, the front door shop was ringing, so he went downstairs to open it, but no one was there, so he went back upstairs.

Note: Spelling and punctuation as in original.

Not surprisingly, perhaps, Mr Browning's students were somewhat dismayed by inevitable discrepancies between the examiners' assessments of the other students' work and their own – chiefly, of course, because of the implications of these discrepancies for the assessment of their own examination folders. Their tendency was to overgrade (in terms of likely *actual* grades) the scripts they were being shown, in a way that suggested their own work would comfortably achieve pass grades. When the 'unseen' students' actual grades were shared with them, this resulted in an instant – but very short-lived – sense of demoralization, as illustrated in Dialogue 12.

Dialogue 12: Extract from students' initial response to grading
comparisons

Julian:	Oh. ... How much did Student A get, please?
Mr B:	Grade 3.
	(Silence.)
Winston:	Is it bad? Is that bad?
	[...]
Julian:	*(Very anxiously.)* I don't know what grade I'll get, but I reckon I'll get about a 3. I'm throbbin' now, you know. I reckon I'll get about a 3, boy.
Mr B:	Why? Because you think your work is not as good as this [Grade 1 piece, written by Student B]?
Julian:	Dunno. ... D'you reckon my work is as good as this? Did this get sent off?
Mr B:	Yeah. This [Student B work] is a photocopy of work from a student in another school –
Julian:	That got sent off ...
Mr B:	That actually was given a Grade 1. But they only just got a Grade 1.
Julian:	She only just got –
Mr B:	[...] yeah.
Julian:	And what did Student A ...
Mr B:	Student A, as I said, got a Grade 3. You want to see something that got a Grade 2?
Julian:	And Student A's is as good as this!
Winston:	Let's have a look.
Mr B:	That one got a Grade 2.
Julian:	Shit!
	(Pause while Winston reads.)
Winston:	No way am I getting a Grade 2, boy.
Mr B:	Personally ... I thought it was worth more than a 2.
Winston:	What, like what ...
Mr B:	Like a 1.
Michael:	So what's Grade 1 standard, then? You know, man!
Mr B:	Well, I can show you a good clear Grade 1. This one did well ...
Winston:	Let's have a look.
	(Mr B reads opening of story.)
Julian:	*(Appreciatively.)* Mmmm. ... That's firin', I reckon.
Mr B:	But why? What is – I mean, what is so good about it?

Julian:	Dunno. ... It just depends ... I reckon. ... To me, it depends on the reader ... [...]
Mr B:	Do you think ... from looking at these, there's a difference between what you thought was gonna be good in the exam and what actually is considered good?
Julian:	Yeah.
Winston:	Yeah.
Julian:	I thought that. ... (Incredulous.) Student A got 3! (To *Winston.*) What d'you reckon you'd get? *(Pause.)*
Winston:	2?
Julian:	That's a 2!
Mr B:	What grade d'you think you'll get? 1, 2, 3, 4, 5?
Winston:	5!
Julian:	Have to look at my work, boy. That's serious, boy!

The sharing of criteria in this particular way may have caused momentary discomfort to the students involved; however, Mr Browning clearly thought it was a risk worth taking:

> *At least they now know fairly precisely what they've got to do if they want to pass the exam, and they know it's not just me selling them a line. For some of them, this'll be a wake-up call – it'll push them on from a near-miss to actually passing the exam, which I don't think is beyond any of them.*

Mr Browning's faith in his students' ability – and his own ability to replicate this faith in his students – was clearly important if the risk was to succeed, and he felt that much had already been achieved in this respect through the initial criteria-sharing exercise, in which the students had learned to identify, articulate and appreciate the qualities in their own and one another's writing. Mr Browning's suggestion that

> *they'll be shell-shocked for a little while, but they'll quickly get the message that this is just a matter of building on their existing expertise in ways that are well within their capabilities*

was, indeed, borne out as the students quickly shook off their initial discomfort to set about reappraising the situation in a variety of ways.

Having reached this point, the students' next task was to respond in more elaborate, less 'involved' ways to the scripts they had been shown. Dialogue 13 gives a flavour of these discussions, with reference to the 'Marrige' story, written by Student A and shown as Figure 20. This is the story that one of the students, Julian, had originally been shocked to discover had only been awarded a Grade 3.

Dialogue 13

Leonard:	Why does she say her husband '*come* back' instead of 'came back'? Is that a mistake? Or is it meant to be a style of writing?
Mr B:	Who knows?
Leonard:	'Her husband *come* back ... '
Mr B:	It depends, you see: you can either treat it as style or a mistake. Depends on your point of view and Student A's intention. Which we don't know ... [...]
Leonard:	This ... I reckon this story is just a load of rubbish, Sir. I swear ... I swear ...
Mr B:	So you think a Grade 3 or 4 is -
Leonard:	'He walked in the bedroom to kill her' ... I reckon that's a load of rubbish.
Mr B:	Right ...
Leonard:	It doesn't *(laughing incredulously)*. ... It doesn't prepare you or nothing: he just walks into the ... he walks in through the door to kill her ...
Winston:	In other words, it tells you before it happens.
Leonard:	What's that? ... front door ... ringing ...
Winston:	Do you agree with me? It tells you before it happens.
Mr B:	Yes. ... It takes away the suspense ...
Leonard:	Sir, can I just tell you something. ... Sir ... You know where he goes to kill her, right, then she says the front door bell's ringin', right, and he went downstairs to open it, now ... if you were going to kill someone, don't you think you'd put something in between that? 'He panicked'? 'He sump'n sump'n sump'n'? You know what I mean? She just. ... He went downstairs as if he's still got a knife in his hand ...

Allen:	He ascended ...
Leonard:	*(Scornfully.)* How can he ascend? What you talking about?
Julian:	What did he say?
Leonard:	As he 'ascended' ... !
	'He went back upstairs. ... His wife was reading the paper and eating' ...
	'He went behind her and slashed her throat ... '
	(Laughing.) This is just a load of rubbish, I swear.
Winston:	'He slashed her throat and ... '. And what?
Leonard:	'Blood splashed on the mirror and over the paper and the bedcovers.'
Michael:	Ah, get off with that story, man.
	(Noise as Leonard continues to read, then:)
Leonard:	'He polished everywhere and throw the paper out.'
Luke:	*(Laughs.)*
Leonard:	'First he ... '
Michael:	Primitive!
Leonard:	'And he put the covers in washing machine – '
	[...]
Leonard:	That story is a load of ...
Julian:	Codswallop.
Michael:	Rubbish.
Leonard:	Infantile. I'm sorry to say that, but it is.
Mr B:	What, do you mean it was simple and –
Leonard:	It's so simple, and ... *silly*! You know what I mean, Sir. Silly and rushed and ... no ... as if she didn't think about it, she just writ it and didn't do a rewrite or nothing. ... 'Cos when I do my stories I always have to do a rewrite. I don't think no one can write a decent story first ... I think she did. I think she just writ it first ... first go.

The contrast between these observations and the students' initial responses to Student A's work is notable for more than just its level of detail. From an initial overvaluing of this student's work, the students in Mr Browning's class appear to have swung dramatically the other way in their evaluations, now, perhaps, being overcritical of this student's writing. Such a swing is not without problems, particularly when one bears in mind that Student A was also someone who regularly used non-standard forms of language, and contains a clear warning for teachers undertaking this kind of exercise with their students. That aside, however, there is evidence in this dialogue of Mr

Browning's students arriving at a clearer *understanding* of why it was that Student A 'failed' her examination and (implicit in their now universal condemnation of her work) evidence of a belief that her weaknesses are avoidable or non-existent in their own writing *for the exam* and perhaps, too, in their own writing for themselves and for each other. They also appear to be developing an impressive and potentially very useful ability to *articulate* the examination assessment criteria as well as to *prioritize* them. In their criticisms of Student A's work, for example, it is not so much punctuation, spelling, grammar, or even vocabulary that they choose to home in on; it is, rather, the fact that (to use Barthes' terminology) the story was 'nucleus-heavy' (Barthes 1983): that is to say, there were too many critical incidents in the story, insufficiently woven together by the use of introductions, elaborations, characterization, scene-setting and so forth. This is what Julian was getting at when he said the essay did not 'explain the text' and what Leonard meant when he said:

> It doesn't prepare you or nothing … don't you think you'd put something in between that? 'He panicked'? 'He sump'n sump'n sump'n'? … It's so simple, and … *silly*! … Silly and rushed …

One result of such nucleus-heaviness, which in the students' eyes seems to betray the very protocol of story-writing, is that it eliminates possibilities in the text for what Mr Browning and (on an earlier occasion) Winston refer to as suspense – that is to say, 'a game with structure, designed to endanger and glorify it' (Barthes 1983, p.290). The sentence 'He walked in the bedroom to kill her' is selected by Winston as a classic example of how Student A's absence of distortion, expansion and insertion removes that essential element of suspense (particularly essential in the murder-story genre), that holds its readers' interest by keeping them guessing. As Winston so aptly puts it: 'It tells you before it happens.'

This articulation on the part of 'failing students' of the criteria by which they are judging another student's work not only suggests that they have absorbed very effectively the criteria by which their *own* writing will be assessed in the examination, but invites the question: *why were they labelled failing students in the first place?* Was it, for example, because they knew about the criteria but were simply unable to translate them into practice in their own writing? Or was it, rather, because no one had thought to share the criteria with them in the first place, leaving them with only their own 'independent' criteria of what made a good piece of writing, even though (as conversations with the students very clearly indicated) there were major discrepancies between their own values and those of their examiners? This issue was subsequently approached by Mr Browning through engaging the students in discussions about writing 'style', in the hope that this would clarify the extent to which fundamental differences in criteria existed between the students and their 'official' assessors and the extent to which they were *willing or able* to sacrifice independent criteria in the interests of examination success. Dialogues 14 and 15 give some sense of how these discussions began.

Dialogue 14

(Following their demolition of 'Marrige', the students discussed at length another piece, in which the same student had been asked to write two 'Agony Aunt' responses to letters sent in by people with problems: a girl whose fiancé had been told he only had five years to live and who still wanted to marry him against her doctor's advice; and a girl going out with a younger boy who was being teased and called 'cradle-snatcher' by her friends.)

Leonard:	No ... I. ... This doesn't look like it's come from any agony aunt.
Julian:	That's exactly what I said.
Leonard:	You know why? 'Cos it doesn't kinda go into no kinda depth. You know what it looks like? It's like you asked my advice, Julian asked my advice, and I'm telling him as a friend. It doesn't look like someone who's a profes-sional. It doesn't have any professional touches to it, that's why. ... It just looks like as if friends are saying it to each other. [...]
Winston:	She doesn't express her views *clearly*.

Dialogue 15

Mr B:	Leonard, I've often heard you use the word 'style', when you've been talking about other students' work. But I wonder if you could tell me – in a few words. ... What is style?
Leonard:	Suppose you write five different stories and they're all the same style, it would be boring. That's why when I write I try ... to do different things, you know what I mean. It's true ... I. ... You know, it's boring. My 'Fear' story and my 'Fugitive', when I read it they're the same style, so – know what I mean? – So that's why I took out my 'Fear' [from my folder] and done something else. ... 'Cos I like to change ... I like to change ...

166

As far as Student A's 'Agony Aunt' writing is concerned, there is no single view as to what is 'wrong' with it ('it doesn't kinda go into no kinda depth', 'she doesn't express her views clearly'). Uniting the criticisms, however, is Leonard's view that it 'doesn't have any professional touches': in short, Student A's work has failed to achieve what Leonard refers to in other conversations as 'the standard' as demonstrated in the printed word. This failure is, in effect, a failure successfully to imitate the relevant *genre*, either in content or in style. To use the students' terminology, her essay lacks 'full-ness', it does not 'explain the text'; it mirrors the same kind of failings more obviously observable in Student A's *stories*, while at the same time bringing a new element – of *inappropriateness* – into consideration.

The suggestion in this first set of exchanges that the students not only have a developing awareness and understanding of assessment criteria, but that there may be a growing, if incomplete, convergence between their own notions of what is 'good' and those enshrined in the criteria published by the examining board is supported by Leonard's remarks to Mr Browning. Leonard's observations seem to suggest something more, however: not only a concern in his own mind that genres need to be accurately reproduced and that some genres may be more 'appropriate' in certain situations than in others, but an awareness on his part that a 'good' writer needs to be able to demonstrate reproductive skills in a *variety* of genres and, furthermore, that *within reproduction of the genre they find scope for individuality and origi-nality*. This last point is critical and was to become a feature not only of Leonard's but of several other students' responses when pushed on the matter of stylistic and generic issues. Another student, Michael, for example, was to argue with some passion both for the need to conform to generic forms and styles and for the need for the writer's 'voice' to shine through – a debate picked up with equal enthusiasm by other members of the group.

Dialogue 16

Michael: [Y]ou can't write the same style for every piece of work. If people read my school uniform essay [a piece of trans-actional/persuasive writing carried out earlier in the year] and I'd writ it like a story, what would they think?

Leonard: Not much ...

Mr B: So is that what it's all about, then? Copying certain ways of expressing things?

Michael: It is. ... It is. ...

Mr B: But what about other things, then? Like what you actu-ally put into your essay ... what you say. ... Or originality, feeling, things like that. ... Making the essay

	more kind of personal, so that people recognize it as one of yours – they recognize your style …
Michael:	I'm not saying … I'm not saying that's not important. … But the way it's set out has to be in a certain *style*.
Mr B:	So let me ask you this. Is it possible, do you reckon, to actually have two different kinds of writing – one for the exam, say, and one for you … I mean, is one right and one wrong? …
Julian:	One is right.
Leonard:	No.
Mr B:	You think one is right, Julian?
Julian:	Yeah: the exam is right.
Mr B:	But that's not quite what you were saying at the beginning of the year, is it? … Before we started looking at all these old exam scripts and the criteria … I remember you saying quite clearly that you didn't think there was a right way to write stories and essays – and didn't you say to me that you thought the exam board had a cheek telling people how they should write things?
Leonard:	You did, Julian …
Julian:	I've changed. Right. … Now I've seen these other essays, I do think they're better …
Leonard:	That's rubbish, man.
Julian:	It's not rubbish. … I think they're better than what I was writing before, then. … Than some of them … I still think my *stories* are as good as any of these. … But – you think of my A.I.D.S. essay. Before, it was rubbish – that was rubbish – but now I think I've done a much better job.
Mr B:	Better for the exam?
Julian:	Yeah.
Mr B:	But is it better anyway – I mean, even if there wasn't an exam?
Julian:	Yeah.
Leonard:	I disagree.
Mr B:	Why do you disagree, Leonard?
Leonard:	I thought Julian's A.I.D.S. essay was good – you mean that one you writ about your uncle, innit?
Julian:	Yeah.
Leonard:	That was good – but this one – I'm not saying it's not good, right … but … it's like anyone could of writ it … you know what I'm saying?

Mr B:	Yeah, maybe. ... But is that maybe the whole point? I mean is that what you're supposed to be doing? You know, making it look like anyone could have written it?
Leonard:	No – I don't think it is. ... My 'Suez Street' essay [descriptive piece written earlier in the year] – I still think that was good, but ... maybe I shouldn't say this, but I think it would get a good mark in the exam – I think it stands up to any of them others – in the vocabulary, and all the punctuation and thingummybobbin'. ... But you read that, and you know it's mine. ... It couldn't be anyone else's in this class. ... Could it, Julian? It's *original*, because of the way I've set it out, and the words I've used. ... And I've shown my way of seeing something.
Mr B:	So what would you reckon – do you think looking at these grades and stuff has helped you at all?
Leonard:	Yes.
Julian:	Yes.
Michael:	Yes.
Mr B:	And how then has it helped? I mean has it helped –
Leonard:	It's helped me to know what's expected in the exam.
Michael:	Me too.
Julian:	And me.
Mr B:	Right. ... But has it made you better *writers*?
Julian:	Yes.
Michael:	No. ... Maybe ...
Leonard:	No.
Mr B:	Leonard?
Leonard:	It hasn't helped that ... I *know* I can write ...
Michael:	You're so modest, man ...
Leonard:	I *know* it ...
Mr B:	But you seem to be suggesting that looking at the grades has made you change your writing in some ways ...
Leonard:	In some ways, yes. ... But not in others ...
Mr B:	Can you explain that a bit more fully?
Leonard:	Some writing I do – and I think this is for the examination ... just for the examination. ... It's good – but it might not be my best stuff ... other times – if I'm writing something for pleasure or just for myself, I don't care what the examination – the, er, examiners – think about it – because I know what I'm trying to do and I know if it's working or not.

Compliance, Resistance and the 'Third Way'

Leonard's observations seem to suggest an awareness on his part of a certain danger in the development of writing in educational settings – a danger that he seeks actively to avoid. Although he has no doubt that he must extend his language repertoire if he is to succeed in this important subject at examination level, and although there is evidence of an ability to bring about that extension, he is equally clear that in learning to 'control the genre' (the genre, that is, that is favoured within the system) he must be careful that the genre does not come to control him (Kress 1982, p.11) – that he does not, in fact, become like Harold Rosen's middle-class children, who 'have often to pay a price for the acquisition of certain kinds of transactional language, and that is loss of vitality and expressiveness, and obsession with proprieties' (Rosen 1972, p.19).

This danger that Leonard sees is evident in his criticisms of Julian's work – in particular, in his observation that Julian's formal essay on A.I.D.S. is less effective than an earlier, more 'personal' version of the same essay – that 'it's like anyone could of writ it'. To understand what Leonard is getting at here, it is useful to look at the openings of both versions of Julian's essay, which are given as Figures 21 and 22 below.

Figure 21 Introduction to Julian's 'A.I.D.S.' essay: first version

Last summer holiday one of my cousins came to visit us from America. We went out for dinner, and he told us that one of our uncles had AIDS. I didn't know what AIDS was at the time. I had heard of it in the newspapers and television, but I just thought it was something that gay people got. I remember my mum being totally shocked. 'How long?' she asked my cousin. My cousin said he thought my uncle had contracted the disease on a holiday about five years ago. 'No, how long before he dies?' my mum asked him. But my cousin just went quiet then. Later, when my mum wasn't there he told me my uncle was gay. 'Whatever you do, don't tell your mum,' he told me. 'Your uncle don't want nobody to know.' He then told me what it was like to have AIDS, and about all the kinds of help my uncle was having.

Figure 22 Introduction to Julian's 'A.I.D.S.' essay: second version

A.I.D.S. – WILL THERE EVER BE A CURE?

ACQUIRED IMMUNE DEFICIENCY SYNDROME.

WHAT IS AIDS?

AIDS is a complete breakdown or partial breakdown of the bodys natural ability to fight off disease which leaves the individual susceptibel to some rare cancers and infections. Such infections are usually called 'Opportunistic infections.'

The flurry of press comment on AIDS in recent weeks has focused on how to prevent it. The principal means, is a public education about safer sex. I once read in a newspaper that AIDS was first developed in Africa. A green monkey was said to have bitten a man and it was passed on through his intercourse. Another article said that AIDS was developed in a laboratory experiment in the U.S.A. and broke out accidentally. What really matters is a cure.

As in the case of Winston's 'Nuclear War' essay, described in the previous chapter, Julian had written his 'A.I.D.S.' essay initially in response to Mr Browning's instruction to: 'Write about a topic that is very important to you.' Julian had selected A.I.D.S. precisely because it *was* important to him – because it had recently touched his own life in a very particular, very personal way. It is hardly surprising that his immediate response was to *write* about it in a personal way, which entailed adopting the voice, the 'genre', of an autobiographical piece of writing. It was only after reading the 'successful' scripts of other students writing about important topics that Julian rejected his initial effort as 'rubbish', producing the second version which he felt was far better and far more likely to go down well with his examiners. Whether or not this was an accurate assessment is debatable, and it is easy to see why the first version was so popular with his friend Leonard. While the 'uncle' version does, indeed, have Julian's own 'voice' running through it, the second piece is highly derivative and gives the impression of having been cobbled together from 'voiceless' textbooks and newspaper articles. The worrying thing here is not just that Julian appears to have become constrained by the genre in which he seeks to develop the necessary expertise, but, through believing *himself* that the second way of writing is better than the first, *is complicit in the symbolic marginalization of his own originally favoured expressive style and form*. To put it bluntly, Julian has actually come to believe that his first essay was 'rubbish' and that his second essay is 'good' (a danger, it will be remembered, that Ms Montgomery saw in relation to Mashud's autobiographical essay, described in Chapter 6). In this we see the potential irony of genre-reproduction and replication implicit in Kress's formulation: empowerment of one kind (for example, doing well in public examinations and the various doors opened up by that kind of success in future life) is achieved at the very high cost of disempowerment of another (arguably, much more fundamental and important) kind – *the silencing, that is, of Julian's already marginalized voice, and with it the partial silencing of the much larger field of cultural practices that Julian has inherited.*

The contrast between Julian's and Leonard's attitudes may be seen as offering an interesting example of the difference between *servitude* to dominant genres on the one hand (Julian) and repertoire extension on the other (Leonard) – the first example resulting in a form of cultural genocide (in this case, inclusive of an element of assisted suicide), the second a pragmatic addition of new, dominant cultural forms alongside the continuing practice – and faith in – existing, non-dominant ones. Another way of looking at this is through Fordham's notions of 'acting white' and 'selling out' (Fordham 1990, p.259). Fordham describes how, in school settings, black adolescents 'consciously and unconsciously sense that they have to give up aspects of their identities and of their indigenous cultural system in order to achieve success as defined in dominant-group terms.' For many students, argues Fordham, 'the cost of school success is too high': that is to say, they are unprepared to sacrifice their favoured cultural forms and practices – their 'blackness' – in order to achieve academic success, since to do so would be to accept an unwanted change of identity and to risk rejection by their peers (Fordham 1990, p.259; see also Cummins 1996, p.145). Such students may find that their deliberate and conscious *resistance* to dominant white cultural practices, however, results in severe restrictions to their 'upward mobility, often culminating in students dropping out of school prematurely': in other words, they may find themselves in a no-win situation.

While it is undoubtedly the case that many minoritized students do end up 'becoming white' (complying)[4] or by effectively rejecting the dominant culture of the school (resisting),[5] it is equally clear from observations of students such as Leonard that there is another way – we might say, to use a current catchphrase, a 'third way' – for marginalized students and their teachers to approach the situation, and that is precisely through the notion of repertoire extension argued elsewhere in this book. This particular third way bases itself on the notion of an additive rather than a subtractive biculturalism, and gives fuller recognition to the possibilities for *agency*: that is to say, for the possibility that students – often acting with their teachers – can make informed decisions about these matters, including – as with Leonard, and in stark contrast to Julian – *the decision to combine academic success with the preservation and development of non-dominant cultural preferences, despite clear differences between these preferences and those espoused by and reproduced in the school.*[6]

The notion of student choice should not, either, be left out of considerations of minoritized students who submit work for public examinations that clearly does not meet the examination criteria though it may well meet their own. After showing Winston's 'Nuclear War' essay (see Chapter 7) to my own student teachers, I am invariably asked the questions: why did Winston's teacher allow this student to submit a piece of work such as this, knowing that it did not meet the non-negotiable criteria for one of the three pass grades? Was Winston simply incapable of replicating the 'appropriate' genre? Had the teacher just not made the criteria clear? Or had Winston *known* about the criteria and simply chosen to ignore them? The answer to these questions tends to take students by surprise. Discussions with Winston and his teacher revealed that Winston had, indeed, had the assessment criteria for all his assignments very carefully explained to him by his teacher, and had been shown examples of other students' essays from previous years where high marks had been awarded; in short, he had taken a full and active part in Mr Browning's criteria-sharing project, including the 'trial marking' sessions. Mr Browning had also taken great care in his evaluation of the first draft of Winston's essay to indicate (1) that he thought the piece was enormously powerful and beautifully written, (2) that it was unlikely to get a very high grade in the examination, not because it was not good but because for this particular essay the examiners would be demanding a somewhat different *kind* of essay.[7]

Why, then, did Winston persevere in submitting an 'inappropriate' essay in his examination portfolio, and why did Mr Browning let him do it? *The answer is that Winston, in full consideration of the information he had at that time at his disposal, made a conscious decision to ignore the official criteria – to act oppositionally both to and within the dominant discourse.* In his own words:

> *I know this is my best piece in my folder. Michael knows it, Amina knows it, Leonard knows it, Julian knows it – you know it, Sir. And I want to submit my best work. I don't care if it doesn't meet up with the require-ments. Why should I change it? Why* should *I?*

As principled as Julian and Leonard were pragmatic, Winston's choice appears to have been taken *regardless* of its likely consequences. There is no doubt that Winston, like Julian and Leonard, wanted to succeed academically, despite what some of his school reports may have indicated to the contrary: however, there was evidently a line which, if crossed, would (so Winston believed) turn him into someone else. Winston was not prepared to do this.

To summarize, we might say that Winston and his friends – and indeed all the other young people described in this book – did not set themselves up in deliberate cultural opposition to their school. It is true that in the cases of some of the bidialectal students described in this chapter oppositional elements were to be found (for instance, smoking spliffs in the toilets or occasionally setting fire to waste-bins near fire-alarms); however, these acts were always carried out within a street-cred-driven discourse of compromise. Winston and his friends were not like Willis's 'lads', who established their own 'counter-culture' groups and directly confronted the educational endeavours of their teachers (Willis 1977). They were, rather, in their different ways, all actively involved in negotiating identities and making decisions about what they were and were not prepared to do in order to achieve ends that had varying degrees of importance for them. Whereas Willis's 'lads' think they are offering resistance to the system but are, in practice, simply strengthening systemic coercions and marginalizations through internalizing them, the conscious nature of Winston's decision gives it more of the nature of a genuine risk. Whether it is a risk that he will, in future life, regret taking (or not being persuaded more forcefully to take) is another question. It is a question which raises, again, the issue of how far teachers can or should go with students like this in terms of helping their decision-making through a more radical, direct politicization.

Notes

1 There are, of course, other reasons for developing expertise in these 'standard' forms than that of 'getting on'. One that springs readily to mind is the increased opportunity for learning to enjoy a wide range of literature, much of which is 'standard' in style and form.

2 Ms Ainsley provided several reasons for not telling her students about the test scores. These included: the need for confidentiality; avoiding counter-productive competitiveness; 'protecting' the students; confusing the students.

3 There are many schools, of course, who do make a point of sharing examination criteria with their students. Many go as far as to provide simplified versions of these to distribute to and discuss with their students.

4 The movement from physical to symbolic exclusion is here mirrored by a corresponding movement from coercions of which the coerced subject is conscious and coercions which are, as it were, internalized through processes of complicity (see also Foucault 1977). This, perhaps, is what Kress is getting at when he talks of expertise in genre-reproduction resulting in domination by the genre. Winston, as we shall see, appears to reject expertise in a dominant genre, refusing to become complicit in the process of his own marginalization: effectively, he will not admit to his particular way of approaching a subject as being the 'wrong' way.

5 See also Ogbu (1992) on 'voluntary' and 'involuntary' minorities.

6 There remains an issue, of course, about students being put into the position of having to make such impossible choices – choices which students with 'majority culture' backgrounds do not have to make. Far preferable would be an education system that is more pluralistic and equitable, as well as being more tuned in to what is happening in the world in general.

7 Mr Browning had raised a number of other issues, which there is no space to explore here: for instance, Winston's use of sexist language.

9 Afterword

Issues of Responsibility and Choice

> As a child in the Caribbean I was filled with awe at the complexity of the world in which I found myself: the dazzle of tropical colour, the abundant variety of plant and animal life, the power of the sea. It was a rich environment in which to explore and make discoveries. But my sense of wonder at the world was amplified by the miracle of technology: the elegant beauty of schooners in full sail, the power of cane trucks as they crisscrossed the island at harvest, the mystery of cinema. Indeed western science and technology were, to many, testimony of the genius of the white world and a mute justification for its colonial authority. Black inventiveness was not evident in this way. We had no access to information on black travellers or inventors, had no sense of history outside that of Columbus and the British Empire. The black population operated in the long shadow of white power, our minds and perceptions shaped by its formulations of who we were and what we should become. We were acculturated to an environment which constructed us as inferiors.
>
> (Dash 1998, p.79; see also hooks 1992, p.167)

Obstacles to Teacher Activism

At the beginning of this book, I said that I wanted to focus on pedagogy: to show examples of ineffective and culturist practice as well as of effective and anti-culturist practice, in the hope that this would help teachers develop their own anti-culturist strategies for working with multicultured students. I also identified the school curriculum itself, along with its attendant bureaucracy, as a major *obstacle* to teachers developing their practice in this way. Through first legitimizing, privileging and itemizing a very narrow, culturally determined range of skills and areas of knowledge (Usher and Edwards 1994), and then assessing students' acquisition of these through essentially quantitative, summative testing procedures, this obstruction works on teachers' practice in two ways. First, it impels teachers to devote inordinate amounts of their time and energy to the development of these particular skills and areas of knowledge – usually at the expense of (and often to the exclusion of) *other*, non-legitimized skills and areas of knowledge.

Second, it constrains teachers to *teach* in certain related *ways* – for example, to adopt more 'transmissive' modes of pedagogy or (collectively) to introduce setting and streaming. As teachers in English schools repeatedly complain, it is becoming increasingly difficult to sustain progressive teaching methods within the constraints of a still fundamentally 'traditional' (and more maximally detailed than ever before) National Curriculum.

I have tried to illustrate how these curricular constraints work on teachers' practice through case studies of teachers working with bilingual and bidialectal students at various stages in their school careers. In some cases (as exemplified in the study involving Mrs Green), teachers were unable or unwilling to offer resistance to the constraints, or to the cultural biases inherent in the curriculum. In other cases (as with Ms Montgomery and Mr Browning), teachers were able to locate 'action spaces' in which to challenge, with their students, the biased criteria by which they were being judged, in ways that might simultaneously help their students toward higher academic achievement. Even these more successfully anti-culturist teachers, however, were only able to go *so far* within an overarching system dedicated to the perpetuation of culturally dominant tastes, values, understandings and interests. I have suggested that only a radical change in the curriculum itself can open up the path to truly and fully inclusive education for large numbers of our minoritized students. Although teachers can – and really should – militate cogently and persuasively for such change (see also hooks 1994, p.5), we have to accept that this is a long-term project, demanding high levels of patience and self-sacrifice: one that may well not come to fruition within current teachers' lifetimes and that continues to take place in something of a theoretical void as to what, precisely, a revised, 'emancipatory' curriculum might look like.[1] It may well be the case that, in the meantime, teachers may be compelled, as Shor and Freire have suggested (1987), to focus their anti-culturist activity on what they, personally, do in the classroom with their students and in cooperation (or sometimes in conflict) with other professionals in their schools.

If the curriculum itself – and the monitoring of its 'delivery' through regular government inspection – presents one major obstacle to anti-culturist, emancipatory pedagogy, it is not, however, the only obstacle. The external, legal and highly visible constraints presented by the curriculum, which do not support flexibility or recognize contingency (Moore, in press), are in turn supported by – or may be better regarded as the tip of the iceberg of – other, less visible constraints. One set of such constraints, which is very clearly associated with more 'obvious' curricular constraints, concerns funding and issues of *economics*. With reference to this issue, Bernstein has drawn a useful distinction between two modes of pedagogy and school/classroom organization: the 'competence' model and the 'performance' model. The former – not to be confused with the competencies discourse that currently plagues so much of sixteen-plus education and initial teacher education in the UK – is deliberately student-centred, emphasizing, in the evaluation of students' work, 'what is *present*', while the latter is strictly *curriculum*-centred, emphasizing 'what is *missing* in the product' (Bernstein 1996, pp. 59–60). As we have seen in the case studies, these two models can lead to very different ways of working with students and to very different student outcomes. (Mr Geddes' work with Abdul, for example, was very curriculum-centred, focusing on what was absent from Abdul's work rather than what was in it, while teachers like Ms Montgomery began by identifying and valuing students' existing skills and understandings.)

The difficulty with the competence model, Bernstein argues, is that it is relatively expensive to set up and maintain, containing many 'hidden costs' to do with the extra time teachers have to commit to the model to make it work (a suggestion often articulated with reference to the kinds of student-centred pedagogy implied in Vygotsky's writing: see, for instance, Baumann et al. 1997, p.67). These hidden costs 'are rarely explicitly recognized and built into budgets, but charged to the individual commitments of teachers'. This lack of recognition of hidden costs 'may lead to ineffective pedagogic practice because of the demands of the practice, or, if these are met ... , to ineffectiveness because of the fatigue of the teachers' (Bernstein 1996, p.63). According to Bernstein's analysis, the larger social system makes it far harder to establish and sustain student-centred pedagogies (demanded by, for example, 'in-house' anti-culturist projects) than it does to establish and sustain curriculum-centred ones that unproblematically reproduce and communicate a culturist, externally fixed national curriculum. Thus, in what is still sometimes called 'progressive teaching', there is always a disproportionate *possibility* of things going wrong, which can then be interpreted by the principal carriers of dominant ideologies as evidence that the progressive approach *itself* is wrong. It is precisely this kind of analysis that may help us understand the ineffective outcomes of some of the teachers in the case studies, who individually and collectively espoused student-centred views, only to be constrained into letting their marginalized students down in practice because the overall circumstances – including the financial constraints within which they worked – let *them* down. In days when schools are increasingly being funded – directly and indirectly – on 'performance indicators' related almost exclusively to students' results in public examinations, such a situation seems likely to get worse before it gets better.

Both the curriculum and the financial constraints under which schools and teachers work represent what, to follow Bourdieu, we could call 'the objective relations' within which pedagogy operates – that is to say, the actual legal, social and economic structures and circumstances that exist independently of the individual actor and, in that sense, 'outside' them (Young 1971a, 1971b, Wacquant 1989). These objective relations are described by Bourdieu in terms of 'field' – 'as social arena within which struggles or manoeuvres take place over specific resources or stakes and access to them' (Jenkins 1992, p.84). Pedagogy, however, is not simply structured through the teacher's conscious reactions and responses to external circumstances and relations. As Bourdieu reminds us, teachers, like everyone else, also carry with them *internalizations* of these objective relations: what Bourdieu, effectively offering a reading of the workings of hegemony as it operates at the personal level, calls our 'habitus' (Bourdieu 1977, 1990a, 1990b). 'Habitus' refers to the *hidden* attitudes, perspectives and aspirations – the 'dispositions' – that we all carry with us in our heads without normally knowing that we do so: ways of seeing and responding to the social world, that is, which are themselves formed *by* and out of that social world and which in turn inter-react with it. They are, effectively, an aspect of our *culture*: internalizations of 'external' structures and ideologies (class structures, 'received wisdoms', power relations and so on) that predetermine our responses to the behaviours and cultural products (as well as our *expectations*) of ourselves and others.

Such an analysis has clear implications for the issue of teacher choice. In its most deterministic configuration, for instance, the habitus controls our every act, so that we only *think* we are making choices with regard to, for example, our style of pedagogy or our degree of subversive activity, whereas in fact we are carrying out wishes and interests initiated 'elsewhere', typically for reasons we do not remotely understand. The notion of habitus, however, also sheds light on the differing behaviours of teachers, including those described in the case studies. We might suggest, for example, that Mrs Green, who was able to articulate anti-racist perspectives and opinions in interview, still included what might be termed racist perspectives and strategies in her teaching precisely because of her internalization – invisible to herself – of racist perspectives and racist power-relations in the broader society of which she was, willy-nilly, a part. It is, moreover, this 'unconscious' character of her racist practice and perception that renders it different, and arguably harder to get at, than 'prejudice', which implies a higher degree of *consciousness*. Other teachers, by contrast, such as Ms Montgomery, were able, through the awakening 'of consciousness and socio-analysis' (Bourdieu 1990a, p.160), to 'get at' these internalized attitudes and to adopt different perspectives and strategies as a result. Whatever else we might make of this, there are clearly practical implications here for the *professional development* of teachers.

In addition to his hypothesis of the 'habitus' and the implications of this for pedagogy, Bourdieu provides us with one other, perhaps surprising, source of opposition to teacher activism – and that is our students themselves. This opposition is explained partly through a recognition of the habituses of the students themselves, who may carry self-images, self-expectations (often very low self-expectations) and common-sense views of teaching and schooling that can conflict with the attitudes, ambitions and methods of their would-be anti-culturist teachers, and partly through the elaboration of two further concepts – those of *pedagogic action (PA)* and *pedagogic authority (PAu)*. Pedagogic action (Bourdieu and Passeron 1977) is what teachers do – and can do. Pedagogic authority is the manner in which they are presented and (more importantly) are perceived by their students as *curriculum legitimizers* – an understanding which leads Bourdieu to suggest that teachers who are critical of the curriculum and who wish to share this criticism with their students, telling them, for example, that a particular piece of work is not intrinsically 'wrong' just because it does not meet National-Curriculum or public-examination requirements, are doomed to failure in their enterprise. This is because, in Bourdieu's words, pedagogic action is inseparable from pedagogic authority, which stands as the '*social condition* of its exercise' (Bourdieu and Passeron 1977, pp.11–12; my emphasis). According to this analysis, the teacher who tries to 'come clean' by exposing the system to their students is bound to fail, since to do so would involve stepping outside the teacher's authoritative role – and, indeed, outside of the whole legitimizing process that produces and supports that role. Once you are working as an active agent within the system, it seems – as one effectively supporting the system through your social and pedagogic position – you can do nothing to change the system from within.

Possibilities for Action and the Issue of Responsibility

Whatever we may think of Bourdieu's notions of habitus, it must be said that his notion of pedagogic authority and the limits it sets on teacher action are not entirely borne out by the case studies described in Chapters 5 to 8. In some of these, teachers have been shown to engage their students, in appropriate and sensitive ways, with the political dimensions of the school curriculum, and appear to have had considerable success in getting their arguments over. Other commentators, too, have been more optimistic about the viability and possible effectiveness of joint deconstructive exercises between teachers and their students. Giroux, whose work has already been referred to, is an obvious case in point – but Bernstein, implying an insepa-rability of, rather than an antagonism between, student emancipation from teacher emancipation (that is, from their mutual 'inscription' in the domi-nant discourses of partiality and privilege), has also chosen to describe what he calls a 'radical mode' of teaching, that 'focuses upon inter-class/group opportunities, material and symbolic, to *redress* its objective dominated positioning' (Bernstein 1996, p.64; my emphasis).

Bernstein suggests that:

> [t]he pedagogic practices and contexts created by this mode presuppose an emancipatory potential common to all members of the group. This can be actualized by the members' own exploration of the source of

their imposed powerlessness under conditions of pedagogic renewal.

(Bernstein 1996, p.64)

While Bernstein accepts that this radical mode of teaching is 'more often found in adult informal education', that it is 'absent from the official recontextualizing field' (that is, from official policy), and that its presence in the mainstream teaching of young people 'depends upon the autonomy of [the mainstream school] field' (Bernstein 1996, p.65), it is significant that it is not dismissed by Bernstein as an 'impossibility'. Bernstein seems to suggest that, given appropriate levels of autonomy, teachers can be successful in achieving a degree – however limited – of *self*-empowerment, leading them to be able to pursue curricular and pedagogic practices which, in turn, may empower their students.

In terms of teacher choice – and, indeed, teacher *responsibility* – where does this leave us? The point has been made that transformative pedagogic action is not easy and must overcome very powerful resistance from a range of sources (Figure 23). *It would clearly be wrong for teachers to be made to feel guilty because they were not taking on a coercive, culturist system single-handedly* – as wrong as central government holding (or claiming to hold) that teachers are principally responsible for the difficulties experienced by so many of our young people inside school. Ultimately, the main responsibility for defeating culturist attitudes and practice must lie with central governments, which cannot be allowed to let racist, exclusionary *policies* hide behind the scapegoating of the institutions – or individual members of the institutions – that they establish and control. Nevertheless, teachers clearly do have a considerable degree of responsibility, not only for what happens in their classrooms but in terms of the possibilities for shaping better futures for their students – and my suggestion, supported by the case studies we have considered, is that they do also have some measure of choice in how they respond to this responsibility. Andy Hargreaves, who has often spoken up sympathetically for teachers (for example, Hargreaves 1994), has offered his own blunt statement about this matter. Teachers, he says, are

the immediate processors of the curriculum for the child. They are the evaluators of pupils' academic work ... the assessors of their overall

Figure 23 Opposition to anti-culturist pedagogy

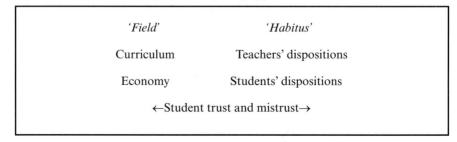

'Field'	*'Habitus'*
Curriculum	Teachers' dispositions
Economy	Students' dispositions
←Student trust and mistrust→	

ability … the immediate adjudicators of children's moral worth and the direct arbiters of the 'appropriateness' of their everyday behaviour.

(Hargreaves 1984, p.65)

While recognizing the social constraints within which teachers must operate, Hargreaves' suggestion, in line with that of 'symbolic interactionists' (for example, Mead 1934, Woods 1979, 1983, 1992), is that teachers are sense-making individuals whose active choices and *interpretations* can make significant differences to the young people with whom they work. Such a view, as we have already seen, enables other radical commentators to argue that teachers can still mount effective *local opposition* to discriminatory *state practices*, effectively acting as agents of social change (Giroux 1988, McLaren 1988).

In the end, teachers' choices as to how they respond to systemic and insti-tutional culturism will, inevitably, be partly dependent on how they perceive the operations of hegemony and central government. If they see hegemony as a one-way coercive street, for example, flowing in an unadulterated way from the dominant classes into the minds of the dominated classes, they may feel that the limited forms of local action (for example, pursuing practices associated with *multicultural teaching* within their own classrooms) promoted by, among others, Shor and Freire (1987) represent the very most that it is reasonable to attempt. If, on the other hand, they see hegemony as more of a dialectical process, as commentators increasingly do (see, for example, Gramsci 1985, Giroux 1988, Martin-Barbero 1993),[2] they may take a more optimistic line, both 'introjectively'[3] (in classroom activity that is more directly *anti-racist*) and 'projectively' (that is, aimed at influencing the thinking and operations of the 'world outside the classroom' and of the educational *system* itself).[4] The Paul Dash quotation with which this final chapter began is, I believe, very useful in addressing these considerations. Dash describes a childhood of inscription in the dominant Western European cultures and discourses of an occupying power. Inserted within – but never totally or comfortably within – these cultures and discourses, his own identity is shaped within *their* terms: his very habitus, with its own self-regulating ambitions, self-expectations and perceptions of relative self-worth, is constructed out of the occupying power's 'formulations of who we were and what we should become'. The indigenous black population of his Caribbean island operated, says Dash, 'in the long shadow of white power. … We were acculturated to an environment which constructed us as inferiors' (Dash 1998, p.79).

The pertinence of Dash's words lies partly in the questions they invite. For example, if a child such as this is so convinced of his and his people's own inferiority, how can he grow up to recognize and to articulate so eloquently and persuasively the processes of enculturation and coercion to which he was subjected? What is the story behind this change – the story of this individual's 'awakening of consciousness' and consequent 'socioanalysis'? There may be many answers to this question, and many contributory factors. Some of these may connect with the fact that, as a child, this particular individual moved away from a situation of being the member of an indigenous population, experiencing an occupying force purely through certain very limited, specific and seemingly miraculous manifestations of that force's culture and capability, to one of being a non-indigenous player on that same power's 'home turf'. The questions raised by Dash's testimony, however, remain critical for teachers working with all black students, regardless of where they or their parents were born, prompting other questions, more directly linked to matters of responsibility and pedagogy: to what extent do young minoritized people perceive aspects of their cultures as inferior to the dominant (white) ones? How can these youngsters be supported in schools, in the development of their understanding that no such inferiority exists other than in the minds of people and in the culturally biased systems that those minds (re)produce? How, exactly, does a (typically) white teacher negotiate with their black students that very difficult and dangerous terrain between achieving some measure of empowerment and equality of opportunity through the absorption and replication of dominant cultural forms and styles, while at the same time promoting, celebrating and developing preferred, currently non-dominant forms and styles? These are not easy questions and there are no easy answers: however, they are questions that teachers owe it to their multicultured, minoritized students – and indeed to themselves – to consider in the most serious way.

Conclusion: The Two Domains of Teacher Activism

As has been suggested already, the anti-coercive choices available to teachers can operate in two domains and in two directions, neither of which is exclusive but both of which need to be contextualized and considered within constraints that are externally fixed and internally experienced. In Figure 24, I have tried to illustrate this situation, taking as my starting point Bernstein's notions of 'official' and pedagogic 'recontextualizing fields' (Bernstein 1996). The official recontextualizing field relates to dominant government views and policies towards educational change in the context of wider socio-economic change, while the pedagogic recontextualizing field refers to dominant schools', teachers' and teacher educators' views and practice in this area. As Bernstein observes, there are moments – as with the Plowden Report – when in certain areas of educational philosophy and practice there exists an 'unusual convergence' between the two fields (Bernstein 1996, p.57). Typically, however, the two fields are oppositional in many critical respects. (A simple example of this might be the current divergence of thinking in the UK on the issue of formal assessment, where schools appear to continue to seek to prioritize continuous and formative assessment, in the face of growing pressure from central government and the examination boards to prioritize end-of-course and summative assessment.)

To the left of Figure 24 I have placed the two major domains of resistance to teachers' anti-coercive action – the curriculum and its attendant bureaucracy, imposed by central government, and the internalized habitus or common-sense perception of the social (and indeed the 'natural') world that is fundamentally conservative in nature and that operates like a cultural fifth-columnist to further the interests of the dominant classes (an example already given of this force in action is that of Mrs Green's dismissal of her student's drawing ability as non-existent simply because – though this was not her self-understood reason – it did not conform to a certain privileged genre). To the right of Figure 24 I have placed teachers' perceptions and practice: the domain of the pedagogic recontextualizing field. The arrows moving from left to right indicate the various ways in which the curriculum and the habitus inform, affect and constrain classroom practice and philosophy. More important, perhaps, are those moving from right to left, which are indicative of *the ways in which teachers might respond to those powerful forces emanating from the official recontextualizing field.* Those responses can be of two kinds: the kind that is essentially 'accommodatory' – ranging from doing what one is told to undertaking minor local subversions (making sure that spaces are found to teach non-standard poetry, finding ways of interpreting the National Curriculum that make possible the teaching of genuine political awareness, and so on) – and the kind that is essentially resistant. Both responses recognize the centrality of human *agency* and both are resistant to straightforward deterministic views of the workings of hegemony: the latter, however, emphasizes the potentiality of agency to influence or effect societal and attitudinal *change.* We might say that while the more resistant varieties of the former kind of response are able to promote limited

Figure 24 Habitus, curriculum, practice

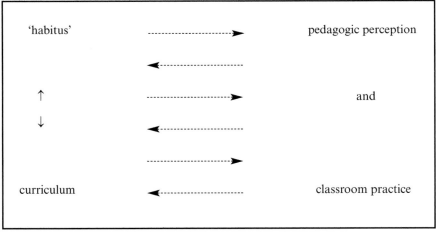

help for students like Mashud, Leonard and Julian, in order to be of *further* help – not just to these students but to students like Nozrul and Abdul – teachers will need to include an *'outward'-oriented* dimension to their activity, seeking ways of making their own professional voices and authority more central and persuasive to debates on the nature and future of public education.

There is, as I have already indicated, a central problem about this notion of agency. On the one hand, one does not want to present teachers – and teachers do not, generally, want to perceive themselves – as powerless victims of the System, any more than one would want to present students as passive vessels. On the other hand, once one has foregrounded teacher agency it becomes much easier to introduce the idea of teacher *blame*. This is one reason why the notion of agency, linked to a politics of the *symptom*,[5] has always been popular with the political Right: the notion of free will and choice, that is, makes it easy to pathologize the individual person, institution or even country, rather than to address inequalities and inadequacies in the *System*. The intellectual Left, however, has begun to reclaim agency through a more subtle interpretation and understanding of the workings of hegemony, that does not deny the coercive, privilege-led aspects of its character but that opens up possibilities for action and resistance and speaks with guarded optimism of the possibilities for fundamental social change (see, for example, Walkerdine 1990, Martin-Barbero 1993). Such a reclamation problematizes *determinism* for its potential 'absolution' of the individual from responsibility (as bad as holding the individual principally responsible for social injustices). *It might also be seen to imply, in the area of teacher responsibility, that, regardless of how we feel about central government's role in this matter, if teachers themselves do not, somehow, mount an effective opposition to coercive, exclusionary policies and practice then no one else will.*

This last suggestion is central to the arguments I have tried to put forward elsewhere in the book, all of which have been underpinned by a critical sense that teachers must not lose hope nor let their oppositional discourses wither and die under the weight of a compromise multiculturalism and a time- and energy-sapping bureaucracy that allows systemic culturism to prosper. If education's current *limits* rest within externally fixed curricula, rules and financial constraints, its improving, empowering qualities lie, as they always have done, with teachers themselves.

Notes

1 There are notable exceptions to this – for example, Usher and Edwards 1994, Edwards and Kelly 1998. Also useful are Giroux 1992, Hamilton 1993, Hargreaves 1993, Carr 1995, Green 1995. For Giroux, the new educational project entails a serious debate not about the 'management and economics of education', as is so often the case, but that addresses 'the most basic questions of purpose and meaning. What kind of society do we want? How do we educate students for a truly democratic society? What conditions do we need to provide

teachers … and students for such an education to be meaningful and workable?' (Giroux 1992, p.241).

2   Giroux usefully talks of the need, in educational research, to problematize 'how teachers and students sustain, resist, accommodate those languages, ideologies, social processes and myths that position them within existing relations of power and dependency' (Giroux 1988, p.200).

3   I have borrowed the terms 'introjective' and 'projective' from Bernstein (1996), but used them in a different way. Bernstein uses these terms to describe different kinds of pedagogic *identity* – the 'introjective' identity, which draws upon traditions and educational goals and ideologies located essentially within the school (the school's 'ethos' and own worked-out educational philosophy) and the 'projective' identity, which constructs itself increasingly on such 'external' situations and developments as market forces and government policy.

4   Similarly, if they see central government as supporting and promoting the needs of all the people, and militating for a fairer, more equitable society (as governments often profess to do), they may take a very different view than if they perceive the prime function of central government and its advisers as legalizing the demands, needs and wishes of the dominant classes. This latter view might suggest that any attempt to change government thinking is quite useless as long as those demands, needs and wishes themselves remain unchanged.

5   Similarly, a certain determinism, linked to a *causal* politics, has found more favour with the Left. Polarities of this kind are not necessarily helpful, however, to the furtherance of the Left agenda: indeed, as Willis has observed, they may lead to untenable positions resulting in inertia (Willis 1977). It is by no means impossible for the Left to reclaim agency without compromising a view that people are, indeed, coerced and conditioned and that our choices may not, in reality, be as wide and far-reaching in their consequences as we might like them to be.

References

Appel, R. and Muysken, P. (1987) *Language Contact and Bilingualism*, London, Arnold.

Apple, M. (1979) *Ideology and Curriculum*, London, Routledge & Kegan Paul.

Atkinson, D. (1991) 'How children use drawing', *Journal of Art and Design Education* 10(1), pp.57–72.

Atkinson, D. (1994) 'Discourse and practice in the Art curriculum, and the production of the child', unpublished paper, Goldsmiths University of London.

Atkinson, D. (1998) 'Teachers, pupils and drawings: Extending discourses of visuality', unpublished paper, Goldsmiths University of London.

Au, K.H. (1980) 'Participant structures in a reading lesson with Hawaiian children: Analysis of a culturally appropriate instructional event', *Anthropology and Education Quarterly* 11, pp.91–115.

Bakhtin, M. (1981) *The Dialogic Imagination*, translated by C. Emerson and M. Holquist, Austin, University of Texas Press.

Bakhtin, M. (1984a) *Problems of Dostoevsky's Poetics*, translated by C. Emerson, Minneapolis, Minnesota Press.

Bakhtin, M. (1984b) *Rabelais and His World*, translated by H. Iswolsky, Bloomington, Indiana University Press.

Bakhtin, M. (1986) 'Extracts from "The Problem of Speech Genres" (1929)', in Morson, G.S. (ed.) *Bakhtin: Essays and dialogues on his work*, Chicago and London, University of Chicago Press, pp.91–7.

Ball, S.J. (1981) *Beachside Comprehensive*, Cambridge, Cambridge University Press.

Barthes, R. (1973) *Mythologies*, London, Granada.

Barthes, R. (1975) *S/Z*, London, Jonathan Cape.

Barthes, R. (1983) 'Introduction to the structural analysis of narratives', in Sontag, S. (ed.) *Barthes: Selected writings*, London, Fontana, pp.251–95.

Bartle-Jenkins, P. (1980) 'West Indian pupils and Art education', in Loeb, H., Snipes, D., Slight, P. and Stanley, N. (eds) *Projects and Prospects: Art in a multicultural society*, Birmingham, Birmingham Polytechnic Papers, pp.15–26.

Baumann, A.S., Bloomfield, A. and Roughton, L. (1997) *Becoming a Secondary School Teacher*, London, Hodder & Stoughton.

Ben-Zeev, S. (1977) 'The effect of bilingualism in children from Spanish-English low economic neighbourhoods on cognitive development and cognitive strategy', *Working Papers on Bilingualism No.14*, pp.83–122.

Bernstein, B.B. (1971a) *Class, Codes and Control*, vol.1, London, Routledge & Kegan Paul.

Bernstein, B.B. (1971b) 'On the classification and framing of educational knowledge', in Young, M.F.D. (ed.) *Knowledge and Control*, London, Collier-Macmillan, pp.47–69.

Bernstein B.B. (1977) *Class, Codes and Control*, vol.3, London, Routledge & Kegan Paul.

Bernstein, B.B. (1996) *Pedagogy, Symbolic Control and Identity*, London, Taylor & Francis.

Bleach, J. and Riley, S. (1985) 'Developing and extending the literacy of bilingual pupils through the secondary years', *English in Education* 19(3), pp.28–40.

Bourdieu, P. (1968) 'Outline of a sociological theory of art perception', *International Journal of Social Science Research* 20, pp.589–612.

Bourdieu, P. (1974) 'The school as a conservative force: Scholastic and cultural inequalities', in Eggleston, J. (ed.) *Contemporary Research in the Sociology of Education*, London, Methuen, pp.32–46.

Bourdieu, P. (1976) 'Systems of education and systems of thought', in Dale, R., Esland, G. and Macdonald, M. (eds) *Schooling and Capitalism*, London, Routledge & Kegan Paul for Open University, pp.192–200.

Bourdieu, P. (1977) *Outline of a Theory of Practice*, Cambridge, Cambridge University Press.

Bourdieu, P. (1990a) *In Other Words*, Cambridge, Polity Press.

Bourdieu, P. (1990b) *The Logic of Practice*, Cambridge, Polity Press.

Bourdieu, P. and Passeron, J. (1977) *Reproduction in Education, Society and Culture*, London and Beverley Hills, Sage.

Bourne, J. (1989) *Moving into the Mainstream: LEA provision for bilingual pupils*, Windsor, NFER-Nelson.

Brice Heath, S. (1983) *Ways with Words: Language, life and work in communities and classrooms*, Oxford, Oxford University Press.

Britton, J. (1975) 'Reading the game', *The English Magazine* 1, pp.18–21.

Brown, T. (1998) 'Memories are made of this', unpublished paper, Manchester Metropolitan University: Department of Education.

Brumfit, C. and Johnson, K. (eds) (1979) *The Communicative Approach to Language Teaching*, Oxford, Oxford University Press.

Bruner, J. (1976) *The Relevance of Education*, Harmondsworth, Penguin.

Bullock, A. et al. (1975) *A Language For Life*, London, HMSO.

Burgess, A. and Gore, L. (1985) 'Developing bilinguals and secondary school', *English in Education* 19(3), pp.41–52.

Burgess, E.W. (1929) 'Basic social data', in Smith, T.V. and White, L.D. (eds) *Chicago: An experiment in social science research*, Chicago, University of Chicago Press.

Burgess, R.G. (1984) *In the Field*, London, George Allen & Unwin.

Burt, C. (1921) *Mental and Scholastic Tests*, London, Staples Press.

Carey, S.T. (ed.) (1974) *Bilingualism, Biculturism and Education*, Proceedings from the Conference at Collège Universitaire Saint-Jean, University of Alberta.

Carey, S.T. and Cummins, J. (1983) 'Achievement, behavioural correlates and teachers' perceptions of Francophone and Anglophone immersion students', *Alberta Journal of Educational Research* 29, pp.159–67.

Carr, W. (1995) 'Education and democracy: Confronting the postmodernist challenge', *Journal of Philosophy of Education* 29(1), pp.75–92.

Central Advisory Council for Education (1967) *Children and Their Primary Schools* (a.k.a. The Plowden Report), London, HMSO.

Chomsky, N. (1995) 'A dialogue with Noam Chomsky', *Harvard Educational Review* 65, pp.127–44.

Christopherson, P. (1973) *Second Language Learning: Myth and reality*, Harmondsworth, Penguin.

Coard, B. (1971) *How the West Indian Child is made Educationally Sub-normal in the British School System: The scandal of the black child in schools in Britain*, London, New Beacon.

Coleman, J.S. et al. (1966) *Equality of Educational Opportunity*, Washington, D.C., Department of Health, Education and Welfare: Office of Education.

Collier, V.P. (1987) 'Age and rate of acquisition of second language for academic purposes', *TESOL Quarterly* 21, pp.617–41.

Commission for Racial Equality (1986) *Teaching English as a Second Language: A report of a formal investigation by the CRE into the teaching of English as a Second Language in Calderdale Local Education Authority*, London, Policy Studies Institute.

Culler, J. (1983) *On Deconstruction: Theory and criticism after structuralism*, London, Routledge & Kegan Paul.

Cummins, J. (1978) 'The cognitive development of children in immersion programmes', *The Canadian Modern Language Review* 34, pp.855–83.

Cummins, J. (1979a) 'Linguistic interdependence and the educational development of bilingual children', *Review of Educational Research* 49, pp.222–51.

Cummins, J. (1979b) 'Cognitive/academic language proficiency, linguistic interdependence, the optimum age question and some other matters', *Working Papers on Bilingualism* 19, pp.121–9.

Cummins, J. (1980a) 'The construct of language proficiency in bilingual education', in Alatis, J.E. (ed.) *Georgetown University Round Table on Language and Linguistics 1980*, Washington, D.C., Georgetown University Press.

Cummins, J. (1980b) 'The entry and exit fallacy in bilingual education', *NABE Journal* 4, pp.25–60.

Cummins, J. (1984) *Bilingualism and Special Education: Issues in assessment and pedagogy*, Clevedon, Multilingual Matters.

Cummins, J. (1989) *Empowering Minority Students*, California, CABE.

Cummins, J. (1996) *Negotiating Identities: Education for empowerment in a diverse society*, California, CABE.

Cummins, J. and Swain, M. (1986) *Bilingualism in Education: Aspects of theory, research and practice*, London, Longman.

Dalphinis, M. (1988) Keynote address to National Anti-Racist Movement in Education annual conference, April, Manchester.

Dash, P. (1998) 'Critical studies, diaspora and museum education', *Journal of Museum Ethnography* 10, pp.79–86.

Dewey, J. (1939) *Freedom and Culture*, New York, Putnam.

DFE (Department For Education) (1995a) *Art in the National Curriculum*, London, HMSO.

DFE (Department For Education) (1995b) *English in the National Curriculum*, London, HMSO.

Dillon, D. (1985) 'The dangers of computers in literacy education: Who's in charge here?' in Chandler, D. and Marcus, S. (eds) *Computers and Literacy,* Milton Keynes, Open University Press, pp.86–107.

Dulay, H., Burt, M. and Krashen, S. (1982) *Language Two*, New York, Oxford University Press.

Dunn, R. (1987) 'Do students from different cultures have different learning styles?' *International Education* 16(50), pp.3–7.

Eagleton, T. (1983) *Literary Theory*, Oxford, Blackwell.

Edwards, D. and Mercer, N. (1987) *Common Knowledge: The development of understanding in the classroom*, London, Routledge.

Edwards, G. and Kelly, A.V. (eds) (1998) *Experience and Education: Towards an alternative National Curriculum*, London, Paul Chapman.

Edwards, V. (1987) 'Clever people speak proper', *Guardian*, 5 May, p.13.

Exton, R. (1984) 'The language of literature', in Miller, J. (ed.) *Eccentric Propositions*, London, Routledge & Kegan Paul, pp.70–9.

Fordham, S. (1990) 'Racelessness as a factor in black students' school success: Pragmatic strategy or pyrrhic victory?' in Hidalgo, N.M., McDowell, C.L. and Siddle, E.V. (eds) *Facing Racism in Education*, Reprint Series no. 21, Harvard Educational Review, pp.232–62.

Foucault, M. (1977) *Discipline and Punish*, Harmondsworth, Penguin.

Freire, P. (1970) *Pedagogy of the Oppressed*, New York, Seabury Press.

Freire, P. and Macedo, D. (1987) *Literacy: Reading the word and the world*, London, Routledge & Kegan Paul.

Garfinkel, H. (1967) *Studies in Ethnomethodology*, Englewood Cliffs, Prentice-Hall.

Giddens, A. (1991) *Modernity and Self-Identity: Self and society in the Late Modern Age*, Cambridge, Polity Press.

Ginzburg, C. (1980) *The Cheese and the Worms*, London, Routledge & Kegan Paul.

Giroux, H. (1988) 'Critical theory and the politics of culture and voice: Rethinking the discourse of educational research', in Sherman, R. and Webb, R. (eds) *Qualitative Research in Education: Focus and Methods*, London, Falmer Press, pp.190–210.

Giroux, H. (1992) *Border Crossings: Cultural workers and the politics of education*, New York and London, Routledge.

Giroux, H. and McLaren, P. (1992) 'Introduction', in Stanley, W.B., *Curriculum for Utopia: Social reconstructionism and critical pedagogy in the postmodern era*, New York, State University of New York Press, pp.xi–xv.

Gonzalez, V. (1993) 'How to differentially diagnose normal second language learning from true handicapping of conditions: A qualitative–developmental approach', paper presented at the Annual Meeting of the National Association for Bilingual Education, 24–27 February, Houston.

Goodman, K.S. (1967) 'Reading as a psycholinguistic guessing game', *Journal of the Reading Specialist* 4, pp.126–35.

Goodson, I.F. and Walker, R. (1991) *Biography, Identity and Schooling*, London, Falmer Press.

Gramsci, A. (1985) *Selections from Cultural Writings*, London, Lawrence & Wishart.

Green, B. (1995) 'Post-curriculum possibilities: English teaching, cultural politics and the post-modern turn', *Journal of Curriculum Studies* 27(4), pp.391–409.

Gregory, E. (1996) *Making Sense of a New World: Learning to read in a second language*, London, Paul Chapman.

Gregory, E. (1997) *One Child, Many Worlds: Early learning in multicultural communities*, London, David Fulton.

Guthrie, L.F. and Hall, W.S. (1983) 'Continuity/discontinuity in the function and use of language', in Gordon, E. (ed.) *Review of Research in Education* 10, pp.55–77.

Hacker, A. (1995) *Two Nations: Black and white, separate, hostile, unequal*, New York, Ballantine Books.

Hamilton, D. (1993) 'Texts, literacy and schooling', in Green, B. (ed.) (1993) *The Insistence of the Letter: Literacy studies and curriculum theorizing*, London, Falmer, pp.46–57.

Hammersley, M. and Atkinson, P. (1983) *Ethnography: Principles in practice*, London, Tavistock.

Hargreaves, A. (1984) 'The significance of classroom coping strategies', in Hargreaves, A. and Woods, P. (eds) *Classrooms and Staffrooms*, Milton Keynes, Open University Press.

Hargreaves, A. (1993) 'Professional development and the politics of desire', in Vasquez, A. and Martinez, I. (eds) *New Paradigms and Practices in Professional Development*, New York, Teachers College Press.

Hargreaves, A. (1994) *Changing Teachers, Changing Times: Teachers' work and culture in the postmodern age*, London, Cassell.

Hester, H. (1989) 'Stages of English learning', London, Centre for Language in Primary Education.

hooks, b. (1992) *Black Looks: Race and representation*, Boston, MA, South End Press.

hooks, b. (1994) 'Camille Paglia: Black pagan or white colonizer?', in hooks, b. *Outlaw Culture: Resisting representation,* New York and London, Routledge, pp.83–90.

hooks, b. (1994) *Outlaw Culture: Resisting representation,* New York and London, Routledge.

Hunt, M.P. and Metcalf, L.E. (1968) *Teaching High School Social Studies*, 2nd edn, New York, Harper & Row.

Ianco-Worrall, A. (1972) 'Bilingualism and cognitive development', *Child Development* 43, pp.1, 390–400.

ILEA (Inner London Education Authority), Division 2 (1985) *The Education of Bilingual Learners: Towards a coherent policy*, ILEA Division 2.

ILEA/ILECC (Inner London Education Authority/Inner London Educational Computing Centre) (1986) *Developing Tray* computer software, London, ILEA.

Jakobson, R. (1971) 'Two aspects of language and two types of aphasic disturbances', in Jakobson, R., *Selected Writings II*, Mouton, The Hague, pp.239–59.

Jenkins, R. (1992) *Pierre Bourdieu*, London, Routledge.

Keddie, N. (1971) 'Classroom knowledge', in Young, M.F.D. (ed.) *Knowledge and Control*, London, Collier-Macmillan, pp.133–60.

Klesmer, H. (1994) 'Assessment and teacher perceptions of ESL student achievement', *English Quarterly* 26(3), pp.8–11.

Krashen, S. (1982) *Principles and Practice in Second Language Acquisition*, Oxford, Pergamon Press.

Kress, G. (1982) *Learning to Write*, London, Routledge & Kegan Paul.

Labov, W. (1972) 'The logic of nonstandard-English', in Giglioli, P.P. (ed.) *Language and Social Context*, Harmondsworth, Penguin, pp.179–215.

Lambert, W.E. (1967) 'A social psychology of bilingualism', *Journal of Social Issues* 23, pp.91–109.

Landes, R. (1965) *Change in American Education*, New York, J. Wiley & Sons.

Lawrence, D.H. (1972) 'Fish', in De Sola Pinto, V. and Roberts, W. (eds) *D.H. Lawrence: The complete poems*, London, Heinemann, p.339.

Leary, A. (1984) 'Assessment in a multicultural society: Art and Design at 16+', *Schools Council Programme 5: Improving the examination system*, London, Longman for the Schools Council.

Levine, J. (1981) 'Developing pedagogies for multilingual classes', *English in Education* 15(3), pp.25–33.

Levine, J. (1983) 'Going back to the mainstream', *Issues in Race and Education*, Summer, pp.1–3.

Levine, J. (1985) 'Culture, bilingual students and the curriculum', keynote address to the 18th Language in Inner City Schools conference, March, London University Institute of Education.

Levine, J. (ed.) (1990) *Bilingual learners in the mainstream curriculum*, London, Falmer Press.

Levine, J. (1992) 'Pedagogy: The case of the missing concept', in Kimberley, K., Meek, M. and Miller, J. (eds) *New Readings: Contributions to an understanding of literacy*, London, A. & C. Black, pp.196–201.

Levine, J. (1993) 'Learning English as an additional language in multilingual classrooms', in Daniels, H. (ed.) *Charting the Agenda: Educational activity after Vygotsky*, London, Routledge, pp.190–215.

Lewis, M. (1987) 'Culture, communication and personal identity', in Loeb, H. (ed.) *Changing Traditions II: Ethnographic resources for Art education*, Birmingham, Birmingham Polytechnic: Department of Art, pp.30–4.

Liedke, W.W. and Nelson, L.D. (1968) 'Concept formation and bilingualism', *Alberta Journal of Educational Research* 14, pp.225–32.

Little, A. and Willey, R. (1981) *Multiethnic Education: The way forward*, London, Schools Council.

Loveday, L. (1982) *The Sociolinguistics of Learning and Using a Non-Native Language*, Oxford, Pergamon Press.

Lowenfeld, V. and Brittain, W.L. (1970) *Creative and Mental Growth*, New York, Macmillan.

Lucas, T. and Katz, A. (1994) 'Reframing the debate: The roles of native languages in English-only programs for language minority students', *TESOL Quarterly* 28(3), pp.537–62.

Lucas, T., Henze, R. and Donato, R. (1990) 'Promoting the success of Latino language-minority students: An exploratory study of six high schools', *Harvard Educational Review* 60, pp.315–40.

Malherbe, E.G. (1946) *The Bilingual School*, Johannesburg, Bilingual School Association.

Martin-Barbero, J. (1993) *Communication, Culture and Hegemony: From the media to mediations*, London, Sage.

Mason, J. (1994) 'Professional development and practitioner research in Mathematics education', *Chreods* 7, pp.3–12.

McCarty, T.L. (1993) 'Language, literacy, and the image of the child in American Indian classrooms', *Language Arts* 70, pp.182–92.

McLaren, P. (1988) 'Culture or canon? Critical pedagogy and the politics of literacy', *Harvard Educational Review* 58(2), pp.211–34.

McLaren, P. (1995) *Critical Pedagogy and Predatory Culture: Oppositional politics in a postmodern era*, London, Routledge.

Mead, G.H. (1934) *Mind, Self and Society*, Illinois, University of Chicago Press.

Miller, J. (1983) *Many Voices: Bilingualism, culture and education*, London, Routledge & Kegan Paul.

Moll, L.C. (1981) 'The microethnographic study of bilingual schooling', in Padilla, R.V. (ed.) *Ethnoperspectives in Bilingual Education Research*, vol.3, *Bilingual Education Technology*, Ypsilanti, Michigan, Department of Foreign Languages and Bilingual Studies.

Moore, A. (1987a) 'From failure to achievement: The story of one pupil's move from remedial classes to public examination success', unpublished paper, London University Institute of Education.

Moore, A. (1987b) 'Pupil evaluation and teacher reception of classroom writing at 16+', unpublished MA dissertation, London University Institute of Education.

Moore, A. (1990) *A Whole-Language Approach to the Teaching of Bilingual Learners*, Occasional Paper no.15, University of California (Berkeley)/Carnegie Mellon University: Center for the Study of Writing.

Moore, A. (1991) 'A whole language approach to the teaching of bilingual learners', in Goodman, Y., Hood, W. and Goodman, K. (eds) *Organizing for Whole Language*, Portsmouth, NH, Heinemann/Toronto, Irwin, pp.231–47.

Moore, A. (1993) 'Genre, ethnocentricity and bilingualism in the English classroom', in Woods, P. and Hammersley, M. (eds) *Gender and Ethnicity in Schools: Ethnographic accounts*, London, Routledge, pp.160–90.

Moore, A. (1995) 'The linguistic, academic and social development of bilingual pupils in secondary education: Issues of diagnosis, pedagogy and culture', unpublished PhD thesis, Milton Keynes, Open University.

Moore, A. (1996a) 'Masking the fissure', *British Journal of Educational Studies* 44(2), pp.200–11.

Moore, A. (1996b) 'KS3 assessment of bilingual students', project report, Goldsmiths University of London.

Moore, A. (1996c) 'Assessing young readers: Questions of culture and ability', *Language Arts* 73(5), pp.306–16.

Moore, A. (1996d) 'Responding to bilingual pupils in the art classroom', *Journal of Art and Design Education* 15(2), pp.179–88.

Moore, A. (1996e) '"Bad at art": Issues of culture and culturism', in Dawtrey, L., Jackson, T., Masterton, M. and Meecham, P. (eds) *Critical Studies in Modern Art*, New Haven, Yale University Press, pp.98–105.

Moore, A. (1997) 'Unmixing messages: A Bourdieuean approach to tensions and helping strategies in initial teacher education', unpublished paper from the International Conference on Bourdieu, Language and Education, University of Southampton.

Moore, A. (1998) 'English, fetishism and the demand for change', in Edwards, G. and Kelly, V. (eds) *Experience and Education: Towards an alternative national curriculum*, London, Paul Chapman, pp.103–25.

Moore, A. (forthcoming) 'Beyond reflection: Contingency, idiosyncrasy and reflexivity in initial teacher education', in Hammersley, M. (ed.) *Researching School Experience*, London, Falmer Press.

Moy, R. (1985) 'Thinking under the influence', in Stephens, J. (ed.) *Devtray: The teaching documents*, London, ILEA/ILECC, pp.4–5.

National Writing Project (1990) *A Rich Resource: Writing and language diversity*, Walton-on-Thames, Nelson.

OFSTED (Office for Standards in Education) (1997) *The Assessment of the Language Development of Bilingual Pupils*, London, Office for Standards in Education.

Ogbu, J.U. (1992) 'Understanding cultural diversity and learning', *Educational Researcher* 21(8), pp.5–14.

Ong, W. (1982) *Orality and Literacy*, London, Methuen.

Peal, E. and Lambert, W.E. (1962) 'The relation of bilingualism to intelligence', *Psychology Monographs* 76(546).

Perera, S. and Pugliese, J. (1998) 'A school for racism: Pedagogy in the face of ethnicity', *Discourse* 19(2), pp.157–70.

Perozzi, J.A. *et al*, (1992) 'The effect of instruction in L1 on receptive acquisition of L2 for bilingual children with language delay', *Language, Speech and Hearing Services in Schools* 23(4), pp.348–52.

Phillips, S. (1972) 'Participant structures and communicative competence: Warm Springs children in community and classroom', in Cazden, C., Hymes, D. and John, V.J. (eds) *Functions of Language in the Classroom*, New York, Teachers' College Press, pp.370–94.

Platero, D. (1975) 'Bilingual education in the Navajo nation', in Troike, R.C. and Modiano, N. (eds) *Proceedings of the First Inter-American Conference on Bilingual Education*, Arlington, Center for Applied Linguistics.

Read, H. (1964) *Education through Art*, London, Faber & Faber.

Ricoeur, P. (1978) *The Rule of Metaphor*, Cambridge, Cambridge University Press.

Ricoeur, P. (1984) *Time and Narrative*, vol.1, Chicago, Chicago University Press.

Rosen, H. (1972) *Language and Class: A critical look at the theories of Basil Bernstein*, London, Falling Wall Press.

Ryan, W. (1972) *Blaming the Victim*, New York, Vantage.

San Diego City Schools (1975) *An Exemplary Approach to Bilingual Education*, San Diego, San Diego City Schools.

Sarup, M. (1986) *The Politics of Multiracial Education*, London, Routledge & Kegan Paul.

Saussure, F. de (1983 edn) *Course in General Linguistics*, ed. Bally, C. and Sechehaye, A., London, Duckworth.

Schutz, A. (1964) *Collected Papers*, vol.2, The Hague, Martinus Nijhoff.

Selinker, L. (1974) 'Interlanguage', in Richards, J.C. (ed.) *Error Analysis*, London, Longman, pp.31–54.

Sharp, R. and Green, A. (1975) *Education and Social Control*, London, Routledge & Kegan Paul.

Shor, I. and Freire, P. (1987) *A Pedagogy for Liberation*, New York, Bergin & Garvey.

Shuy, R. (1978) 'Problems in assessing language ability in bilingual education programs', in Lafontaine, H., Persky, H. and Golubchick, L. (eds) *Bilingual Education*, Wayne, Avery Publishing Group, pp.376–80.

Skutnabb-Kangas, T. and Toukamaa, P. (1976) *Teaching Migrant Children's Mother Tongue and Learning the Language of the Host Country in the Context of the Socio-cultural Situation of the Migrant Family*, Helsinki, Finnish National Commission for UNESCO.

Stanley, W.B. (1992) *Curriculum for Utopia: Social reconstructionism and critical pedagogy in the Postmodern Era*, New York, State University of New York Press.

Stubbs, M. (1976) *Language, Schools and Classrooms*, London, Methuen.

Stubbs, M. (1983) *Discourse Analysis*, Oxford, Blackwell.

Sully, J. (1895) *Studies in Childhood*, London, Longmans, Green & Co.

Swain, M. and Lapkin, S. (1982) *Evaluating Bilingual Education: A Canadian case study*, Clevedon, Multilingual Matters.

Swann, Lord (1985) *Education for All*, London, HMSO.

Taber, A. (1978) 'Art in a multicultural school', *New Approaches in Multiracial Education* 7(1), pp.1–5.

Taber, A. (1981) 'Art and Craft in a multicultural school', in Lynch, J. (ed.) *Teaching in the Multicultural School*, London, Ward Lock Educational, pp.57–75.

Thatcher, M. (1987) Opening speech to UK Parliament, Summer.

Tizard, B. and Hughes, M. (1984) *Young Children Learning*, London, Fontana.

Triandis, H. (1980) 'A theoretical framework for the study of bilingual–bicultural adaptation', in *Bilingualism and Biculturalism*, special issue of *International Review of Applied Psychology* 29(1–2), pp.7–16.

Trudgill, P. (1983) *On Dialect*, Oxford, Blackwell.

Tschantz, L. (1980) *Native Languages and Government Policy: An historical examination*, Native Language Research series no.2, University of Western Ontario, Center for Research and Teaching of Canadian Native Languages.

TTA (Teacher Training Agency) (1998) *National Standards for Qualified Teacher Status*, London, Teacher Training Agency.

Usher, R. and Edwards, R. (1994) *Postmodernism and Education*, London, Routledge.

Volosinov, V.N. (1986) *Marxism and the Philosophy of Language*, Cambridge, MA, Harvard University Press.

Vygotsky, L.S. (1962) *Thought and Language*, Cambridge, MA, MIT Press.

Vygotsky, L.S. (1978) *Mind in Society*, Cambridge, MA, Harvard University Press.

Wacquant, L.D. (1989) 'Towards a reflexive sociology: A workshop with Pierre Bourdieu', *Sociological Theory* 7.

Walkerdine, V. (1982) 'From context to text: A psychosemiotic approach to abstract thought', in Beveridge, M. (ed.) *Children Thinking Through Language*, London, Arnold, pp.129–55.

Walkerdine, V. (1990) *Schoolgirl Fictions*, London, Verso.

Warner, R. (1992) *Bangladesh is My Motherland*, London, Minority Rights Group.

Wiles, S. (1985a) 'Learning a second language', *The English Magazine* 14, pp.20–3.

Wiles, S. (1985b) 'Language and learning in multi-ethnic classrooms: Strategies for supporting bilingual students', in Wells, G. and Nicholas, J. (eds) *Language and Learning: An interactional perspective*, London, Falmer Press, pp.83–94.

Williams, G.A. (1985) *When Was Wales? A History of the Welsh*, Harmondsworth, Penguin.

Willis, P. (1977) *Learning to Labour*, Farnborough, Saxon House.

Woods, P. (1977) *The Ethnography of the School*, Milton Keynes, Open University Press.

Woods, P. (1979) *The Divided School*, London, Routledge & Kegan Paul.

Woods, P. (1983) *Sociology and the School: An interactionist viewpoint*, London, Routledge & Kegan Paul.

Woods, P. (1992) 'Symbolic interactionism: Theory and method', in LeCompte, M.D., Millroy, W.L. and Preissle, J. (eds) *The Handbook of Qualitative Research in Education*, San Diego, Academic Press.

Wright, J. (1985) *Bilingualism in Education*, London, Issues in Race and Education.

Wright, S. (1998) 'Painting as language: Analogy and difference', unpublished paper, Wimbledon School of Art.

Young, M.F.D. (1971a) 'Introduction: Knowledge and control', in Young, M.F.D. (ed.) *Knowledge and Control*, London, Collier-Macmillan, pp.1–17.

Young, M.F.D. (1971b) 'An approach to the study of curricula as socially organized knowledge', in Young, M.F.D. (ed.) *Knowledge and Control*, London, Collier-Macmillan, pp.19–46.

Index

Page references in **bold** refer to figures.